'04

D1001412

THE
UNTOLD
STORY

Iain Calder

THE UNTOLD STORY

My 20 Years Running
THE NATIONAL
ENQUIRER

miramax books

HYPERION

NEW YORK

ISBN 0-7868-6941-0

First Edition
10 9 8 7 6 5 4 3 2 1

*For my beloved wife, Jane, who taught me
the meaning of love and family: I could never
have completed the journey without you at my side.
Thank you for being you.*

*And for my sons, Douglas and Glen,
sources of constant pride.*

My Deepest Thanks . . .

To Miramax Books former chairman Tina Brown for inspiring me to write this book; to Miramax president Jonathan Burnham and editor in chief JillEllyn Riley for their invaluable support and guidance throughout the project.

To my book editor Jan Werner. Her insights and skills made my pages crisper and more dramatic, and her unique talents helped me achieve the "impossible"—cutting my original 240,000-word manuscript in half without breaking my heart.

To reporter/researcher Bill Burt—a dynamo who was my first *Enquirer* reporter and whose prodigious memory added color and history to my work.

To a *great* researcher, Muriel MacFarlane. Fast, accurate, and talented, she's the best. I don't know how I would have finished without her.

To the nearly fifty *Enquirer* staffers, past and present, who generously contributed advice, memories, and wonderful stories of their experiences, including chairman and CEO David Pecker, former editorial director Steve Coz, editor in chief David Perel, and my former boss at American Media, Michael Boylan.

. . . And to the late Generoso Pope, Jr., the most amazing man I ever met. Gene: You were my chariot to the stars.

CONTENTS

FOREWORD

You could make the case that the *Enquirer* almost single-handedly created our celebrity culture.

—*Newsweek* (September 3, 2001)

The *National Enquirer* changed the face of American journalism.

If you enjoy watching *Entertainment Tonight* on TV . . .

If you like to flip through *People* magazine at the hairdresser . . .

If it's fun to glance at the personality section of your local newspaper . . .

If you're happy to have a wide selection of magazines at the supermarket checkout . . .

. . . Just say a little thanks to the *Enquirer*.

Gene Pope was a visionary. When I first joined the *Enquirer* in 1964, GP was the head of a small tabloid notorious for its gory pictures of murder victims, headless horses, autopsies, and other equally graphic scenes.

But he had a vision—an insane vision—of transforming that tabloid into the largest-circulation weekly in the United States.

He made that vision a reality. And I was at his right hand for most of the wild ride.

In the mid-sixties, American newspapers were dull and gray. Editors decided what their readers should read—and that certainly did not include crackling prose or snappy pictures of interesting people.

Television was hot, hot, *hot*. By 1960, some 90 percent of American households owned a set (ten years earlier only 2 percent did), and the competing networks began attracting mass audiences with shows like *Bewitched, I Dream of Jeannie, Star Trek, Gilligan's Island, Mission Impossible, The Flintstones*, and *Hogan's Heroes*—shows that still contribute to the popular culture of today. But in the '60s, outside of *TV Guide* print journalists largely ignored television. Even celebrity magazines like *Photoplay* treated television stars as second-raters and saved their covers for movie stars like John Wayne and Elizabeth Taylor. Television was beginning to steal advertising dollars from newspapers and magazines, which riled up their editors. When I first came to the United States, I was surprised by the many print stories telling readers that too much TV turned their kids into vandals and morons and was bad for the family. They actually called television the "boob tube" and insulted their readers by implying that if you liked *The Beverly Hillbillies*, you were a cretin. Wasn't that smart?

The *Enquirer*'s first break was discovering that covers featuring TV stars sold better than covers with celebrities from the big screen. Lucille Ball was a much better draw than Edward G. Robinson. Looking back, it's all so obvious—but at the time it was a breakthrough.

Our second break started off looking like a potential disaster. During the mid-sixties, most of our sales came from newsstands in the cities, but as more and more Americans moved to the suburbs, the *Enquirer*'s circulation dropped from a high of nearly 1 million per week. Something had to be done.

What Gene Pope did changed the magazine publishing industry forever. At that point, only a handful of specialty magazines were sold at supermarket checkout counters. With an inspired marketing effort, Gene got the *Enquirer* a spot as the first general-interest magazine at the front end. And, as they say, the rest is history.

TV coverage plus supermarket distribution made our sales zoom. A tidal wave of imitators followed. In 1974 Time Inc. launched *People* magazine and the *New York Times* company started *Us* magazine; later Rupert Murdoch began the *Star* tabloid as a direct competitor. Women's magazines followed us into supermarkets, with smiling television stars on their covers. Television got into the tabloid act with shows like *That's Incredible, Hard Copy, Current Affair, Inside Edition,* and *Entertainment Tonight.*

The age of personality journalism had dawned.

But if you believe that the *Enquirer's* success was built solely on celebrities, you're wrong. Throughout the thirty-plus years I spent at the *Enquirer,* fewer than half the stories in each issue covered celebrities. We knew our readers, and we knew that while they liked to read about stars, they were curious about other topics as well. Over the years, by trial and error, we developed an editorial formula that was unique and really successful.

In the 1970s, *Enquirer* stories on subjects such as possible life in space, extrasensory perception, life beyond the grave, and reincarnation were sneered at by the mainstream press. Now, of course, that same mainstream press—including "respectable" publications like the *New York Times* and *U.S. News and World Report*—often cover these subjects. Syndicated TV shows featuring mediums allegedly talking with the dead are ratings hits.

When we ran the infamous photos of Gary Hart and Donna Rice on the good ship *Monkey Business*—pictures that ended a presidential campaign—veteran *60 Minutes* correspondent Mike Wallace said it changed coverage on politicians forever. He was right.

If you're skeptical, ask yourself: Would the media have gone after Bill Clinton for his fling with Monica Lewinsky if the Gary Hart story had never run? I doubt it. Look at how journalists ignored John F. Kennedy's sexual escapades while he was president. He had many affairs, including one with Judith Campbell Exner, who at the time was also sleeping with Mafia boss Sam Giancana. The White House press corps knew about it, but their editors decided to keep it secret. In those days, a small clique of men decided what was fit for you to read. (The *Enquirer* broke the full story years later when Exner decided to write a book.)

Of course, I had no idea I'd be a part of this watershed era in journalism. On the contrary, I believe my participation came about by accident, or through some greater power's design (or sense of humor). But, however it happened, I'm not alone in believing that I've become part of journalistic history.

The Freedom Forum, an organization created by major media companies to promote American journalism, chose to feature the *Enquirer* and me, personally, in the News History Gallery of their $50 million Newseum in Washington, D.C. They have showcased me right alongside some of journalism's leading lights, such as Walter Cronkite, Barbara Walters, and Peter Jennings.

The Ronald Reagan Library in 1995 asked me to attend a journalism conference and participate in a panel discussion they labeled "The Tabloid Republic." The topic: how tabloids (and in particular the *Enquirer*) influenced the media. Hosted by former network correspondent Marvin Kalb, it also featured two famed *Washington Post* writers and other newspaper heavyweights. The consensus seemed to be that our contribution had been significant and—surprisingly—not all that bad.

In 1996, John F. Kennedy, Jr., interviewed me for *George* magazine. He wrote that when I chose my career as a young reporter in Scotland it was "a decision that would alter the future of journalism."

But perhaps *Los Angeles Times* columnist Robert A. Jones said it most directly. In his January 22, 1997, column, he wrote: "The tabloids have won. We now live in a world of JonBenets and Ennis Cosbys, of mysterious ladies in fur coats, of hookers eavesdropping on the President, of [O. J. Simpson's] Bruno Magli shoes. So much fun.

"I remember a day about fifteen years ago, long before the tabloids had begun to win, I picked up a copy of the *National Enquirer.* . . . I remember thinking that the *Enquirer* was an artifact of the past, a vestige. It could not last. . . .

"Who reads this stuff? . . . These days, of course, the answer is everyone. Only no one has to endure the shame of buying the *Enquirer* anymore. The same stuff gets delivered on the nightly news, gets tossed onto the doorstep each morning. The tabloids did not die. They took over."

Clearly Mr. Jones was exaggerating—a bit—for effect. But it does make my point that we undoubtedly changed American journalism.

This is the story of Pope, Calder, and how the *Enquirer* reached more than 20 million readers each week at its peak, how we blazed a path for all the magazines and TV shows that followed. This is the story of how we changed the face of American journalism, for better or worse. And the fun we had on the way.

THE
UNTOLD
STORY

THE BEGINNING OF THE BEGINNING

It was 1964, and life was good.

I was twenty-four years old, with almost nine years of journalism under my belt. I'd covered every kind of story from airline crashes and coal-mine disasters to murders and national elections, and now I was a member of the Glasgow *Daily Record*'s Heavy Mob, the reporters sent out on the front lines of the cutthroat Scottish tabloid wars. I was well paid, with work that was exciting and fulfilling. I was engaged to a special woman, Jane Bell, a hair stylist, who seemed ready to put up with me and the demands of my career.

Yet I was growing too old to be a young kamikaze. My bosses were only in their thirties, so there were no openings for promotion. I was beginning to feel caged.

The next logical step was London. Everything exciting—from Mary Quant's eyeshadow and miniskirts to the Rolling Stones' growls and gyrations—came from London, the center of the world.

With my fiancée's blessing, I asked to be transferred to our parent newspaper, the *Daily Mirror*, the world's largest English-language daily, with a massive circulation of more than 5 million each day. Nobody in Glasgow had ever asked for a transfer before, but my boss agreed. He even said he'd send me down to London for a couple of weeks that summer, to run the *Record*'s London bureau, right in the *Mirror*'s building.

But by my twenty-fifth birthday, my transfer still hadn't been formalized and I was feeling frustrated.

Then destiny stepped in.

During my temporary assignment to the *Record*'s London office, I visited Al Coombes, a short, pocket-Hercules type who tackled life and sports with bulldog-like ferocity. Al and I had met when we both worked at the *Record* several years earlier, and we became good friends. Shortly after I met Jane, I had a blind date with a young woman named Beth. Lovely as she was, I preferred Jane, which was fortunate, since Al was very interested in Beth. Soon, the four of us were socializing together.

While at the *Record*, Al had started freelancing for an unknown American weekly called the *National Enquirer*. Although the *Record* paid very well, Al could make two weeks' salary by doing just one story for this strange publication none of us had heard of.

In 1963, shortly after Al married my former blind date, he announced that he was leaving the *Record* to open the first London bureau for the *Enquirer*. By the summer of 1964, Al was well settled in, and on a visit to London, I went over to visit him at his office. Actually, calling it an office is a gross exaggeration. It wasn't much bigger than an average closet. With Al seated at his desk and myself in one guest chair, and Al's secretary (and only employee) sitting in the other, there might have been room for two more people—*thin* people—to crush in and stand somewhere.

But Al was happy in his tiny domain. He was responsible for building a stringer network across the whole of Europe, able to pay American rates for stories and photos—a huge premium over British magazine payments. At twenty-five, he was lord of his domain.

One strange thing: Al strenuously resisted showing me a copy of the *Enquirer*. I realized later he was too ashamed of his publication, and when I finally got my hands on a copy, I could see why.

The *Enquirer* was in its gory heyday—full of the most graphic black-and-white photos of gruesome murder victims, mangled bodies at crash scenes, charred corpses at house fires. Though I've tried to forget it, I still remember one photo of a horse that had been decapitated in some kind of road accident—its body on one side of the road, its head on the other.

While we sat in his office and talked, Al started to open his mail. Reading one letter, his jaw dropped, his face went white, and he gasped, "I don't believe it." This letter would change my life dramatically.

Al's boss, the *Enquirer*'s executive editor, had written congratulating him on the excellent job he'd done in the last six months. In fact, his work had been so outstanding that the *Enquirer* wanted to bring Al to the United States and promote him to assistant executive editor.

The only delay, the letter said, would be Al's finding a replacement. As soon as he hired someone who could handle the bureau with the same efficiency, Al would have a ticket to the United States.

Al showed me the letter and said: "Do you want my job?"

I said, "How much?"

"Forty pounds"—about $100 a week.

"Not enough."

"Forty-five."

I said, "It's a deal."

When people claim they alone are responsible for their success, I just don't believe them. What if I hadn't happened to be in Al's office when he got that letter? London swarmed with hundreds of fine journalists, and Al might have offered any one of them the job. I happened to be in the right place at the right time. Luck . . . destiny . . . whatever the word, it was not something I controlled.

At that point, I had no idea what I was getting myself into. The world of the *National Enquirer* was different from anything I had ever experienced, or even imagined.

When you tell people in the United States you left school at sixteen, they figure you're some kind of dropout who missed out on a good education. In my case, I feel the opposite is true. I was born in Slamannan, a small village in a coal-mining region in Scotland—on almost the same latitude as Anchorage, Alaska—but I went to Falkirk High School, in the nearest large town. At Falkirk, we took Latin,

French, chemistry, geometry, algebra, geography, history, and other basics—all in my first year, at age eleven. By age fourteen we were reading Chaucer in the original (nearly incomprehensible) Middle English, while at sixteen we were starting calculus. I've never felt I lacked an education.

Falkirk was a good school, but I wasn't an outstanding student, so in June 1955, at age sixteen, I graduated with my Higher Leaving Certificate and left school forever. Now I was in the real world, looking for a job. Although many of my grade-school pals had found high-paying jobs in the coal mines, that clearly wasn't for me. I hoped for a career with a future, and anyway, how could a 6'2" teenager, weighing a Twiggy-like 133 pounds, work in a 5-foot-high coal tunnel?

Within a few weeks, I had two job offers: bank clerk at a major Scottish bank, or junior reporter for a weekly newspaper with a tiny circulation. The bank paid 3 pounds, 7 shillings ($10) per week, and the paper offered 2 pounds, 15 shillings ($8).

Most journalists will tell you they chose their profession because of a noble calling to root out evil, protect the weak, and embark on other equally idealistic crusades. My reason was a little more mundane.

My sixteen-year-old male glands were demanding attention. I was going to dances regularly to meet girls, and sometimes I'd even ask them for dates. I figured that if I told a girl I was a bank clerk, my chances of impressing her were low. But if I told her I was a newspaper reporter, well, then . . .

That was it. I accepted the reporter job. The fantasy of becoming a major babe magnet remained just that—a fantasy. But within a week I knew I'd chosen correctly. I *loved* the job.

The *Falkirk Sentinel* had a circulation of 1,500 copies per week in an area of about 60,000 people; that made us the lowly, distant number-three paper. Our staff consisted of an editor, a chief reporter, and me. They wouldn't exactly make the title official, but I knew on day one that I was the *Sentinel*'s deputy chief reporter.

My first morning on the job, George Hawley, the editor, threw me some plot synopses of films to be shown at Falkirk's movie houses in two weeks' time. We had to review upcoming movies so our readers would know which cinema to choose, but since we couldn't see the films in advance, we had to write our reviews based on descriptions sent to us by the studios themselves.

I wrote them up, pecking out the words laboriously on an old typewriter, and handed them to my editor. He penciled in a few changes and threw the pages into a wire basket on his desk. I timidly asked: "When will my first story actually be published?" His brusque answer: "That *was* your first story, son. We don't have time to baby people here."

I was exultant. Wow—I'm a movie reviewer, and they're actually *paying* me for this!

Day two was even better. I was given my first interview assignment. A local girl, an eighteen-year-old beauty named Nina Moscardini, had won a dancing competition, and since I was now a fully fledged reporter with twenty-four hours experience behind me, I was sent out to get the story. Nina had been a year ahead of me at school, and every boy—and perhaps every male teacher—had lusted after her. At school I would have been happy to stand 10 feet away and worship her; I knew she'd ignore me, an invisible, lowly younger student.

But when I interviewed her as a reporter, she talked to me as though I was a real person. She actually answered my questions and perhaps even worried about what I would write. This was the life!

In the next few months, I traveled around our circulation area by foot and by bus, covering courts, council meetings, flower shows, and soccer matches. You name it, I covered it.

Everyone in my family was impressed with my job except my grandfather, who was partially deaf.

When I told him what I was now doing, a broad grin creased his face. "That's great, son. You'll be able to carry bags for all these nice people," he said.

I was baffled. Then I realized he thought I was a "porter" for the railroad.

When I explained that I was a *re*-porter, a journalist, his smile faded. Clearly the job was suspect, not a good, reliable job like carrying bags at a railroad station.

I, however, was ecstatic. I just couldn't believe anyone would pay me to do this fun stuff.

★ ★ ★

My best story came about three months into the job. It proved to me, and my boss, that I had a real flair for the business.

Looking back from the twenty-first century, it is easy to forget the hardship and unrest behind the Cold War Iron Curtain. In the mid-fifties, groups of miners in Poland, Hungary, Lithuania, and other communist countries began striking and picketing against their Soviet masters, even forming underground resistance movements. After a full-scale rebellion in 1956 in Hungary, the protests ended when Russian tanks killed a number of protesters. Many of the men were jailed, brutalized, and even murdered.

Some of these miners escaped to Britain—and several dozen ended up in a hostel camp in Falkirk. They worked in local mines by day, then returned to their camp and spent the rest of their time with their comrades and a few interpreters. Now the camp was being closed, and the refugees were being split up to live in individual lodgings with local families. All three local papers sent reporters to interview the miners, and I was the baby of the group.

We separately interviewed dozens of men, through interpreters. These miners hadn't learned much English, but despite the language barrier, I began to sense their unease, even fear. I asked the interpreter why they were afraid. He said, "They fear splitting up from their friends. They don't read or speak English. Without interpreters, how will they find how to get a bus to work? How will they be able to buy food? How will they survive?"

It suddenly hit me. Here were these heroes who had battled bullets, bayonets, and tanks to fight communism. Men who had never feared anything were now afraid of leaving their safe little camp.

That's how I wrote my story. The other two rival papers just said the hostel was closing and the miners would move to individual lodgings. Period.

My editor loved my story. Looking back, I could have written it with more pizzazz, but it ran in the *Sentinel* without a change. Mr. Hawley also rewrote the story and sent it to the national newspaper, the *Daily Record*, which published it and sent Hawley a check. He split it with me, and I had my first freelance payment—about $1.50.

I was now sixteen, a nationally published reporter, and unofficial King of the World.

My reign came to an end six months after it began, on February 17, 1956. My paper folded, went bust, vanished, and generally stopped publishing. I was still sixteen, still a nationally published reporter, but now also unemployed and "on the dole," receiving unemployment payments from the government.

Fortunately, I soon got an offer from the *Stirling Journal*, a paper headquartered about 15 miles away. I left home at 8:15 each morning and, with late meetings to cover, usually arrived home on the last bus to Slamannan at 11 P.M. On Saturdays I covered soccer games, which meant a six- or seven-hour day. It was about then I realized that to be a good newsman, work had to come before everything else. For the next forty years, I would work fifty, sixty, or seventy hours, six or seven days a week. And I never regretted it.

Six months later my reputation and my work in Stirling earned an offer to return to Falkirk on the *Falkirk Mail*. So at age eighteen, I was earning the huge sum of 4 pounds, 10 shillings ($13) per week. In addition, the *Mail* editor had a freelance contract with many national newspapers in Scotland and England. He would get his reporters to cover news and sports and pay them 50 percent of the freelance fees. He got 50 percent for doing nothing. Even so, it sounded like a great deal to me. The freelance earnings would double my salary—I was rich!

I was having the time of my life. I was theater critic, movie critic, court reporter, sports reporter, city council watcher, and the main go-to reporter on all the big stories. I saw movies, theater, and sports events for free—always bypassing any lines, something that really impressed the girls. (I must have been prescient at sixteen; being a journalist did have a certain cachet for young women.) I was also attracting attention from the national editors as a promising young journalist.

My boss, the owner of the *Falkirk Mail*, was the oldest publisher in Scotland. He claimed to be eighty-three, but he looked at least a hundred years old. He had two bits of advice for me, both of which helped me greatly throughout my career.

The first was: "To be a success in journalism your health must come first, then your job, then your family, then everything else." It was harsh advice and not necessarily conducive to happiness. But it turned out to be absolutely accurate.

The second was simpler: "*Listen.* Listen attentively to what people are saying. Others are thinking about what they will say next. If you learn how to listen, you will have an advantage."

That may be the best advice I ever got.

In 1960, I moved from a local weekly to one of Scotland's biggest daily papers—the *Daily Record*, with a circulation of about 500,000, a huge number in a country of only 5 million people. The top news editors at the *Record* knew me because I had freelanced for them for the past four years. However, in the previous thirty years, only four journalists had jumped from Falkirk to the Big City of Glasgow, so it didn't do my ego any harm to enter the "big time" at the age of twenty-one.

Five years of journalism had transformed me dramatically. From a shy, introverted teen—even my little sister once said she felt sorry for me—I had become a brash, cocky newsman. I had even put on 1 stone (14 pounds) in weight and was now 6'2½". And a Hercules-like 147 pounds.

But I soon learned that being a big fish in the little pond of Falkirk was one thing. Landing in the middle of a no-holds-barred newspaper circulation war was another story.

The anything-goes Glasgow newspaper war lasted a decade and created an environment that few journalists anywhere have ever experienced. And it created a few extraordinary reporters who could have been legends in the CIA, MI5, KGB, or any other intelligence agency on earth. As a daily occurrence, these men performed the impossible or played the most ingenious dirty tricks on the opposition. It was always for the story. It didn't matter how small the story, the Glasgow mantra was *beat the opposition*. And afterward the bitter enemy camps would meet in a pub as good friends.

Glasgow forged me into a tougher, harder journalist than I'd ever imagined—and prepared me for the adventure that awaited me across the Atlantic Ocean.

The three men who ran the *Daily Record* news-gathering desk were, in order of authority: Donald Bruce, a fierce, taciturn news editor who, it was said, owed his vinegar personality to years in a Japanese prisoner-of-war camp; deputy news editor Fergie Millar, whose temperament swung wildly between screaming, hyperactive slave driver to understanding, empathetic boss; and Hugh McMenemy, the diminutive night news editor who loved his reputation as a brutal ogre and would use the cruelest psychological intimidation to get his troops to crush the enemy.

One reporter tells of an evening assignment when he visited a house three times to try to get an interview. The first time a hoodlum came to the door and told him to get lost. The second time the hoodlum screamed at him to *get lost*—and showed him a snarling 90-pound German shepherd straining on a leash. The third time, the hoodlum snarled, "Knock again and I'll order my dog to rip your throat out."

Feeling he'd surpassed the call of duty, the reporter phoned McMenemy on the night desk. Mac listened and then ordered: "Go back to that man and tell him the *Daily Record* isn't afraid of any bloody dog."

Opting for survival over obedience, the reporter sat in a bar for twenty minutes, called McMenemy, and lied, telling him that on the fourth visit, no one answered.

I remember covering a small story about a falling roof-tile hitting the head of a little boy who was taken to the local hospital and released. No big deal. Yet on that story, I got to the house first and "cleaned it out"—short for asking the mother for all the pictures she had of her child, taking them off walls, from tables, out of drawers, whisking them away, and returning them the following week. After a house was cleaned out, not a single snapshot was left when a rival reporter arrived.

On bigger stories, if you arrived first you would pick up every photo, then convince the family they needed to escape the pack of bad journalists about to descend on them. Few Scottish families owned cars, so you'd drive them to a relative's house to make it tough for the opposition to find them. Then you would cruise around the homes of all relatives who might have publishable photos—leaving scorched earth for your rivals. No photos, no story.

That was fun when you were first. It was hell when you weren't.

I was proud of inventing one trick that was good for about three months, until our rivals picked up on it. When I arrived at a house first and drove off with the family, I would pin a note on their door saying something like "Gone to 2004 North Street, Paisley," an address thirty minutes away—and, of course, it didn't exist. But while my rivals drove to the address, found nothing, and sped back, I had an extra hour with the family, often vital when the deadline was approaching. Maybe not brilliant—but sometimes little things mean a lot.

By age twenty-three, I had seven years of hard news experience. I had gained respect working on everything from murders to mine disasters. It was time, according to my boss Fergie Millar, to join the *Record*'s Heavy Mob.

I was one of the best, but never *the* best news-gatherer. I was one of the best, but never *the* best writer. But my particular talents combined to make me a respected senior member of a great team. The Heavy Mob was a group of elite *Record* reporters who did tough background reporting on the most sensational crime cases coming to trial. Scotland has a law, strange by almost any international standard, preventing newspapers from publishing the kinds of facts and photographs about criminal trials that would be standard fare in the United States. Before trial, we were banned from printing an interview with the accused—or even publishing a photograph. If Robert Downey, Jr., or Darryl Strawberry had been accused of a crime in Scotland, the papers would not have been able to run his picture in connection with the alleged crime—even though he was world-famous! The logic was that a witness might see the photo in a newspaper and identify the wrong person. Yeah, right.

Thus, all reporting and photographing were done *before* the trial—but held in readiness and published *after* the verdict was in.

The mission of the Heavy Mob was to interview everyone with anything to say about the subject, get their stories and photographs, and, if possible, tie them up with exclusive contracts. We used this approach with both villains and victims—*everyone involved*. This was called "background work," and you could spend weeks on one major story.

All the big dailies had major hit teams working on major stories. These crime reporters were often really tough—sometimes working with Scotland's most violent criminal element. Sometimes they were tough for other reasons, as I learned when assigned to the notorious Acid Blinding Case. Here I was competing with some real star reporters, people who could have shone on any paper in the world.

I'm not exactly proud of this story. My only excuse is having been brainwashed by a work environment that never accommodated failure but deified those who did anything to win. In 1962, I was very young, immature, and eager to climb the journalistic ladder of success at the *Daily Record*. If I'd been even five years more mature, it would never have happened.

In the pending trial, the victim was a teenage standout in football (soccer, to Americans)—a member of the Scottish national under-twenty-one team, a young man marked for stardom in the near future. He was walking peacefully through the streets of Glasgow when his world crashed down in ruins. A gang of vicious hoodlums was running amok and threw a jar of acid in his face for no reason at all.

In an instant, the young man was blinded—his life derailed, his promising career over.

The case was due to reach court in about a month. My job was to get to the kid and his family, obtain a heartrending interview, and persuade him to pose for dramatic pictures. All this could be used only after the villains were convicted.

The assignment didn't sound too hard. The boy came from a respectable family. No depraved scum to deal with. We had no interest in the bad guys. Our readers wouldn't want their stories—just a long, harsh sentence from the judge.

When I knocked at the door of the boy's apartment in a tall tenement building, the family invited me and my photographer in. They were very nice, talked freely about their son's terrible ordeal, and even let me talk with the young man himself. They couldn't have been more cooperative, and I knew it would make a compelling story.

A glitch transpired: The *Daily Express*, our main rival, had beaten me to the house by a few hours. So, while my story wasn't exclusive, I was confident my writing style would give me an edge.

Then I asked the father if my cameraman could photograph his son.

"I'm sorry," he said. "I gave my word to the *Express* that their photo would be exclusive, that nobody else would get a picture of my boy."

Now that was a shot to the solar plexus. The *Express* would have a great posed picture and we—if lucky—would print a "grab" shot, a snapshot of the teenager walking into court. It just wasn't good enough.

I pulled out every stop, I argued every position known to mankind—and I still struck out. This family wasn't rich, but they were proud, and their word was their bond. If the *Express* had paid them, I could have topped the offer. But the *Express* reporter had been smart. He had invoked their promise, their honor—and the family was immovable.

Even as I left, I knew it wasn't over yet. I *had* to get a posed picture of the boy. He seldom went outside, but even if he had, a walking photo in the street would *not* tug at the heartstrings. It's said a picture is worth a thousand words? Well, I *had* the thousand words, and the picture was worth a hell of a lot more than that.

Over the next couple of weeks, I went back four more times. Lots of talk, lots of quotes—the dad, the mom, and the son really did like me—but still no photo. By now, I was an adopted member of the family. They even fed me dinner one night—and they agreed to let a *Record* car take them to the court trial in a few weeks so we could have their personal story following the verdict. But still no photo. I could have been their long-lost prodigal son, but they still would honor their word to the *Express*.

Defeated, I was forced to go to my old pal on the Heavy Mob, the legendary Hugh Currie. Hugh was the *Record*'s Rembrandt of reporters, Picasso of professionals. "Can't crack this one," I confessed, and described the circumstances. He thought for a few minutes and then said: "Here's what we do . . ."

The next day Currie and I drove in separate cars to a spot near the boy's home. I waited while he walked toward the tenement and disappeared inside. The plan was under way.

After ten minutes, I followed Currie, and when I knocked on the door the family welcomed me as usual—and introduced me to the man inside, who was, of course, Currie. We shook hands as if we had never met, and the father explained that Currie was from the city youth authority, discussing training programs for blind youngsters. But when the dad told Currie I was from the *Record*, Currie exploded. "I *hate* these newspapers!" he ranted. As I stood there mesmerized, Currie gave an Oscar-worthy performance. What had they told the press? Were there interviews? Had they allowed photographs?

The father stammered that his son had given interviews to the *Express* and to me, the *Record*. Currie then ordered me into another room and—as I strained to listen through the closed door—he delivered his *pièce de résistance* to the family. The interviews were okay—as long as there were no exclusives.

"Why?" asked the dad. Explained Currie: "An exclusive will give the city council the impression that you sold the photo rights—that you were cashing in on your son's blindness, and that might affect your son's training and the blind program."

The shocked father then described the exclusive photo shoot given to the *Express* and explained that no money had passed hands. Currie was adamant: "When that photograph is printed with the word 'exclusive' on the caption, the city will think you took money."

Suddenly the dad had a great idea. What if the photo wasn't exclusive? What if he asked his friend Iain in the next room to take pictures—it wouldn't be exclusive then, right? Currie hesitated. It wasn't perfect, he said, but it was better than the situation now. Currie shrugged. "It's your decision," he said, and walked out.

Now the dad was opening the door to the room I was in, telling me what had happened—and asking me if the *Record* would please take pictures of his son. Of course, I was only too happy to oblige, and, by chance, my photographer was nearby. Almost immediately, the photographer was in the house, snapping away.

I wasn't able to breathe again until I finally walked out that door.

About two weeks later, I took the whole family in a *Record* car to the courthouse, where the gang members were quickly convicted and jailed. The *Express* reporter who thought his "exclusive" was safe just stood with his mouth open as I walked past, almost like a member of the family.

The next morning, as my bosses compared coverage from the *Record* and the *Express*, I was receiving all kinds of accolades and feeling pretty good. Then a call came from the doorman of our front lobby.

It was the father of the blind teenager, wanting to see me.

This was it. I *knew* it had been too good to last. The dad had found out about Currie and me. It meant being fired, and perhaps a criminal charge. Mild panic set in. I rushed over to Currie, briefed him quickly, and told him to hide in the men's room while the dad was brought upstairs to the news desk.

My mouth was dry, I was feeling hot, then cold as I waited for the dad to walk into the newsroom. When he did, I couldn't believe my eyes. He wore the biggest smile, and in front of the whole newsroom, he walked over and gave me a huge hug.

"We all enjoyed your story this morning," he said. "My wife loved it, my son loved it, and I loved it. It was so much better than the *Express*, and I'm glad we gave you the pictures," he said.

I have no idea what I said to him. In a daze, I showed him around the newsroom, introduced him to a couple of colleagues, then walked him back down to the front lobby. As he left, he hugged me again and said, "Consider yourself one of the family. Anytime you're passing, just drop in for a meal."

I finally rescued Currie from the men's room and told about the dad's response. We just looked at each other and laughed, slightly hysterically. Afterward, we contacted the right people at City Hall to make sure the boy and his family got help from their department for training the blind.

I didn't discuss the story with Hugh Currie for years, not until the trauma and guilt had faded. I had really crossed the line on that one, and I knew I could never do anything like that again.

I have never revealed this incident to the public before, but I'm doing it now to illustrate one of the best examples of how tough it was to thrive, or even survive, in the great circulation war of Glasgow.

Gene Pope believed *nothing* was impossible in journalism and had fired every single executive editor and editor before I came along. I believe one of the reasons I survived so many years with him was that I knew he was right, having lived out Pope's philosophy every day in Glasgow, years before I had ever heard of him.

The excesses of the Glasgow circulation wars peaked in the early '60s. In a notorious murder trial under way in Glasgow High Court, the country's highest court, a local criminal named Walter Scott Ellis was charged with the shooting murder of Glasgow taxi driver John Walkinshaw. The case got national attention because murder of any kind was rare in Scotland; murder by shooting was even more rare, and no taxi driver had *ever* been shot to death.

Every newspaper geared up for action. If Ellis was cleared, they wanted his personal story; if he was sentenced to death, they wanted the story of the victim's widow. Reporters had been working for weeks trying to tie up all kinds of relatives for exclusives. One paper thought they had Ellis's brother, another thought they had the father—and everyone believed they'd get some exclusive angle from the famous lawyer leading the defense.

On the day the jury announced its verdict, almost eighty newsmen were swarming around the steps of the High Court.

Unbelievably, the verdict was "not proven"—a judgment unique to the Scottish justice system. It meant the jury believed that Ellis had probably committed the murder but lacked enough proof to find him guilty. Its legal effect is the same as a verdict of not guilty.

Ellis was about to walk free—and every Scottish daily paper wanted him. The *Express* had nearly forty reporters and photographers outside the court, the *Record* had more than twenty, and the other papers provided another dozen or more.

As Ellis started to walk down the courthouse steps, all hell broke loose. A mass of journalistic humanity surged toward him, pushing, shoving, fighting, and clawing to get to Ellis. They all wanted to get him into one of their cars, to speed him away for an exclusive interview. Tempers flared, and reporters began slapping and punching each other. My *Record* colleague Bruce Camlin, who later became an editor at the *Enquirer*, had one leg in a cast, but that didn't stop him from whacking the opposition with one of his crutches.

The few police at the site tried to restore order, but they were no match for the crowd of journalists who were now pulling and pushing a terrified Ellis down the steps.

The *Express* team had the most men—and one key advantage. They had hired three strapping tough guys to get Ellis into their car. And this stratagem was working. They physically propelled the protesting Ellis into one of the cars waiting at the bottom of the steps.

One problem—it was the *wrong* car. In the midst of the screaming and struggling, Hugh Currie, leader of the *Record* team, had caught the eye of one of the toughs and pointed at our car. Confused by the melee, they assumed ours was the car to aim for.

That day I had been given the plum assignment of covering the court proceedings for a cover story. I was in the *Record* office, writing my story when over the office radio came the voice of our reporter in his radio car: "We've got him. We've got Ellis!"

But as we listened it was obvious a fight was going *inside* our car. Ellis, thinking he had been kidnapped by revenge-seeking friends of the murdered taxi driver, was punching and scrapping to get away. In the front seat, our reporter was screaming at our driver to speed off. But the thugs had figured out that they *weren't* in the *Express* car, after all, and every time the driver put the car in gear they'd kick it back out. On the sidewalk, mayhem raged as reporters kept struggling to get to Ellis and the cops tried to regain control.

The terrified Ellis finally broke free, threw open a car door, and escaped. He ran for his life, pursued by the three toughs and a mob of reporters. It was a real Keystone Kops moment.

Just then, reporters for a tiny afternoon paper with *no* hope of an exclusive, the *Evening Citizen*, happened to be stopped at a red light. They saw the fleeing Ellis racing toward them and opened their car door. He jumped in, and they roared off with their prize catch. The little *Evening Citizen* ran their exclusive the same afternoon, but that night they handed Ellis over to our rival, the much-larger *Daily Express*, because they both belonged to the same newspaper chain. The archenemy beat us in the end.

The *Record* was forced to go with my report of the trial plus another reporter's story about Ellis's pregnant wife, who'd fled a local maternity hospital for fear Ellis would harm her. Of course, one of our reporters had engineered the "escape" himself, when Mrs. Ellis revealed she wanted to hide from her husband, who was furious that she wanted a divorce.

The weird thing was, the next day our circulation went *up* while the *Express*'s numbers went *down*. Scotland's readers, disgusted that Ellis had walked free, blamed the *Express* for taking his side. Our anti-Ellis story won the day . . . even if it *was* our second choice.

The mayhem following the Ellis trial marked the beginning of the end of the Scottish tabloid wars. Several people had been injured in the melee, and a policeman's hand was broken by a slamming car door. Stories of the rampage ran throughout Europe, and it made Scottish journalists look like savages (wonder why?) and embarrassed every major newspaper editor.

The local journalists' union condemned the disgraceful scene, and the High Court judges threatened editors with jail for contempt if anything like this happened again. No editor was willing to serve jail time for the sake of boosting his paper's readership. The circulation war went on, but everyone knew there were now limits.

I have to say, however, for all its excesses, that anything-goes climate was the best preparation possible for a career with Gene Pope and the *National Enquirer*.

When Al Coombes left the *Enquirer*'s London bureau for New York, I inherited his apartment off Speakers' Corner, one of the classiest areas of London. The building even had uniformed doormen round the clock. For this I paid $20 per week.

My fiancée, Jane, was thrilled at the prospect of living in one of the world's most dynamic cities. I was too. I was twenty-five and running the whole of Europe for an American newspaper. By U.S. standards I was pretty young, but I had nine solid years of news-gathering behind me. Besides, I'd decided, the *Enquirer* job was worth doing for two or three years, just to get the experience.

Al, in his new position of power, allowed me to lease a bigger and better office and hire a deputy bureau chief. I hired Bill Dick, who had been in the *Stirling Journal* reporting job just before me. He was another veteran of the Glasgow circulation wars and had graduated to London, where he was a top staffer on the *Daily Sketch* in Fleet Street.

The *Enquirer* expected a lot from its London bureau. Our "beat" was immense: the British Isles, of course, plus the Commonwealth countries (including India, Australia, and New Zealand), and all of Europe. We were assigned to gather fascinating stories and eye-catching photos from about half the globe.

Fortunately, Bill and I made a really good team. From our new office off Bond Street, also one of London's toniest areas, we set out to achieve three objectives: widen our freelancer base throughout Europe, get great stories and photos for the *Enquirer*, and recruit journalistic talent for the *Enquirer*'s head office in New York.

We didn't take long to succeed at all three. I went on a two-week European jaunt through France, Belgium, Holland, Germany, Austria, Switzerland, Italy, and Greece. And I came back having signed up some great reporters, many of whom freelanced for us for ten years or more. One reason was that the American dollar was remarkably strong, and $250 for one story might be two or three weeks' salary for European journalists. So an executive for Agence France Presse, the great French news agency, was happy to moonlight for us. So was the news director of Switzerland's largest daily and the managing editor of the biggest newspaper in Norway. Even in Britain, the editors of the biggest newspapers had no idea that some of their best people were also working for the *Enquirer*.

Every week, we gingerly opened the pages of the latest *Enquirer*, fearful of what new gory picture would bleed across the page. Like Al Coombes before me, I took care about who had access to our copies.

Tough guy Bill, who would brave fire, storm, and personal danger to get a story, had a weaker stomach than I did, so he often asked me to open the paper first, to warn him in advance. Whether it was a dead burn victim or a driver with a pole rammed through his windshield *and* his head, I usually could handle seeing the photos.

Until one day. The cover was headlined THE UGLIEST MAN IN THE WORLD . . . HE GETS PLASTIC SURGERY TO LOOK BETTER. This picture was unspeakable. The poor man's face was like a huge blob of lumpy, cooked oatmeal, the eyes set 18 inches apart in places I'd never seen eyes. And it was just a guess as to which orifice was his nose and which his mouth. Or possibly an ear.

I dropped the paper in shock. Then I tentatively picked it up again and realized with horror that this was the *after* picture, when the guy looked good! The caption invited readers to look inside at the "before" picture. Well, I tensed up enough nerve to take a peek.

I'm not going to describe the inside photo. Enough to say that I skipped lunch that day.

The story was from Switzerland, our area of coverage. Normally, I would have been embarrassed to lose a page one to someone else. In this case, I was relieved that we were never asked to handle this kind of stuff. Our bureau specialized in great human-interest features, good celebrity interviews when American stars visited Britain, and terrific photos.

Before long, Bill and I were filling a quarter to one-third of the whole paper each week. The London bureau was a winner.

Oddly enough, however, unlike other newspaper bureaus, we had to use the telephone as seldom as possible. Calls to and from Europe were very expensive, so stringers sent ideas for possible stories by mail; we'd select the best and mail these to the United States. Then America would okay some and return them by mail, and we'd mail the assignment to our stringer. If you think that was a snail's pace, just imagine if America or London had queries. Everything came and went by the postal service. We spoke to our bosses in New York maybe once a month or less, and even then, calls had to be kept to a minimum.

Despite this, we prospered. Bill and I both kept getting raises that, by British standards, were *great*. It wasn't until later we learned that our earnings were what secretaries in New York made.

Within a year, Bill and I were well along the way to achieving two of our three goals. We had established a strong stringer base throughout Europe, and we were sending a steady stream of exciting stories to the United States. Now we concentrated on being the eastern recruiting office for the *Enquirer*.

It was really tough getting good American journalists to work for the *Enquirer*. Nobody wanted their names anywhere close to these gory photographs. Many *Enquirer* staffers in America didn't tell their friends or neighbors where they worked. And it was a joke (perhaps) that no ex-*Enquirer* journalist applying for a job would mention their years with GP. If a would-be employer asked about the two- or three-year gap in the résumé, I was told that the journalist would rather claim to have been in Attica or Leavenworth Prisons than confess to being an *Enquirer* staffer.

Given that background, I could understand why GP wanted to recruit Brits. Bill and I could make a reasonably attractive offer. A good Fleet Street salary was about 40 pounds per week. We could offer double that, plus moving expenses and the chance of adventure in New York City.

The all-or-nothing work ethic I'd learned during the Glasgow circulation wars hadn't changed a bit with my move to the *Enquirer*. Work took precedence over everything else—even my honeymoon.

My marriage to Jane was set for April 17, 1965, and we planned a honeymoon in Spain. I had been in London for about eight months, while Jane stayed in Glasgow. We saw each other only every six weeks or so and were eagerly looking forward to getting away together.

One problem: When the wedding date came around, Bill Dick was in America on assignment. I couldn't leave the London office unattended except for our secretary. It never crossed my mind to call America and ask permission to take a week or so off. That would have been deserting my post, which was unthinkable.

So I told Jane the wedding was on but the honeymoon was off. We had been serious now for nearly four years, so she knew this was a sign of what the future would bring. She should have called the whole thing off but didn't, thank goodness. She was as sweet as could be, said all the right things, and we were married in a lovely ceremony in Glasgow, as scheduled.

After a slow, three-day drive, I was in my office in London. So much for the exotic honeymoon.

★ ★ ★

Soon after I got married, Bill Dick and I got a new direct boss, Bill Condie, who, oddly enough, was one of the British stars Bill Dick and I had recruited to the paper.

A few months later came a call from New York. Condie was taking an extended trip through South America to find stringers, and in his absence, they wanted me to spend a few weeks in New York helping out the editors.

It was April 1966, and going to America meant missing my first wedding anniversary. I'd given up my honeymoon for the paper, so what was a first anniversary? Jane, as usual, was a saint about it, so off I flew across the Atlantic.

After a few days in the office, Condie dropped a bomb on me. He wanted me to stay in New York for three months as an editor. I had proved my devotion to the *Enquirer* many times over, but three months away from my wife of one year was too much to ask. I said no.

Condie was to be gone a long time; he had no deputy, and he wasn't sure the editorial department could survive with him gone. So he made me an incredible offer. The *Enquirer* would fly my wife over, rent us a luxury apartment for the summer, keep paying my full salary, and also give us a generous living allowance while we were in New York.

Wow. I called Jane, who whooped in excitement. She quit her job as a buyer for a major London store and boarded the next plane to New York.

Condie was as good as his word. He rented a plush apartment on the Upper East Side and walked us through it. For Jane and me, it looked like the American movies we'd watched back home—two huge bedrooms, two bathrooms (in Britain if you wanted two bathrooms, you had to buy two houses), and white wall-to-wall carpets throughout. There was a top-of-the-line black-and-white TV on a trolley that could be wheeled about the apartment—you could actually watch TV in bed! The refrigerator was the size of our closet in London, and the kitchen had an electric dishwasher, whatever that was.

If only our editorial offices at prestigious 655 Madison Avenue had been nearly that exciting. Within hours of taking over one of the news-gathering desks, I could hardly believe the Mickey Mouse atmosphere.

Our editors were a mix of kids, has-beens, and never-weres, with a couple of good journalists thrown in. The newsroom was at the back of the office, and few executives ever visited. Editors would spend the day flying paper airplanes, playing baseball with paper balls and little sticks, and generally acting like unruly kids in class when the teacher was gone. Any decent reporters could hardly operate in such a disorganized environment.

No wonder our little two-man office in London had filled 30 percent of the paper or more. I quickly learned that one enterprising freelancer was handling another 35 percent. So this group of maybe six or seven New York editors was responsible for only *one-third* of all the stories in the paper.

These guys came in at nine and left at five o'clock on the dot, with long lunch hours in between. One journalist had been promoted to assistant executive editor almost solely because of his devotion to the job, demonstrated by his staying till 5:15 some evenings. When he was finally fired, his next job was lab assistant for a chemical company.

I was flabbergasted. I had given up my honeymoon; I had given up my first wedding anniversary; Bill Dick and I worked nights or weekends whenever necessary. And we thought nothing of it. You did the job, no matter what obstacles stood in your way. These Americans thought it heroism for an editor to stay an extra fifteen minutes.

This was no way to run a newspaper. I decided that when I got home, I'd better start looking for another job because this lot couldn't support a successful publication. But meanwhile, I was in the most exciting city in the world with my wife, we had money in our pockets, and time on our hands. One way or another, we'd have fun.

I worked pretty hard five days a week until five o'clock, I had every weekend off—and I loved New York. The *Enquirer* employed some great characters to drink with. There was Joe Dean, a 5-foot-tall, 300-pound headline writer, who spat out the most amazing insults ever heard and who was destined to become an *Enquirer* legend. There was Bill Bates, a photo editor with a glittering State Department past, who entertained audiences with a host of believe-it-or-not stories of foreign escapades. Bill used to pay his teenage daughter to come to the bar at 9 P.M. to remind him to go home, so he wouldn't drink himself into oblivion. Then we had Barney (real name Baldissari) Giambalvo, a charismatic Italian-American pool shark who'd turned down a numbers job with the Mafia to join the *Enquirer* as production chief. One night Barney gave me a 98-point start in a pool match to 100. He won—playing with *one hand*.

Damon Runyon would have been jealous of these characters. The *Enquirer*'s news-gathering staff might have been a colorless bunch, but the support staff could make after-work sparks fly.

The greatest character of all was Generoso Pope, Jr. But to the average staffer, he was the feared, seldom-seen apparition who at any moment might step out of the elevator and spirit himself into the hidden holy space known as GP's private office. If you saw him, the lore went, don't look him in the eye; just find a way to change direction and stay unnoticed. Nobody actually said the evil eye would turn you to stone, but word was that a wrong look could get you fired. Even worse, new workers were warned, he had the power to get you rubbed out through his "connections."

Word was that one young man had walked in front of him into an elevator. Pope stopped, looked him in the eye, and said, "You're fired." The young guy supposedly stared back at Pope and said, "I don't work for you. I was just delivering lunch." True or not, many people believed it.

I never heard that Gene had actually had anyone rubbed out, but back then it wouldn't have surprised me. It *did* surprise me that I was GP's London bureau chief, churning out 30 percent of his paper each week, but in the three months I was in New York I was never even introduced to him.

Summer in New York City went quickly. We made lots of friends and took a lot of fun journeys. But the trip that topped all others was the weekend that Jane felt very sick and started throwing up. New York, with some help from me, had made her pregnant. A local doctor confirmed the diagnosis, and we were thrilled.

However, our last two weeks in the city were agony for Jane. The heat trapped the smells that, until then, had given New York character and charm. Now they made her nauseated, and all she wanted to do was get home.

Condie finally returned from South America with a Rolodex full of new stringer names. We said good-bye to that wonderful apartment and returned to London . . . now three souls instead of two. The little American fetus was destined to return to his home country a lot faster than anyone could have imagined.

Back home, Jane and I and baby-to-be knew our life had changed forever, but we had no idea how much. Our apartment wouldn't be suitable for our new family, so we started looking for a house in the countryside, within commuting distance of central London.

Business in the London bureau went on as usual. Bill had done a great job in my absence, and my long stay in Manhattan had, I perceived, simply strengthened our clout with head office.

Meanwhile, back in America, a storm was brewing. Circulation, once close to a million, had slipped to below 700,000. Readers were now moving to the suburbs, and city newsstands all over the East were shutting down due to lack of customers. Something had to be done to save the *Enquirer*.

Bill Dick and I had no inkling of this, but Gene Pope was developing a plan that would eventually make his gory tabloid a real powerhouse in American media.

The first step—change the editorial team. Out with the second-rate hacks and in with an expensive, professional team of first-rate journalists. Pope started by recruiting senior newsmen from respected publications with big money. With great stories and excellent writing, he'd have an editorial package he could sell to the supermarkets.

Finally he calls in executive editor Condie and asks, "What are these two guys in London like . . . Calder and Dick?"

"They're really good," replies Condie, so GP gives the order: Bring 'em over.

One problem: A few months before, editor Nat Chrzan had offered us jobs in New York at a salary of $210 a week, not enough to cover the higher cost of living, so we'd politely declined. When Condie tells

GP that we'd already turned down one offer, Pope says, "Here's how we'll do it."

The plan was simple and ruthless. Condie would close down the London bureau and tell Bill and me that we'd be out of work in a few weeks. After we'd had time to think about unemployment, Condie would jump on a plane, fly to London, and make the job offers.

That's what happened. It came as a shock—especially since by this time Jane and I had both a new house and a new baby—but I knew I'd get another job without too much trouble. Bill felt the same. It had been a good ride, but it was over.

Two weeks after the bad news, Condie arrived in to London with orders from the boss: "Make them an offer they can't refuse." (And this was long before the *Godfather* movies made the phrase famous.) GP had given Condie no salary limit, and failure was *not* an option. When Condie took me aside and offered me a New York job at a whopping $350 a week, I jumped at the chance. An hour later Bill signed on at $300 a week. Condie was surprised at how easy it was, since nobody over in America realized we'd turned down the earlier offer because of the lousy pay. But it worked out great for Condie. He was making $400 weekly as executive editor, not much more than my new salary, so when he returned to New York, GP immediately gave him a $100 raise.

Jane was ecstatic. She loved America, and even today, you'd have to kidnap her to get her to live anywhere else. It was a wonderful moment—a chance for a big adventure with a big salary. And our best friends Bill and his wife Margaret would be with us.

In October 1967 I emigrated to the United States. Jane stayed behind with eight-month-old Douglas to sell our house and wait until I found a home in the States. Bill Dick went on to the States while I finished closing the office.

The *Enquirer* paid our moving costs, including cash to ship our furniture across the Atlantic. But we didn't ship the furniture. We put it into storage and kept the cash—to pay for return air tickets in case the job didn't work out. I told relatives that we'd be gone for maybe five years, but I knew it could be five weeks. Gene Pope was already infamous for his firings. On my last trip to the United States, the editor's secretary, Helen Gray, had told me how she once survived a purge—because she happened to be sick on the right day.

Helen had been at the *Enquirer* for about two weeks when she came down with a sore throat and called in sick. She didn't know it, but for some time there'd been a rumor in the office that the members of the editorial staff were talking about joining a union. GP happened to pick Helen's sick day to make sure no one joined a union. He fired everyone in editorial —innocent and guilty alike—except his top two executives. Editors, writers, secretaries—they all went. Helen wasn't around that day, and because she was so new, people forgot about her.

So it was into this Stalinesque environment that I plunged. Still, I was cocky, confident, and just twenty-eight years old, so the excitement of starting a new life in the world's most dynamic country overcame any trepidation. Or most of it.

IT ALL STARTED WITH *MADONNA*

It's a story that might eclipse even Mario Puzo's extraordinary epic *The Godfather.*

A young boy from Sicily arrives in America at the age of fifteen, unable to speak English and with $6 to his name—yet within a few decades he becomes the most powerful Italian-American in the country.

He has New York judges and cops in his pocket; the friendship and respect of governors, mayors, and even the president of the United States; almost total control of the Italian vote in New York; a major fortune from owning many businesses, including Italian-language media; close ties with the country's top Mafia families; the power to influence elections, not only in his new home, but back in the old country.

It sounds like fiction—but it's all true.

Born in 1891 in the Sicilian province of Benevento, Generoso Papa escaped impoverished Italy in 1906 aboard a ship named *Madonna.* He landed in New York, where the immigrant community got him a job painting pianos, but that lasted just four months. He was hired as a shoveller and driver for a construction company, Colonial Sand and Cement, where he quickly climbed the promotion ladder and became superintendent within a few years.

By 1916, however, Colonial was on the brink of bankruptcy. Papa, who by this time had Americanized his name to Pope, made the owners and creditors a brash offer: "Let me try to save the company. If I do, you make me president and fifty-percent owner." He did—and Pope was on his way. Eventually, he'd own the entire company.

In the following years, Colonial provided most of the sand, gravel, and concrete for such New York landmarks as Rockefeller Center and Radio City Music Hall, and became the nation's largest building supply materials company. By 1928, Pope was rich enough to pay $2 million for America's number one Italian-language daily, *Il Progresso*, with a circulation of 100,000 readers.

He'd already made his fortune. Now he had *power*.

Pope organized the Italian-American vote to help Jimmy Walker become mayor of New York, and, in return, he was given all kinds of awards, plus access to yet more major construction projects. Through the years, his enormous influence with city administrations wasn't hurt by his very close ties to the Mob. One of Pope's best friends was Frank Costello, Mafia boss extraordinaire, known as the Prime Minister of the Underworld, and arguably the guy who called the shots in New York City.

By this time, Pope had married the beautiful, socially prominent Catherine Richichi and had three sons, Fortunato, Anthony, and Generoso, Jr. His youngest son, his favorite, would ultimately have an even greater impact on America than his old man.

In 1929, Pope took his family on a triumphal return to his old village. While in Italy, Pope had private meetings with Pope Pius XI, with the last Italian monarch, Victor Emmanuel III, and, most important, with the man the king had appointed prime minister, Benito Mussolini. Mussolini charmed the powerful, now-American tycoon. For the next decade, Pope used his influence to back the Fascist government of Il Duce, turning against him only when World War II broke out and Pope declared his allegiance to his new country. In the '40s, he became friendly with President Harry Truman and arranged for his sons to visit the White House and meet Truman.

My boss, Gene Pope, Jr., was very proud of his father. He talked about him often, once telling me, "My father controlled the judges and the cops for the 'families.'" Was Pope senior actually in the Mafia? During his lifetime there were many charges and many rumors, but nothing was ever proved. Clearly *I* have no proof either way, but writer Leonard Katz gives a clue in *Uncle Frank*, his biography of Frank Costello. Katz says that Costello "greatly admired Pope because he was a man who made it legitimately." Regardless of whether Pope was ever a "made man," he controlled politicians, could get judges appointed to the superior court, and had major Mafia bosses as his pals.

And while he always remained loyal to his adopted home, he also maintained close ties to his birthplace. After World War II, concerned about Italy's political situation, Generoso mobilized Italian-Americans to send hundreds of thousands of letters back to their homeland, urging friends and relatives to vote against a communist government. The Commies lost. When you can influence a national election in a foreign country, that's *power.*

Generoso Pope, Jr., was born on January 13, 1927. Frank Costello must have been a *very* close friend of Generoso, Sr., because he was asked to be Gene's godfather. The man Gene called "Uncle Frank" really was like an uncle to him, and he would later play a vital role in GP's career.

But the most important influence in Gene's life was his dad. It was obvious to everyone, including his mother and brothers, that Gene was his father's favorite. While still a teenager, Gene was running *Il Progresso*. GP once told me, "When I was just fifteen, my father put me in charge of all the bills at the company. Not one invoice could be paid without my approval."

Heady stuff—but the youngster couldn't see the storm clouds on the horizon.

I never knew GP's mother, and he rarely talked about her to me. Lois Pope, GP's widow, remembers her mother-in-law as an angry, bitter woman, nicknamed "The General" by the family. Apparently Catherine Pope resented her husband's favoritism for Gene. She could do nothing to protect her other sons, not then, but she was a strong, powerful woman, and she bided her time.

Unlike his father, Gene Pope grew up a pampered rich kid. He was driven from his palatial home at 1040 Park Avenue to the exclusive Horace Mann school, where his best friends were Si Newhouse, current publishing powerhouse; Anthony Lewis, destined to become a *New York Times* columnist; and the infamous Roy Cohn, who became Senator Joseph McCarthy's chief counsel during his House Un-American Activities days. After graduating from Horace Mann, Gene took only two and a half years to earn his engineering degree from M.I.T. At age nineteen, he returned to New York, and Generoso officially named him editor of *Il Progresso*. Soon Gene would become vice president of Colonial Sand, still one of the largest building-supply companies in the United States, and a director of radio station WHOM, another Pope property. Gene began to follow his father into New York politics: He was named one of the city's honorary deputy police commissioners and appointed to the Board of Higher Education. He also backed a friend of his Uncle Frank's in the mayoral race.

In 1950, at age fifty-nine, Generoso Pope, Sr., was stricken with either a heart attack or a stroke. In the hospital, he asked his wife for a manicurist (he had always been proud of his fingernails). GP's widow, Lois Pope, remembers, "I'm told on good authority that his wife said, 'You're dying. You don't need a manicure.'"

And so one of New York's most powerful figures—a man who could break politicians and make judges snap to attention—died with ragged fingernails.

His father's death was a double blow to twenty-three-year-old Gene. Not only had he lost someone he loved, he'd also lost his protector. It wasn't long before family rivals pounced.

Mama Pope and brothers Fortune and Anthony demoted him from his corporate titles; the new mayor ejected Gene from his police post. Even his Board of Higher Education membership went down the drain.

Gene stormed out of the Park Avenue apartment and "divorced" himself from his family—a schism that was never healed. Gene told me once, "If my mother died, I would not attend her funeral." As it turned out, Catherine Pope outlived her youngest son.

At Gene's funeral in 1988, his mama and brothers were obvious no-shows.

Several years after GP died, I was introduced to Fortune Pope at the Westchester Country Club in New York. I nervously wondered how he would react to his estranged brother's closest associate. Fortune gave me a huge smile and an even bigger hug. "Iain, you were very loyal to my brother for many years. That's a good thing," he said. We met on several later occasions, and he always treated me like an old friend. Sicilian families, I guess, honor loyalty.

The Pope family feud sent Gene off on a journey that was to set journalism on its ear. First, he joined the Central Intelligence Agency for "adventure" but quit after a year or so—"bored to death," as he said often. By 1952 Pope was back in New York, nearly penniless. His decision to buy the *New York Evening Enquirer* for $75,000 seemed idiotic. Circulation for the Sunday-afternoon paper had dwindled to 17,000 per week, and it was virtually bankrupt. But Gene must have seen an opportunity everyone else missed, and he took it.

He reportedly borrowed the $25,000 down payment from his Uncle Frank. Years later, in an interview with *Editor and Publisher* magazine, Gene said, "I had no money. I borrowed a lucky silver dollar from my lawyer to pay for cab fare down to the contract signing. Next day when I went down to the *Enquirer* office, I discovered nobody had been paid in months and I was a week away from bankruptcy." GP told me that when his first wife gave birth to their son Generoso III, the hospital wouldn't allow them to leave until the bill was paid. "I had to smuggle my wife and new baby out of the hospital, since I was totally broke," said Gene.

GP soon renamed his paper the *National Enquirer* and put together an editorial mix of gossip, sports, and some hard news, such as the Soviet invasion of Hungary. In the beginning, running the *Enquirer* was one long nightmare of debts, unpaid bills, borrowing from one person to pay another, and staying one step ahead of bankruptcy. Within a few years, Gene got the *Enquirer*'s circulation up to 250,000—but that still wasn't enough to pay all the bills.

Dino Gallo, Gene's loyal aide for forty years, from *Il Progresso* to the *Enquirer*, remembers the early days well. An office landlord once locked up all their files and typewriters for non-payment of rent. Dino and Gene sneaked into the office after midnight and took their equipment out through a window. "We needed the typewriters to get the paper out," said Dino.

The breakthrough came in one of GP's flashes of intuition. Around 1957, Gene was caught in a traffic jam and observed motorists rubbernecking to see the mangled bodies of crash victims. If that's what they want, he thought, that's what I'll give them.

He certainly did. The *Enquirer* became a gore tabloid, with such memorable headlines as MOM USES SON'S FACE AS ASHTRAY and I CUT OUT HER HEART AND STOMPED ON IT. Photos of drivers impaled on steel rods, horses with their heads torn off in auto crashes, and—famously—the autopsy picture of Lee Harvey Oswald made copies fly off the stands. By the time I joined the company in 1964, some issues sold more than 1 million copies. Gene finally clawed his way out of debt.

Still, cash flow remained a problem, and he needed help from his godfather for years. Reports were widespread that Costello gave Gene $10,000 cash each week to pay the printer, and Gene repaid the interest-free loan a few days later when the cash came in from newsstand sales.

I have one eyewitness to the other end of the transaction, the Mob loan being handed over. Barney Giambalvo, who joined Gene as a production manager in 1960, has become the unofficial historian of the *Enquirer*. From Barney's first day on the job to the day he retired, nobody remembers more about what went on.

When Barney joined up, the paper was printed in Tenafly, New Jersey. Barney recalls interesting Italian-American characters coming around the plant to talk with Gene, including a curly-haired tough named Mickey Zupa. Mickey, built like a tank and always reeking of cologne, worked for Uncle Frank. "Mickey was very friendly to me," says Barney, "but he never smiled. And he had a look like he'd enjoy killing people."

By this time, Pope's credit history was notorious. *Enquirer* employees knew that the printer wouldn't start the presses unless he had his money up front. On a number of occasions Barney watched Mickey fish in his pocket for a really thick roll of banknotes that he passed on to Gene. So the word around the plant was that Uncle Frank was definitely bankrolling the *Enquirer*, but there were two other theories as well:

- Mobsters were collecting Gene's unpaid bills from newsstand operators, who were known to be difficult about paying on time.
- The *Enquirer*'s sports section was the only one to publish results and scores of that weekend's Italian soccer games. These games were used in a highly profitable numbers game in the Italian community, and maybe the cash was a thank-you for printing the scores.

No one will ever know the real story.

Dino Gallo says he was personally involved in the yo-yo movement of cash. In a *Talk* magazine article, he describes his weekly errand for Gene, delivering an envelope of cash from newsstand sales to Costello's right-hand man, "Big Jim," at the Waldorf-Astoria hotel.

Mickey Zupa was also very helpful with marketing problems in New York. Sometimes a newsstand wasn't displaying the *Enquirer* prominently enough to please Gene. Mickey would have a little chat with the owner, explaining that the *Enquirer* was the favorite paper of the truck drivers union. So? Well, the persuasive Mr. Zupa would explain, if a delivery driver didn't see his favorite paper displayed *very* prominently, he might become so upset that his attention might stray, and the truck might smash into the newsstand. An unfortunate accident. If the owner happened to be inside, it would be *very* unfortunate.

One chat was usually sufficient, and the *Enquirer* was easy to spot all around New York City.

The delivery drivers didn't just haul newspapers around; they also handled quite a lot of cash for the *Enquirer*. Each week, they'd deliver new *Enquirers* on their route, then pick up last week's leftover papers and cash for the copies that sold. If a driver delivered fifty copies to a store last week and twenty-five of them sold, the driver would get cash for the twenty-five sales and return the twenty-five unsold copies to the *Enquirer*, where all the numbers were added up and balanced.

Those drivers, a tough bunch, came up with a scheme to cheat Gene. After the printing plant closed in the small hours of every Sunday morning, some drivers would sneak in, start up the presses, and print several thousand more *Enquirers*. The following week, if they got twenty-five returns, they'd add another ten pirated copies, claim there were thirty-five returns, and keep the extra cash.

Gene finally hired Gene Canevari, his bodyguard when he was a kid, to keep watch on the plant after it closed, and that solved the problem. Even those truck drivers weren't tough enough to take on a Mob-friendly bodyguard.

That episode must have stayed with GP the rest of his life. In the '80s, when we were printing millions of copies in reputable plants around the country, Gene always insisted on having his security men on site to ensure all the papers were counted correctly. We were the only publication in the country hiring our own private plant security.

Guy Galiardo, another *Enquirer* old-timer, remembers dealing with its trucker/bankers. In 1964, Guy was hired as assistant comptroller and given the job of collecting the sales proceeds. Each week, the circulation department gave him a list of how much was due from each driver, and that night, he'd go downtown to a cellar on Front Street, near Manhattan's East River docks and the Fulton Fish Market—not exactly Park Avenue. Accompanying Guy was one Angelo Lespinosa, rumored to be connected with the wiseguys and definitely connected to the drivers' union.

Into the cellar came a parade of unsavory characters, carrying wads of cash. Money just *poured* in. Most weeks, the total topped $25,000. During the New York newspaper strike, however, for several months the weekly take was far bigger since the *Enquirer* was selling out to readers who couldn't get their *Post* or *Daily News*.

Have you ever seen $25,000 in cash? That's a lot of greenbacks, and handling that many bills made Guy *very* nervous. At the end of the night, Guy would carry the cash back to the car, Lespinosa at his side, and they'd drive away. A New York Police Department cruiser followed them all the way to the bank, where Guy stuffed the money into the night drop-off.

This type of accounts-payable transaction wasn't covered when Guy was studying for his accounting degree.

As I said before, I doubt that Gene's father was a "made" member of the Mafia. I have no doubts about Gene himself: He was not, absolutely *not*, a member. For nearly twenty years no one spent more time with Gene than me, other than his wife. We talked for hours about everything and anything. I knew the finances of the company, the problems we had, and how they were solved.

Never once did I see or suspect help from any "mystery" source.

Gene did have connected friends, but he made it clear to me—without saying it directly—that he had never been tempted to join.

Gene's daughter Maria remembers her father as both a ruthless, demanding executive and as a loving family man, an ordinary guy sitting in bed eating and watching shows like *Hogan's Heroes* (his favorite) and *Car 54, Where Are You?*

Maria says that she wanted to ask a family friend to be godfather to her first child. When Gene found out, he called her into a private room and told her she couldn't do that. Maria protested that it was her decision. Gene's response: "My granddaughter can't have that man as her godfather." He actually raised his voice, Maria says, which was unusual. "It's guilt by association," he said. "Do I have to spell it out for you?"

Mystified, Maria agreed, and then went to her mother for a fuller explanation. The family friend was a member of the family . . . not their family but *the* Family.

Like me, Maria believes that Gene was never involved with the Mafia. Some of his friends from the old days were—but Gene was squeaky clean. He once told Jane and me over dinner, "The only time I'd ever take a favor is if one of my children was kidnapped. Then I'd make the call, but *only* then. If they do you a favor, you are hooked forever." How that philosophy calibrates with the earlier loans from Costello, I can't figure. Maybe the loans were personal transactions, favors from a man who considered his godson real family.

In the early days of the *Enquirer*, Gene continued to have weekly dinners with Uncle Frank and occasional meetings at the *Enquirer*'s new offices at 655 Madison Avenue. Gene's most publicized episode with Frank Costello took place on May 2, 1957, the evening Uncle Frank was shot. That night Costello dined with his wife, Bobbie; Gene Pope; *Enquirer* gossip columnist John J. Miller and his wife, Cindy; and Gene's lifelong friend Al Minaci and his wife, Rose. They had dinner at L'Aiglon, a favorite restaurant, and then moved on to a nightclub called Monsignori for drinks.

Close to 11 P.M., Costello announced he had to go home for a telephone call from Edward Bennett Williams (a lawyer who would later have a historic role defending the *Enquirer*). When Frank reached the elevator of his building a tall, fat man called out: "This is for you, Frank." Whirling around, Frank saw a gun pointed at his head. It went off with a loud boom.

The would-be assassin was either a crack shot who didn't want to kill Costello, or he needed new glasses. The 32-caliber bullet grazed Frank's skull, splitting the skin behind the right ear. Bleeding, the Mob boss was rushed to Roosevelt Hospital, where he asked an associate to get the news to Mrs. Costello.

The associate called Gene Pope at the club Monsignori. Gene returned to the table and, not saying why, told the group it was time to go home. Gene took Bobbie Costello into a cab and, as gently as possible, broke the news to her and went to Roosevelt Hospital.

The Mafia chief had escaped assassination, but he got the message and gradually gave up the reins of power, leaving a vacuum that was soon filled by bosses like Vito Genovese.

As the paper continued to prosper, Gene grew more uncomfortable with Uncle Frank, and in the mid-sixties he dropped Costello. The aging gangster told friends he thought he'd become an embarrassment to the increasingly successful publisher.

All this happened before I came to the United States. I did, however, witness several later examples of Gene's touchiness about anything to do with the Mafia. Probably the most dramatic story is the one about the "Mafia Myth."

In the late '60s, University of Buffalo criminologist Professor Robert E. Ford concluded that the Mafia was a myth and a slur on Italian-Americans. He gave an interview to local reporter Dominick Merle, and the story made the cover of the Buffalo daily newspaper.

Several months later, Merle was working as an *Enquirer* staff writer and suggested this story through the usual process: He wrote up a lead sheet, which was approved by higher-ups, and the story was assigned. Soon after, Merle submitted the story along with a photo of the professor.

The "Mafia Myth" article got a prominent place on page five—one of the most highly visible pages in the paper—and that week's issue went to press. As always, Gene Pope received his early copy of the *Enquirer* while the presses were still running.

Then all hell broke loose. Gene exploded in fury. He called his editor, Nat Chrzan, and yelled, "Stop the presses! Get this @%&* story out of my paper and destroy all the papers printed!"

The trucks speeding to Los Angeles, New York, Chicago, and everywhere else were halted. Papers were destroyed, and the presses were quickly replated with a new page five. The day was saved, at a cost of well over $100,000, in 1960s dollars.

Retribution was swift and ruthless. Gene stormed into the office the following morning and ordered Chrzan to fire the reporter who'd written the story. "They [meaning the Mafia] got to him!" ranted GP. "Get him out of here!"

Dominick Merle had no idea what hit him. He'd redone a story he'd originally written for his previous newspaper; he'd suggested the idea in writing and submitted it to his bosses, who had approved it. If the Mafia had gotten to Merle, then they had gotten to *all* the bosses who approved the story, edited it, slotted it for page five, and wrote the headline. But the bosses walked free, while Merle bit the dust.

Years later, Gene told me he knew the Mafia existed and that his father had worked with the kingpins. When his new wife, Lois, saw the story, she had commented, "Huh, they finally got to you!"—meaning the Mafia had persuaded him to run the story.

He told her, "I never saw that story. It somehow slipped past me."

Right! GP saw every page proof, with headlines, photos, and copy, before it could be printed. While going through some files, I found Merle's original lead sheet. And there was Gene Pope's unmistakable writing in the red ink reserved only for him—*6/15 OK*.

Gene had *personally* approved the story idea. Why, then, a mere two months later, did he spend a fortune to kill the story and fire an innocent victim?

Was he really wounded by Lois's comment? In other versions of the story, perhaps some underworld figure called Gene to say thanks.

As with so much about Gene, we'll never know.

★★★

In 1967, as I prepared to make the move across the Atlantic, I didn't know *any* of this—the cash-flow problems, the extent of the tough-guy involvement. Would I have made the same decision if I *had* known? You bet.

A NEW START

An hour or so after my plane from London arrived at Kennedy Airport, I checked into the Courtesy Inn Motel in Fort Lee, New Jersey, not far from the *Enquirer*'s new offices in Englewood. Since my summer in New York, the paper had moved from Madison Avenue to New Jersey, about a mile from the George Washington Bridge and a mile from Pope's massive house in Englewood.

Bill Dick was at the motel to greet me. He had emigrated several weeks before me while I closed up the London office. As we sat down in my room he dropped a bombshell: "I have bad news. So bad that if I'd called you in London, you might have decided not to come. Then I would've been left here alone."

Bill's news *was* really bad. Bill Condie, the executive editor who'd hired us, was about to be fired. His replacement's task was to hire a brand-new team of editors,

I was stunned. I'd known my American adventure might not last five years, but now it looked like I might be on my way home in five *days*.

Bill and I did the only logical thing. We went out for a drink. Actually, a *lot* of drinks.

★ ★ ★

Trying to make the best of our situation, Bill and I threw ourselves into our work, and after hours we looked for a place to live.

We both settled on two-bedroom apartments in a huge Fort Lee luxury complex called Mediterranean Towers—Bill in one tower, me in another. Rent was high, $271 per month, but at $350 a week, I could afford it. We later discovered that Fort Lee was the safest little town in America. Big-time mobster Tommy Eboli, aka Tommy Ryan, lived in one of the high-rises, and other hoods were scattered through the community. I'm sure the local no-goods figured that if you mugged somebody, it could be a Mafia wife or mom—which would get you a swim in the Hudson with concrete boots. So women and kids walked Fort Lee in perfect safety even after dark.

Around the time I got to America, Mr. Pope stopped being a mysterious eminence and would occasionally walk through the newsroom; once in a while he'd actually hold an editorial meeting.

GP was physically intimidating—about 6'2" and maybe 240 pounds—and his employees kept their eyes downcast when he was around. The thought was, keep looking down and maybe he wouldn't see you, wouldn't ask you a question, and wouldn't pick you out to be fired. Whatever you do, don't ever, *ever* look him in the eye.

Another element of the intimidation factor was the occasional "special visitor." A well-dressed Mediterranean-looking man would arrive in a black limo with a big, tough-looking driver and disappear into Gene's office. The office whispers identified the visitor as Vito this or Vinnie that—always someone with a Mob reputation. The guy could have been his architect or a librarian, but those in the know would tell you they really *did* know.

Then there was Gene's haircut routine. Every week, on the same day at the same time, a barber would show up, go into Gene's office, then leave thirty minutes later. I asked why Gene didn't just go to a barber. The answer I was given was that Gene had been talking with Murder Incorporated killer Albert Anastasia in his barber's chair on October 25, 1957, just before he was shot to death. I didn't know if the story was true, but I had to admit such an incident might have influenced my own haircutting arrangements. Gene continued this haircut practice in Florida, right up until he died.

I had never worked with anyone like Gene Pope before. It was like stepping into a movie plot—exciting, but a little scary.

For years, the *Enquirer* was organized like no other publication I've ever seen or heard of.

Most magazines or newspapers have news departments run by one top editor. He may have several deputies reporting to him, and then there's a group of reporters who report to them. There is one channel of control up and down the system. Everyone is working on the same team.

Not at the *Enquirer*. When I arrived in 1967, we had an editor in overall charge of editorial, a managing editor who ran page layout, headlines, and design, plus an executive editor who supervised news coverage and photo-gathering. Under the executive editor was a group of articles editors—like individual city editors—who worked independently of each other. Each articles editor had to initiate story ideas, get them approved in writing, assign the stories to freelancers—and, in later years, staff reporters—before submitting the final version, which then went to one of the rewrite men, who'd rework the copy into a polished, finished gem.

With this system, every editor was in competition with every other editor. As an articles editor, I would be fighting the ten or so others for the best ideas, the best stringers, and the most stories. It created *tremendous* competition. Let's face it: If Bill Dick produced 20 covers and 300 stories in one year and I produced 5 covers and 150 stories, guess who'd be gone the next year?

The flaws in this system are obvious inefficiencies and high costs. Yet it's also the engine that powered the *Enquirer*'s ability to break amazing stories and drive our circulation up until we became America's number-one weekly.

After Gene died, we were sold to more traditional publishers and the system was changed drastically. Why? Two main reasons: financial considerations and lobbying from editors, who hated the added pressure.

You can't fight progress, but I know that without this system of internal competition and fierce infighting among our own staff, the *Enquirer* would never have reached the top.

In January 1968 my wife and son finally joined me in Fort Lee.

Jane and I were *very* happy to see each other after three months apart. But I had bad news. I was leaving the next morning to cover a story in another state. The apartment I'd rented wasn't ready to move into yet, so she'd have to stay in my temporary quarters in a motel right on a highway. Actually, *in* a highway—one lane wrapped around one side of the motel and the other lane circled the other. It was designed for car traffic, not for walking. So here was Jane in a new country, with a baby less than a year old, no car, living in a motel where you couldn't walk across the road. Also, they were in the middle of a snowstorm, actually a blizzard. Alone. For days. They both survived, but I still hear about it from time to time.

All was forgiven the following week when I showed my wife our new home, a beautiful two-bedroom apartment complete with impressive twelfth-floor view, twenty-four-hour doorman service, and an Olympic-size swimming pool. No furniture and little money to buy any, but Jane found warehouses and discount stores, so in no time at all we were very comfortable and happy.

Outside of the constant specter of being fired on a whim, life was pretty good. I worked hard but only nine to five, five days a week—an *Enquirer* custom that lasted for years, until I became executive editor. Bill Dick's wife, Margaret, had given birth to a little girl, Morag, and our two families were very close.

Bill and I were beginning to love America, but we couldn't live like most Americans. We were making good money, but neither of us could bring ourselves to go into debt. We refused to buy cars, even when our colleagues laughed at our old-fashioned mores and called us "cheap Scotsmen."

This meant that when Margaret and Jane went shopping for groceries, they walked to the supermarket with the infants and took a taxi back. For trips to department stores, there was always the bus. I was told this was often a chore, especially in the dead of winter.

These arrangements did not last long, as our wives became more and more Americanized.

Looking back, I can see that Gene Pope was beginning his two-pronged attack in the fight to make the *Enquirer* America's biggest weekly. He knew we had to break into America's supermarkets, where the readers were, and to do that, he had to create the right editorial formula. The *Enquirer* was destined to be an incredible success at both, something to be copied and emulated by America's publishers in the years and decades ahead.

But in the late '60s, the guys in the trenches didn't know they were about to make journalistic history. In editorial, it was enough of a struggle just to keep our jobs, leaving little energy to dream about a glorious future. We knew about the plans for breaking into supermarkets from the occasional meeting with Mr. Pope and from barroom gossip with circulation executives. But nobody believed Pope's dream had much chance. The *Enquirer*'s circulation was well under a million. None of us, maybe even including GP, could envision that just about ten years later the *Enquirer* (with me as editor) would sell 6.7 million copies of the Elvis's coffin issue, eclipsing publishing heavyweight *Time* by more than 2 million.

This, I believe, was the genius of Generoso Pope, Jr. Against the better judgment of magazine experts, his employees, his friends, and the world around him, he believed, he *knew*, that he could forge a disreputable paper into the country's biggest weekly *and* make it famous around the world. All alone, spending money he didn't have, Gene pushed ahead through sheer will, and he made it all happen.

The march into supermarkets, which I'll address later, was a tour de force of marketing, one that should be a case study at Harvard B-school. The editorial changes were a slower evolution, a weekly hit-and-miss experiment to find what attracted readers and what didn't. But Gene's editorial approach was just as revolutionary as the supermarket move, and I think journalism students—and a lot of journalists—could benefit from studying it.

By the late '60s, Gene had the genesis of a sharp, hard-working editorial department able to come up with new ideas or execute

Gene's own concepts. We were a pale precursor of the powerful editorial team assembled ten or fifteen years later, but slowly we began to believe in ourselves, and in GP's dream.

Gore was definitely out. So was lurid sex. These kinds of stories would kill us in supermarkets. Celebrities were in, but we needed all sorts of other features to make us unique.

For the first time, Pope began to get involved at the idea stage so he could guide the editorial content from the beginning. In 1968, that got me involved with the boss one-on-one for the first time in my four years of employment with him.

It was a high-stress experience. I remember the first time editor Nat Chrzan called me into his office to explain that Mr. Pope wanted to see me. He had given a story assignment to another editor, who'd blown it and was now being fired for being "an idiot."

Now it was my turn to enter the tiger's den and receive the same assignment. I asked Nat for some guidance, but he threw up his hands in horror and said, "Not me. Just listen to Mr. Pope."

I always remembered my old Scottish editor's advice, and I was good at listening. So, with sweaty hands and knocking knees, I ventured into the luxurious, wood-paneled office and sat down opposite Mr. Pope at his massive desk.

Mr. Pope showed me a clipping about a man who had made millions making shoes, but whose family couldn't afford to buy him shoes when he was a boy. "Get me the story and pictures. Find out this man's guiding philosophy."

I came out shaking my head. That wasn't so tough an assignment. I called a stringer and a couple of weeks later, the story arrived. It was okay, but it lacked dramatic quotes about how the millionaire felt now and what advice he had for others who were poor. The stringer mentioned that the millionaire's house had a stunning pool and overlooked a scenic valley. "Get me a photo of him at the pool," I ordered. "And get more quotes."

The stringer went back, and the millionaire gave us some great new quotes. But the photo showed a man lying on a deck chair with a wall behind him. No pool, no view. The man could have been next to a parking lot. I screamed down the telephone at the stringer, who calmly said, "You told me you wanted a photo of the guy *at* the pool. You didn't say anything about *seeing* the pool or the view."

I learned a lesson about dealing with journalists out in the American hinterland: *Be specific.*

Anyway, we got a good new photo, and I turned in the story. Three weeks later it ran with the logo "Rags to Riches"—and became the first in a series that lasted twenty-five years.

Nobody said good job, bad job, or anything else. When I asked Nat if Mr. Pope had liked my story, he just shrugged and said, "You're still here, right?"

GP had begun to completely reshape the editorial content of the *Enquirer* to match his vision. He wanted stories that didn't just give information but triggered *emotions* in his readers—anger, laughter, gratitude, fear, love, even hate. In the 1980s, the *Enquirer* commissioned a study on the psychological reasons that readers liked our stories. The experts' research confirmed what GP had discovered by instinct. In the '60s, we were just searching for stories that worked, driven by the force of Gene Pope.

The "Rags to Riches" story, I now know, wasn't just another story. It was a message to our readers, many living dull, humdrum lives: *If this man can get rich after a childhood of poverty, then maybe you, too, have a chance.* We were selling dreams.

Our readers wanted dreams, but they also wanted to feel they were helping someone who needed it. We discovered that when we ran a series of stories on an eleven-year-old girl named Norma Gallant who was dying of old age.

A stringer in the Maritime Provinces of eastern Canada sent us a local newspaper clipping about the tragedy-struck Gallant family.

A terrible disease, called progeria, a Greek term for "prematurely old," strikes young people and causes mechanical defects in the aging system. They become old, frail, and infirm before they reach their teens. This tragedy is rare, but the Gallant family had *two* children fall victim to progeria.

In the early '70s, the *Enquirer* still didn't have staff reporters, so the articles editors who had reporting experience often covered stories themselves. I was sent to the little town of Moncton, New Brunswick, to get Norma's story.

On my way to Canada, I read all the clippings available. The Gallants had been normal, hard-working blue-collar Canadians until the first blow came. Their son Ricky began to grow old in front of their eyes. Local doctors had no idea what was wrong, and within a few years little Ricky passed on.

And before he died, to the utter horror of the parents, their second child, a little girl named Norma, started to show the same symptoms of premature aging.

Now doctors were paying attention to the family. It was the first time in medical history that two children from the same family had developed progeria. But despite the medical interest and reports in the medical literature, nothing could be done. No operation, no medicine could stop the disease's progress. The parents had to wait for old age to take their second baby.

That was the situation when I arrived at the Gallant home, a small cabin on a lonely road, miles outside the little town of Moncton. And that's when I first met Norma.

I had to hide my shock. She wasn't a little eleven-year-old girl. She was a tiny eighty-year-old woman, with shriveled limbs, an emaciated face, and enormous staring eyes. She moved with the effort of an arthritis victim. When she spoke, it was in a barely audible whisper you had to get close just to hear. But in spirit she was a lovely, lively young girl, upbeat and happy to see a visitor.

Her parents were both fine, uncomplicated, and uncomplaining people who were obviously hurting inside and trying to bear up under the strain.

The situation was heartbreaking, and lack of money made it worse. The family was on welfare. There were no jobs this far out in the country, and the father couldn't leave his family to find work elsewhere. To help feed his family, Mr. Gallant shot one moose every two years, the maximum the local authorities allowed. The meat didn't last for two years, but he'd never even thought about sidestepping the hunting limit to shoot a moose every year. "That would be wrong," he said. So his wife made do with their meager income, which afforded few treats for her dying child.

"What does Norma really like to eat or drink?" I asked. Mrs. Gallant said that Norma loved Mountain Dew soda. They could afford only four cans per month, so sips of her favorite drink were a wonderful luxury.

Moncton was an area of extreme cold—sometimes 30 below zero, and walking just 100 yards outside could cause frostbite or even death.

"How," I asked, "do you stay warm in this house?"

"We don't," was the reply. "Norma really feels the cold," said her mom, "and we just can't heat the house enough to keep her warm in winter."

To this day, when I think of these good people, I get emotional.

As I wrote my story back in New Jersey, my eyes teared up. This little girl would die happy if she could just stay warm and sip some cans of Mountain Dew. It was so little to ask for. I planned to call the Mountain Dew company after the story ran and suggest they send some cases to Norma for promotional purposes.

But I didn't have to. Gene Pope read my story, and before we even went to press, he called me into his office. No words of praise for my prose, but something even better. "We have to do something for this kid," he said. "How about an appeal for money to our readers?" That, of course, wasn't a question but an order.

We started an appeal for little Norma Gallant—and over the next few months we raised more than $35,000. Enough to build a really warm little house right in the town of Moncton . . . and to buy an unlimited supply of Mountain Dew. Gene's idea was to print the name of every single donor, even the kids who sent in 50 cents, and so we ran pages of names with amounts. The total grew and grew.

Our readers loved the idea so much that we kept running "Money Appeals" into the '80s—raising hundreds of thousands of dollars for many poor, unfortunate children. Gene *loved* these stories. He could be a ruthless employer, but he was a soft touch for people, especially children, in real trouble.

About a month after the first story on Norma ran, a team at America's National Institutes of Health (NIH), in Bethesda, Maryland, called me and offered to examine her. There was little chance they could reverse the damage, they said, but they might learn something that might help other children. The only hitch—they couldn't pay Norma's travel expenses. The *Enquirer* covered the cost. We seldom saw Gene excited, but this got him smiling. We were finally making a move away from the gore days.

Norma and her mom were to fly to the NIH, and I knew I needed help looking after them. The *Enquirer* allowed me to take Jane and Douglas along, and they provided me essential emotional support.

Douglas, at sixteen months of age surely the youngest journalist ever, really made a difference. By this time, Norma could no longer walk, but when she saw our son, she really lit up. Douglas would toddle toward her bed and "talk" to her as if she were a healthy, normal girl, and Norma would pat him on the head like an older sister—or, sadly, like an eleven-year-old grandmother. We have some memorable pictures of them together.

We spent a week at Bethesda, and the medical staff looked after Norma like she was their own. Even as they took blood, prodded, and probed, they treated her like a little princess and kept her smiling.

The doctors' pessimistic predictions were correct. They could do nothing but thank Norma and Mrs. Gallant for helping in the fight for a cure.

Then it was back to Moncton. Somehow, the family seemed happier. The trip had been an adventure for Norma and her mother. Money from *Enquirer* readers kept flowing in, and *Enquirer* lawyers set up a trust fund with a local bank manager as trustee. Now Norma could have all the food and Mountain Dew she wanted. It was spring, so cold was no longer a problem, and the new house would be finished by the end of the next year.

On one visit in the fall of 1968, snow had come early, and I saw that Mr. Gallant had planted a small tree in his yard, its thin trunk sticking out of a 5-foot snowdrift. He said, "We've picked out a nice spot to bury Norma when she goes. I need the tree to mark the place so I can dig down through the snow and find the place for her grave."

Try writing that story without tears in your eyes.

Norma didn't make it to the new house.

Football fans remember January 12, 1969, as the day of Super Bowl III, when Joe Namath took his New York Jets to a dazzling 16–7 victory over the favored Baltimore Colts. I remember it as the day of Norma's funeral. I'll never forget standing on frozen, crunchy Canadian snow, saying good-bye to that brave little girl who had touched the hearts of so many *Enquirer* readers.

The series about Norma wasn't just a tearjerker. By sending money or even prayers and good wishes to Norma's family, readers got that inner glow that comes from good deeds and generosity. Reading about the difficulties of the Gallant family and their simple decency and honesty also put their own problems in perspective.

Gene had a real gift for understanding the kind of stories that touched our readers. By the '70s and '80s, we had this formula down to a science, a balanced combination of stories about celebrities, useful medical information, and tales about heroic everyday people. Now that the cult of celebrity has taken over, I don't see any publication using our simple but powerful approach of giving readers stories that make a difference to their lives.

Another *Enquirer* innovation of the late 1960s was attention to television. It may sound stupid, but at that time, when TV was decried by intellectuals, newspapers, and magazines as "the boob tube" and a "vast wasteland," this attitude was understandable. For the first time, newspapers and magazines were beginning to lose their position as the premier advertising medium. Companies were realizing they could sell their refrigerators, stoves, soap, and beer more efficiently using the boob tube. And publishers fought back, criticizing television every chance they got.

Their response created a vacuum for us. We found that Lucille Ball on the cover sold better than John Wayne. Mary Tyler Moore was bigger than Doris Day. This sounds so obvious these days, but at that time all the fan mags were still focusing on movie stars. *TV Guide*, of course, ran television stars on the cover, but they didn't do *Enquirer*-type stories.

With the combination of TV covers, better stories, and brilliant marketing in stores, the circulation figures started to creep up. GP didn't reveal the actual sales numbers, but we knew they were good—and editorial was humming with new energy and a budget that allowed for high salaries and generous stringer payments.

Job security was still an oxymoron. Whenever editors invited colleagues' families over for a barbecue or a party, the invitation always included the phrase "if we're still here." That wasn't a joke. We really meant it. Editors and writers—multiple dozens of them—came and went in a blur of faces.

Every single Friday all the editorial staff kept watch on Nat Chrzan's office. If anyone was called into that office after lunch, we knew there was a 50–50 chance he or she would be gone. At 4 P.M., if your name hadn't been called, you breathed a sigh of relief and knew you were safe . . . for one more week.

It was brutal at times—but GP's remaining staff was highly paid and becoming more and more efficient and elite as the months and years passed. I guess the Boss figured he had to go through hundreds of journalists to get the dozen or so key personnel he needed to reach his dream goal. And the survivors kept making our team stronger and stronger.

In 1970 Jane and I made a *major* decision. We bought a car, a new Ford Maverick, for $2,000 because we were beginning to realize that—Pope willing—America was becoming our new country.

That same year, my young family again helped me cover a story, one that became the *Enquirer*'s first international exclusive.

The incredible, irrepressible, but doomed Judy Garland died on June 22, 1969, after taking an overdose of sleeping pills in London. Not long before, Judy had married her fifth husband, British showbiz executive Mickey Deans, now her widower.

Judy's body was flown to a New York funeral chapel. On June 26 and 27, more than 20,000 fans filed past her coffin to pay their final respects. Then, after a twenty-minute funeral service with a eulogy by famed actor James Mason, Judy's body was moved to upscale Ferncliff Cemetery in Ardsley, New York. There her casket was placed into a temporary crypt, basically a hole in a wall, awaiting her family's decision on a suitable last resting place for the beloved superstar.

In October, Deans wrote a touching account for *Look* magazine: "I decided she would be buried in a quiet peaceful cemetery outside

New York. . . . She was buried with all the jewelry she wore at our wedding."

Months later, more than a year after Judy's death, I received a telephone call from a source who refused to leave his name. The message: Judy Garland has still not been buried.

I checked the old clippings on Judy's death and went in to see our executive editor, who was very excited by this tip. We still had no staff reporters, so he sent me and a photographer out to the cemetery to investigate.

In a situation like this, the last thing you want to do is to alert the cemetery officials. Maybe they'd been the source of the telephone tip, but maybe not, so I couldn't take the chance they'd try to cover up the fact that Judy had been forgotten.

I went to Ferncliff posing as a bereaved son of someone who had just died, accompanied by Jane and Douglas, now a journalistic veteran at age three. The family was a great cover. The photographer waited out of sight, until I knew whether we needed him.

We respectfully entered the main building and, when approached by an attendant, asked about the temporary crypts. He led us to a plain wall in the basement of the mausoleum with plain squares of marble arranged in three long rows. The squares, each with its own plastic nametag, marked the crypts.

The attendant was apologetic: "It doesn't look like much, but remember, the loved ones are only there for a few days or weeks. Just until the family decides on the permanent resting place."

After he left, we slowly walked along the wall, staring at each marble block. In moments, my eye stopped on one square in the middle row. Near the top of the square was a 3-inch plastic name tag that read JUDY GARLAND DEANS. My heart nearly stopped. I touched the marble—and it wobbled enough for me to fear it might fall out.

Behind this unstable slab of stone, just inches away, lay one of the world's greatest performers, a star who'd electrified audiences and moviegoers all over the world. In life, she had wanted to go "over the rainbow" but, in death, she hadn't even been given the respect of a proper burial.

We now knew the anonymous tip was true, and we had to find out why no one had buried Judy. But first, we *had* to get a photo, to show the world evidence of this travesty.

The problem was that the crypts were in a long, straight hallway. If anyone walked around the corner unexpectedly, they'd immediately see us shooting. We needed at least three or four minutes to make sure we got good photos.

I placed Jane and Douglas as lookouts at the corner, where danger might lurk. "If you see anyone coming, just whistle," I said. Jane gave me a "how-stupid-are-you?" look. "Iain, you *know* I can't whistle," she said. Jane decided that if she saw anyone coming she'd send Douglas running down toward us. The clatter of his feet on the marble floor would alert us.

I told my photographer the plan, and he sneaked his equipment down into the basement. He shot the crypt, the wall, and the name tag a dozen times, then said, "I need something with more action. Just stand there and point to the crypt." So I did.

Now that the story and photo were in the bag, I approached the top executives of the cemetery. They reluctantly admitted that there were still no plans to bury Judy. Their vice president told me that temporary crypts were free for sixty days, after which the charge was $20 per month. He added, "It's very unusual for anyone to leave a body in a temporary crypt for as long as a year."

The Ferncliff execs told me that visitors came to Judy's crypt daily. Flowers arrived from all over the world, but there was no place to put them near the crypt. A cemetery employee confided, "Many of Judy's fans are quite upset . . . they expect something more dignified for Judy."

The fans may have visited faithfully, but the family didn't. The cemetery employees said it had been months since they'd seen Mickey Deans or any of Judy's children—Liza, who was twenty-four, Lorna, fifteen, or Joseph, thirteen. In February 1970, Liza Minnelli was performing at New York's Waldorf-Astoria hotel. Deans had called Ferncliff to say they would visit, but according to a senior employee, "Something must have come up because they didn't come." This was eight months after Judy's death.

Our front-page story was headlined JUDY GARLAND IS STILL NOT BURIED. The photo of me pointing at her crypt dominated the cover. That issue created an international furor. Press from all around the globe called us, magazines bought reprint rights to our words and photos, and both Mickey Deans and Liza Minnelli were bombarded with calls from reporters.

My family in Scotland was pleased to see the story, with a huge byline and an even bigger picture of me pointing at the crypt, in Britain's popular *Reveille* magazine. I never got so much attention when I worked there!

Besides bringing smiles to the Calders back home, this story had two results.

First, Mickey Deans and Liza Minnelli issued a super-fast response claiming that, of course, they had plans for Judy's permanent resting place. (Liza's people pointed out that she would have needed a court order to bury her mom.) Shortly afterward they kept their vow. That gave me a glow of satisfaction. I wasn't curing cancer, but I did help Judy Garland get a proper burial.

Second, the *Enquirer* had broken a big international exclusive for the first time. The story rocked America and was reprinted around the world, picked up by international media with full credit. Suddenly, other journalists were paying attention to this emerging editorial powerhouse.

BREAKING INTO
THE SUPERMARKETS

Question: Which of the following helped the *National Enquirer* break into supermarkets in the 1960s and early '70s?

- President Nixon
- Former Vice President Hubert Humphrey
- Senator Robert Dole
- Vice President Spiro Agnew
- Congresswoman Shirley Chisholm
- Secretary of Defense Melvin Laird
- Joan Crawford
- Michael Caine
- Lorne Greene
- Jayne Mansfield
- NBC anchorman Chet Huntley
- Tony Randall
- Lord Litchfield, cousin of Queen Elizabeth II

Answer: All of the above.

In the mid-sixties, when the *Enquirer* was still in its gore-and-crime period, circulation peaked and started to decline. In 1965, we boasted circulation of 1 million (which in reality was probably closer to 800,000 or 900,000). But, as mentioned earlier, by 1967 circulation was down to 700,000, or even less, per week. City folks were moving to the suburbs, and supermarkets were emerging as the place to get groceries. Newsstands and little stores began to fail—and with them went our sales.

This was bad news *and* good news. The sales slide was bad, but it sparked the Great Idea—selling the *Enquirer* in supermarkets. Everyone I ever spoke with, including Gene, always credited the original idea to GP. Everyone except the amazing Henry Dormann, who can recall the exact moment it all began.

Henry and Gene were dining at Gene's favorite New Jersey restaurant, The Opera, not far from his home in Englewood Cliffs.

Henry had been friends with Gene since the 1950s and had even written a column for the early *Enquirer*. Born on a humble Erie Railroad barge during the Depression, he now ran a successful public relations company in New York. Even as a young man, he'd become famous in Manhattan for his political connections, and when Gene asked him to write a political column for the then *New York Enquirer*, Henry agreed.

Henry told me later: "I knew almost nothing about New York political gossip, but I went to Mayor Robert Wagner, and each week he gave me the inside story of what was going on. The column, under the name Joe Grant, gave Wagner a forum to write what he wanted in secret, I had a great column, and *Enquirer* readers got many scoops that beat out the New York dailies."

Among *Enquirer* staffers, Henry was known simply as "Mr. Fixit." In later years, Gene paid Henry $1 million per year plus unlimited expenses for executing the occasional task—usually a task that appeared virtually impossible.

This was a man Gene listened to—and at The Opera restaurant early in 1967, GP was bemoaning the loss in circulation. Recalls Henry, "It suddenly struck me. Go where the consumers are going, whether in the cities or in the suburbs. Sell in supermarkets."

Odd as it seems now, this was a wild idea—"thinking outside the box," in today's phrase. At that time *TV Guide*, *Woman's Day*, and *Family Circle* were the only magazines at checkout counters—*TV Guide* because it was small in size and a huge seller, the other two because they'd been started by the supermarket industry. In some markets you might also find *Good Housekeeping* and *Reader's Digest*, but that was it.

Gene loved the idea of breaking into supermarkets—but how?

Over that dinner Gene and Henry worked out a rough blueprint of a marketing strategy that would change the face of American journalism—and create the modern checkout counter, postered by magazine covers that make millions for supermarkets each year.

To anyone else, the prospect of selling the *Enquirer* in supermarkets must have looked bleak to impossible. Although it was changing, this was still a sleazy weekly filled with gore. Even worse, only a few months earlier the paper had headlined a story about mouse and rat droppings in stores owned by A&P, the premier supermarket chain. Now A&P was going to sell the paper in these same stores? *Sure.*

Here was Gene Pope's genius. When he believed in an idea, he was like a freight train. He forged ahead with a drive and optimism that inspired everyone around him with the same passion. When Gene stated a fact, he expected everyone to accept it. People who doubted him didn't last long.

When you know you're right all the time and you usually turn out to be wrong, that's the mark of a buffoon. When you know you're right and turn out to *be* right, time after time, that's the mark of a genius. Many times, from the mid-sixties until his death in 1988, Gene gambled his company on what seemed to be perilous decisions. But on the big things he was always right, a trait that turned most of his executives into zealots.

Gene was already in the process of making enormous changes in the paper's editorial tone. But selling in supermarkets . . . Where do you start?

First, Gene named Henry Dormann chairman of the board of the *Enquirer.*

That done, Dormann went to a friend, none other than former United States Vice President Hubert Humphrey, who directed him to the main political lobbyist for supermarkets. The lobbyist was less than thrilled to help a sleazy weekly but, to please LBJ's vice president, he suggested that Gene talk to marketing consultant Bob Foley, who had the best contacts in the business.

Foley met with Gene and said the task was nearly impossible, but after Gene offered him a contract for $100,000 a year, Foley agreed to give it a try. The best way to get accepted, said Foley, was to attend the big annual supermarket conference. All the owners, chief executives, and top bananas attended, where they were courted, cosseted, and coddled by all the big consumer-product firms, such as Coke, Kraft, and Procter & Gamble. But, Foley warned, "It might take years to get an invitation to attend."

Gene just smiled, and Henry Dormann swung into action. The first priority was to make the *Enquirer* name known. For the next convention, Henry persuaded Jayne Mansfield, Hollywood's hottest blonde after Marilyn Monroe died, to help out. Dressed in a low-cut gown, Jayne sashayed into the convention hall uninvited—as if anyone would stop her—and strolled past thousands of conventioneers and up the steps to the platform.

Remembers Henry, "There was a bald-headed chairman who hated us and he just stared, bug-eyed, as Jayne approached. She was holding a copy of the *Enquirer* and walked right up to him. The whole room was in shock as she handed over the copy to the stunned man, flashed her million-watt smile, and purred into the microphone, 'Here's your personal delivery of the *National Enquirer.*' Then she walked out."

The chairman might have been speechless, but the room erupted in a great roar.

Less than a year later, Foley called to say that the conference was looking for a big-name speaker. "Right up our alley," said Gene.

One phone call to Dormann and the next keynote speaker at the supermarket conference was . . . Vice President Spiro Agnew. Agnew not only gave a speech, but he also held an informal party afterward. Naturally, if you wanted an invitation, you had to ask the *National Enquirer.* "After that," said Gene, "we *ran* the conference." A proud, but mildly exaggerated, boast.

One year, when the conference was in Washington, D.C., Dormann concocted a special treat for the twenty or so conference board members—a visit to President Nixon's White House with a special domestic policy briefing by Vice President Agnew, Treasury Secretary Bill Simon, and Secretary of Defense Melvin Laird. When the group left the briefing, they were met by an official photographer for individual photo sessions.

Dormann recalls, "By this time, most of the supermarket chiefs were on our side. One holdout had always been Schnuck Markets in Kansas. Don Schnuck always told me, 'You'll never get into my stores.' After being photographed in the White House, Don told me, 'Henry, you finally win. The *Enquirer* gets in.'"

Between 1968 and the early '70s, we were sewing up the upper level of supermarket executives. But we had to do the same thing in the trenches.

Our consultant Bob Foley introduced Gene to Bill Hall, vice president of the huge Kroger food chain. Hall, making just over $21,000 per year, was in charge of buying all non-food items. He became our first executive vice president at a salary of $80,000. Hall's job was to build sales forces all over the country that would persuade stores to accept the *Enquirer*.

His most inspired choice as lieutenant was Neil Carey, who came aboard in 1968 and was soon vice president, sales. Neil worked with us for nearly thirty years and became probably the best-known, most popular business executive working with the supermarket chiefs, so much so that he was often invited to their family weddings and funerals.

With an okay from the supermarket bosses, Neil and his guys went store to store, persuading often skeptical managers and regional bosses to give us a chance. Putting *Enquirer* pedestal stands in stores, they'd guarantee that at least 50 percent of the papers would sell, bringing in a big profit. If we *didn't* sell half the papers each week, we'd pay the store the difference.

Neil says, "As soon as we put the *Enquirer* in these stores, they'd sell like hotcakes. We never once had to pay a guarantee."

Once the pedestal racks were a success, the *Enquirer* began to get permission to build racks for the checkout counters. We had to pay for the whole thing, but Neil Carey comments, "It was just the cost of doing business."

This is where Gene's genius arose again. All of this cost several millions, more money than he had, so he went into hock with banks all the time. Friends and family told him he was crazy, that he'd go bankrupt, but he kept going, wildly spending money that wasn't there.

Gene always wanted an edge, something to make us stand out from the crowd.

As the sales force went out on its messianic mission of placing the *Enquirer* in every supermarket and chain store around the United States, Henry Dormann put together an amazing video to show regional managers and decision-makers. If executives kissed us off as second-rate, our guys would show them this video—and their eyes would pop.

It was an endorsement message from the most influential people in the country. Hosted by Chet Huntley, co-anchor with David Brinkley of the *NBC Nightly News*, the video featured Senator Bob Dole; Shirley Chisholm, the charismatic African-American U.S. congresswoman; Joan Crawford, legendary movie star and board member of Pepsi; and Merv Griffin, talk-show host and one of the best-known television personalities. They and others of similar stature all talked about the *Enquirer* in glowing terms.

When, along with other editors in the newsroom, I first saw that video, we were all mesmerized and sky-high with enthusiasm. If GP could get these big names to endorse us, who knew what other miracles lay ahead?

We'd dazzled the supermarket guys with America's top politicians. Now we were going to top ourselves, with an array of Hollywood celebrities. Gene called me and said, "Let's give a great Hollywood party."

I turned to Henry Gris, the most unlikely *Enquirer* reporter you could imagine. A tall, urbane, imperious-looking gentleman of indeterminate age, Henry had an aristocratic air developed over years of running news bureaus in Europe for the United Press International wire service. Henry had friends among Hollywood royalty, both old and new. On this Hollywood party assignment, he was *brilliant*.

The first *Enquirer* celebrity FMI (Food Marketing Institute) convention, in 1973, was a smash hit in Los Angeles. We had a big crowd of celebs, including Tony Randall and Jack Klugman from the TV hit *The Odd Couple*, Michael Caine, Cesar Romero, Glenn Ford, Anne Francis, Loretta ("Hot Lips") Swit from *M*A*S*H*, *Bonanza*'s Lorne Greene, and a whole host of others.

Neil Carey, now running our sales force, was ecstatic: "The supermarket chiefs were like little kids in a candy store. In these days, some of them were quite unsophisticated. They had built little stores into multi-million-dollar empires, but they were still plain, hard-working, regular guys—and they were awed by these stars they'd only seen on TV or in films."

As always, GP wanted more. The following year, the convention was in Las Vegas, a tougher sell since many of the celebs would have to travel from L.A. We came up with the idea of an awards ceremony—we'd invent an award for *anybody* who would agree to attend. *And* we snagged Jerry Lewis as our master of ceremonies. The *Enquirer's* second party, in October 1974 at the MGM Grand in Las Vegas, was an even bigger hit than the first.

The same group from L.A. came, plus Johnny "Tarzan" Weissmuller, Connie Stevens, Shirley Jones, Ernest Borgnine, Raquel Welch, Hugh O'Brian, plus dozens of others. We also had an English blueblood to add some class—Patrick, earl of Litchfield, first cousin to Queen Elizabeth II. Surprisingly, the evening's biggest hits were Jeane Dixon, then America's most famous psychic, and Charo, the curvy coochie-coochie girl, who spent the evening perched on the knees of those old supermarket kings and kissing them on their bald spots, to the delight of the crowd.

We had thirty-five genuine celebrities; maybe names that don't create excitement now, but at the time they were *big*. We gave the supermarket bosses' wives autograph books and silver pens, and they went *mad*, gathering as many signatures as they could, giggling like teenagers.

Another smash hit. The place was wild. Two other lavish parties were being hosted on the same floor of the hotel at the same time. One, I think, was Coca-Cola, and they were doing their best to compete against us. No chance. Most of their guests abandoned their parties to "crash" ours and see the stars.

Our only problem was that we ended up with *too many* celebrities. We'd expected twenty to attend and had had twenty-five awards made. Not enough. How were we going to keep from disappointing someone? Henry presented the awards, and he was brilliant. He'd announce the celebrity's name, offer congratulations and the award, then immediately take *back* the award, whispering, "We didn't have time to inscribe it properly. We'll do that later and send it to you." Then he'd hand the same statuette to the next star.

Gene didn't attend either party, because he refused to travel more than 30 miles from his home. As with everything else, he'd pushed everyone to achieve beyond their capabilities in organizing these parties. His only comment to me when we returned was, "Heard it went okay."

Neil Carey was more enthusiastic. He recently told me, "Those two celebrity nights really helped put us on the supermarket map. Twenty-five years later, major chain executives and owners still talked about them."

They had cost the *Enquirer* big, *major* bucks and used literally hundreds of hours of editorial time. But Pope knew that key positions in supermarkets were vital to our success—and keeping the store bosses happy was worth almost anything.

SUNNY DAYS AHEAD

Jane and I loved our new life in the States. We were just half an hour by taxi from New York City, and from time to time we were able to have dinner and see a Broadway show there. It was the late '60s, I was making well over $20,000 a year, more than many senior reporters on the *New York Times*, and I really enjoyed my job.

We liked our new surroundings, so when our apartment lease was almost up, we began looking at houses in some of the beautiful small towns nearby. We found a small house that was within our budget and a half-hour's drive to the office. It had a little garden and a small picket fence, and it was within walking distance of the town center.

I asked my boss, editor Nat Chrzan, who lived nearby, about the area. His response: "The area is great, but don't buy; there might be an announcement. We may be moving."

So Jane and I signed a new apartment lease and waited for the big news.

We got it in a major meeting of all staff with GP. Several years earlier, he'd moved our printing plant from New Jersey to Florida, and now Gene began the meeting by telling us that the printing plant people were so happy in Florida, especially in winter, and maybe—just maybe—we should be thinking of moving to the Sunshine State.

Clearly Gene wanted to move south but was playing it cool because he needed to find out how many employees would follow him.

If he lost half his editorial staff, the paper's expansion would be set back for years. He told us that *if*, emphasizing *if*, we moved, it wouldn't be for a year or two.

The Boss's reasons all sounded good to us. Barney Giambalvo added another, one that applied only to GP: As the *Enquirer* grew nationally, Gene wanted to shake off any rumors about Mob links. In Florida, "connected" people wouldn't just drop in at his office.

Whatever his reasons, Gene needn't have worried about our reaction. It sounded like a great adventure. At that time, most workers in Florida were paid so little that they grumbled about being paid in sunshine. The *Enquirer* would be paying top New York salaries, so our lifestyles should be great.

That was in the fall of 1970. When Gene learned that most of the staff would follow him, his "one to two years" turned into nine months, and the *Enquirer* moved to Florida by June 1971. For Bill Dick and me, it was no big deal. After crossing the Atlantic, relocating to Florida was *nothing*.

The company was generous. It paid each family for a week's advance trip to find a place to live, then picked up six weeks of motel bills when we arrived. Our family's checkout trip was in May. For Scots like us, who thought 80 degrees was a Sahara heat wave, it was like stepping into a sauna going full-blast. The three of us drove around drinking gallons of water and soda each hour. Jane and I kept telling ourselves, "It'll be great in winter—there's no snow." In retrospect, it was the best-ever move, but it did take some acclimatization.

On returning to New Jersey, we immediately sold our little Ford with no air-conditioning and bought a big red Buick Skylark with an eight-cylinder engine that seemed to zoom from zero to 100 in two seconds flat. Most important, it had igloo-strength air-conditioning.

As the date of the move to Florida approached, our excitement grew, but the whole thing was marred by one of the most stupid, cruel incidents in *Enquirer* history.

Articles editor Robert Johnson had joined us from Los Angeles, and his wife had adjusted to the East Coast, although she hated it. When word of the Florida move broke, Bob's wife refused to go. If

Bob went to Florida, the marriage was over and she was returning to Los Angeles.

Bob made his choice: His marriage was over. His car and remaining furniture were shipped down to Florida with the belongings of all the other *Enquirer* employees. On our last day in New Jersey, Bob joined Bill Dick, myself, and another editor for lunch at a famous local restaurant called Sid Allen's, a sometime haunt of Frank Sinatra's. We helped ourselves to some of their signature large martinis, and we were all in good spirits as we left to pick up our families to head to the airport.

Three of us had airline tickets in our pockets, but Bob, a bit surprised, said he hadn't gotten his yet. A taxi dropped him back at the *Enquirer* office while the rest of us went home, calling out, "See you at the airport!"

At LaGuardia, we saw many *Enquirer* families—but no Bob Johnson.

Then one of the writers approached us, ashen-faced. "Have you heard about Bob?" he asked. We shook our heads, and he dropped the bad news.

When Bob had returned to the office after lunch, he breezed into the office of executive editor Mel Snyder and said, "You forgot to give me my plane ticket." Mel asked Bob to sit down and then announced, "You're not going. You've been fired."

Johnson almost collapsed. He'd dumped his wife for Florida and now he wasn't going?

Why hadn't Mel Snyder told the poor man earlier? Mel was a nice man with a good heart, and when asked this question years later, his only excuse was, "I could hardly bear telling him the news. I kept putting it off . . ."

The result? A dispirited, disillusioned group set off to Florida. If our company had *wanted* to destroy employee morale, it couldn't have done a better job.

Life at the *Enquirer* went on, however, and soon grew sunnier in many ways. Florida was another world. First and foremost, it was hot and humid. Walking 30 yards from your air-conditioned car to your air-conditioned office, you could sweat half a gallon and look like you had fallen into a swimming pool. But at least there *were* swimming pools—nearly all our well-paid employees bought houses with pools or rented apartments in complexes with huge, sparkling, blue-water pools.

Our brand-new office was so spacious and bright you felt good just walking in. We were in the little redneck town of Lantana in the middle of ritzy Palm Beach County. Why? Because Gene had bought land on the Atlantic Ocean and was building an impressive 12,000-square-foot house. Gene told his executives to find land to build new offices no more than four minutes' drive away. They found a site. When Gene tested the distance in his car, it took him five minutes . . . so back to the drawing board.

Lantana was it. The only problem, a minor one, was that we were right next to a railroad track, and a few times a day the roar of the train stopped all conversation. On the track side of the building, you could hardly hear yourself think. But that was no problem for Gene in his spacious, thick-carpeted, teak-paneled personal office. He liked trains and the noises they made. He even had a huge model train set in the basement of his home.

Lantana was a quiet, working-class community, and the social center for a large Finnish population who'd congregated in the central part of Palm Beach County. Many years earlier, the city fathers had passed a law forbidding non-whites to live in town. It was clearly unconstitutional and anathema to later Florida imports like us. The council decided to vote on rescinding the law, but the change did not pass. But when recently asked if the law was still on the books, a council spokesman claimed it had later been rescinded. He couldn't pinpoint the date.

This was our new home, the launching pad for the editorial rocket ship that would soar to new circulation heights.

Florida seemed to free Gene. In previous offices, he had done most of his editorial work behind closed doors. In Lantana, the newsroom was open and all offices (except his) had glass walls, so we saw the Boss walking around the office all the time. It didn't stop the power that seemed to waft from him or the fear that he engendered. But the new visibility allowed him to gain respect from his people, as they saw the enormous work and energy he poured into the dream that was rapidly coming to reality.

One thing I never understood: Here was this freight-train publisher running over employees who didn't produce—he was a man with a manic mission to be the biggest and the best. Yet our editorial department, while hardworking, ran on hours more like a bank or insurance company.

Remember that in Britain, Bill Dick and I had worked in news organizations where fanatically competitive reporters and editors would work long, long hours and then go to the pub and talk about the long, long hours. In Lantana, as in New Jersey, most of us worked 9 A.M. to 5 P.M. with weekends off. Our chief articles editor, Selig Adler, the former managing editor of New York's *Daily Mirror*, came in at 8 A.M. and, at about ten minutes to four, would start preparing to leave. The Dapper Dan of Lantana, Selig wore expensive, stylish, colorful clothes—and just before 4 o'clock he'd put on his perfectly tailored jacket, straighten his collar, and then strike out. You could set your watch to his disappearing through the door.

I just shrugged and accepted that this was the *Enquirer* way, never for a moment anticipating that soon I'd be able to change it . . . losing whatever popularity I had in the process.

Bill and I were fierce competitors in the office, but we were also drinking buddies and best friends. Our wives, Jane and Margaret, were also absolute best friends, filling our new lives in Florida with many happy domestic memories.

After work we'd often go for a drink and talk about how the paper had incredible potential, but the system was creaky and needed a transformation. We fell into being an informal team and gave our suggestions jointly to GP. New proposals could be dangerous. If they were too boring or too wild, Gene was liable to think, "These guys are really crazy," and the predictable consequence would be—two unemployed Scots.

But you only live once, we reminded ourselves, and Bill and I made two suggestions that were pretty obvious, but radical at the time.

1. AEs (articles editors) were bogged down by paperwork and too many phone calls. We kept payment records, logged stories coming in and out, typed out payment cards for accounting, and fielded all kinds of queries from readers and freelancers. Why pay big salaries to do clerical work? Instead we needed editorial assistants.

2. We needed staff reporters. *Badly*. Now that the *Enquirer* was going after major stories, we needed brilliant investigative reporters who would break major exclusives. Part-time stringers would always be necessary, but staff reporters were needed to break into the big time.

Bill and I didn't consider the millions of dollars needed to enact our plan. Apparently neither did Gene because, almost immediately, he okayed both ideas. And, quite quickly, they catapulted the paper into a new dimension.

The articles editors immediately hired assistants to free up more time for creative work. And we began to bring in reporters on four-week tryouts. Most of the tryouts bombed out for many reasons, but some survived. We started hiring bright-eyed, bushy-tailed journalists who were destined to become legends in the tabloid world. Most were British or Australian because, in those early days, top Americans still shunned the *Enquirer*.

Our hard work and ideas paid off for Bill and me. In November 1972 GP called us both into his office.

"You two are my best editors," he announced. "I'm going to promote you, hand you titles to show everyone you *are* the best, and give you big raises."

Bill and I smiled, thanked Mr. Pope, and just sat there.

"Anything else?" he asked.

Since I figured he couldn't be handing out titles and a lot more cash without expecting something in return, I timidly ventured, "Do the jobs come with more responsibility?"

GP sat back as if he had never considered the possibility and responded, "Do you *want* more responsibility?"

Bill nodded vigorously and asked, "Could Iain and I have a chance to talk it over tonight and get back to you with a plan tomorrow?"

When GP agreed, we walked out of his office, out of the building, and headed straight for the nearest pub.

For four hours we drank and talked, talked and drank. Tons of ideas poured out—ideas for streamlining the *Enquirer*'s news-gathering and sharpening the content. The next day Gene okayed our suggestions. Bill and I had twin glass offices on the news floor, and we were pretty much running the news-gathering department. I'm not sure what our nominal boss, executive editor Mel Snyder, thought of the move. It made him dispensable and, in fact, within a year he was gone.

During my time editing the *Enquirer*, we got hundreds of letters *every month* from sick people whose lives had been either saved or improved through our stories. Like Harvey Quick, aged seventy-three, of St. Petersburg, whose doctor had scheduled a foot amputation because of a severe bone infection that wouldn't heal. We ran a story about a new drug that worked where other antibiotics had failed. Mr. Quick showed the story to his doctor, who tried the new medicine. It worked, and his foot was saved.

In June 1991, Sidney Mobell told us we actually saved his life. Mobell, a San Francisco jewelry designer, had weak blood vessels in his brain, and at any moment, one could burst, killing or crippling him. Doctors had no treatment or operation to recommend and told him he was living on borrowed time. Then his wife read the *Enquirer* and learned about a new technique being developed at Stanford University. Mobell contacted the Stanford researcher, who performed an operation that was 100 percent successful. And Mobell wrote: "Thank you, thank you, *Enquirer*."

The *Enquirer*'s groundbreaking medical coverage had actually started long before most general-interest publications bothered with such stories. Our first full-scale mission began as a rather ordinary lead, but Gene's editorial genius turned it into dozens of stories and the beginning of a whole new area of coverage.

In the early '70s, at one of our weekly editorial meetings, articles editor Alan Markfield submitted a lead about a new treatment for cancer. In lab experiments and human trials, doctors had boosted the body's natural immune system to overcome the malignant cells. A drug called bacillus calmette-guerin (BCG) worked with white blood cells to attack cancer cells—with dramatic, promising results.

Within the next few weeks, the National Cancer Institute (NCI), the largest federal research institute, would hold a major conference to present research on BCG. Researchers from all over the world would convene at NCI's Maryland headquarters to share ideas and experiences with colleagues.

Gene's gut told him this was *big*—and Alan Markfield's ideas were too small. Alan wanted to handle this as an ordinary news story and just send a couple of reporters to interview a few doctors.

Gene's instincts were great, but he didn't know quite how to tackle this. He turned to his assembled editors: "This is a major story, so how do we handle it?"

I happened to be the first articles editor to open my mouth. I suggested that Markfield take a big team of reporters to the conference and interview every single researcher they could get their hands on. Get details of the most promising experiments and the results, plus case histories of cancer patients whose lives had been saved. Then we follow a few selected doctors home—and get more great stories of their cures and hopes for the future.

Pope's response: "Great. You've got the story." I wanted to say, It isn't *my* story, it's Alan's! But with Mr. Pope you just said, "Yes, Mr. Pope."

Fortunately, Alan was relieved to get the help, so I put together the *Enquirer*'s first editorial mass attack. GP had made this a priority, so I gathered together seven out of the dozen staff reporters, and off we went to Maryland.

We booked most of one floor of a big hotel and set up a war room in one of the meeting rooms, installing a bank of new telephone lines. Piling into our cars, we headed for the National Cancer Institute in a motorcade longer than the president's—eight cars.

The Institute had set up a special desk to distribute credentials to the 160 doctors expected and to the reporters covering the event. I walked up to the woman handling the distribution and asked for press credentials for the *National Enquirer* team. With a friendly smile, the young lady asked how many we needed. When I said, "Eight," she just about fell off her chair.

"*Eight!*" she spluttered. "You must be kidding!" All the thousands of other media outlets throughout the world, including the networks, UPI, Associated Press, the *New York Times*, and the *Washington Post*, had sent a grand total of seven reporters combined. No wonder she was shocked. "I'm not kidding," I said. "We need eight press passes."

So eight it was.

Back at the hotel, we assembled in the war room for a strategy session. I told my guys that they had to be all over that conference like a cheap suit. I wanted an interview with every single doctor there. In the end, we may have missed a couple who left early. Doctors had come from the United States, Great Britain, France, Germany, Switzerland, Japan, and all over the globe. We buttonholed them after meetings, in lobbies, on elevators, wherever we found them. If we could, we wined and dined them with steak, lobster, champagne, and other consumables a lab doc's salary wouldn't cover. BCG might have been the major topic of this conference, but the *National Enquirer* came in a close second.

The conference lasted three days, with several sessions each day; at least one of our reporters attended each and every session. There was one closed session, barred to the press. Of course, we were at that one too, because Bill Burt and Bob Smith, two canny Scots, bluffed their way in. I doubt they even understood the discussion, but guys like that just don't like being told they *can't* go somewhere or do something.

We ended up with dozens of great stories about real-life "no hope" cancer sufferers who'd won a new chance at life through this treatment. As the conference broke up, we made arrangements with several of the major foreign doctors to visit them in their own countries, to follow up on their patients and gather more detail. In the weeks after the conference, *Enquirer* reporters traveled to research labs in Britain, France, Germany, Switzerland, and Canada, plus various parts of the United States.

For the sake of thoroughness, I even assigned a reporter to fly to the Philippines. We'd learned that their researchers were making significant advances on BCG treatment, but they couldn't afford to attend the conference. Our reporter there got several good stories, ones that *no one else* in the U.S. press was covering. Then the research center in Manila assembled their doctors and had our *Enquirer* reporter lecture them on what he'd learned at the NCI conference. Not only was he treated like a visiting VIP, but he was very happy to play some small part in the fight against cancer.

GP was thrilled with our results. Not that he ever said so, but he showed it by running our stories for *ten weeks* in a row, including several cover treatments.

We were *way* ahead of our time covering BCG. The U.S. Food and Drug Administration finally approved BCG as a cancer-fighter for bladder malignancy, and the "new" treatment got wide press coverage in May 1990—*eighteen years* after we first reported on it.

During the first few years in Lantana, I covered a lot of medical stories, and I noticed that many of the big breakthroughs in cancer treatment came from M. D. Anderson Cancer Center in Houston, part of the huge University of Texas medical system. M. D. Anderson clearly was, or was becoming, one of the world's great cancer research centers.

The Center's legendary founder and director was a physician named Dr. R. Lee Clark. Dr. Clark neither treated patients nor conducted research, but he was the heart and soul of the institution. He spent all his time making sure the state legislature, and every wealthy Texan he could find, continued to pour hundreds of millions of dollars into his "baby." Driven by a desire to cure sick people and save lives, he was enough of a visionary to recognize that the *National Enquirer* could be a powerful ally.

Just as I'd noticed M. D. Anderson and Dr. Clark, Dr. Clark had noticed the *Enquirer*. After several stories by medical writer Lee Harrison had elicited an outpouring of mail to M. D. Anderson, asking about the center's breakthrough treatments, he invited me to Houston to talk about working together.

It was thrilling. Dr. Clark was a major figure in medical and political circles, not just in Texas but across the country. He was lean, with graying hair and spectacles—not the strapping movie-Texan type—but when he spoke, his eyes gleamed with a fierceness no cinema cowboy could match.

He told me, with typical Texan modesty: "This is the greatest cancer research center in the world. We make breakthroughs and discoveries all the time, some big, some small. Our doctors are finding new treatments and drugs to fight cancer.

"But, you know, it takes seven years for our latest proven methods to reach the doctors who treat patients. *Seven years*, while patients are suffering or dying needlessly.

"Your publication reaches these people, millions of them, and if you report on our latest research, the patients will go to their doctors and say: 'Will this help me?' The doctors will call us, we'll give them the information on the new procedures or drugs they can begin using in their practices. And lives will be saved."

The last thing he wanted was to distribute misleading or inaccurate information. How could M. D. Anderson work with the *Enquirer* to publicize its cutting-edge work—and be certain each story was accurate? That was easy. Before I left for Houston, I got GP's okay to offer M. D. Anderson total copy approval on all stories dealing with the Center. They'd give us full access to their discoveries and early notification about their best research—and we'd show them the stories and headlines before they ran, making any corrections they asked for. We'd also advise readers to ask their doctors to call M. D. Anderson for medical information.

The *Enquirer* and M. D. Anderson collaboration was a tremendous success, bringing new hope to innumerable cancer patients.

Over the next few years, Dr. Clark became a friend—to me and to the *Enquirer*. When he visited south Florida to receive awards or commendations for his work, he insisted that I be his guest. I must say, it was intimidating be a lowly *Enquirer* editor surrounded by 50 or 100 of the world's leading physicians and researchers. But I became friends with a few of the most prominent researchers, and on occasion Jane and I were Dr. Clark's honored guests at special hospital galas. Dr. Clark really believed in the relationship we'd built between M. D. Anderson and the *Enquirer*.

So in 1981, when Peter Mathon called Gene Pope on behalf of the Arthritis Foundation to talk about a possible relationship, I was the obvious go-to person. Peter, now owner of a successful public relations company in Atlanta, is one of the smartest "spin doctors"

I've ever met, despite suffering from severe spinal arthritis for years.

He's not alone. More than 31 million Americans suffer from arthritis, and we ran many arthritis stories, all seen by our 20 million readers.

Mathon's organization, however, believed we sometimes interviewed doctors with strong opinions but weak research. Mathon, then head of public relations for the Arthritis Foundation, was constantly handling questions about *Enquirer* articles. Quite often he told patients, reporters, and Foundation staffers that the *Enquirer* doctors were full of it.

One day he had a flash of inspiration: If we can't lick 'em, join 'em.

He didn't know about our relationship with M. D. Anderson, whereby we allowed them final okay over stories and headlines, but he approached his bosses and proposed making just that kind of deal with the *Enquirer*. Then the Foundation could be sure the stories we ran were useful and accurate.

Recalls Peter: "They thought I was totally insane. Our wonderful institution team up with 'that rag'?

"I finally won out. When I left the Arthritis Foundation seven or eight years later, I left a legacy of setting up wonderful events, of persuading Betty Ford and Victoria Principal to be major spokespersons, and of creating a first-class PR department. But doctors and administrators alike told me my greatest single achievement had been creating the bond with the *Enquirer*."

For that first meeting in Lantana, the Arthritis Foundation sent Mathon and his boss, Dr. Frederic McDuffie, senior vice president for medical affairs. McDuffie was the classic absentminded professor, a bespectacled character who wore bow ties and clothes of mismatched colors. With credentials from Harvard Medical School and the Mayo Clinic, he was brilliant, but always feisty and argumentative. He was also smart enough to realize this was a match made in heaven. Gene and I sat down with Mathon and McDuffie and worked out the details.

In 1982, the *Enquirer* ran thirty stories on arthritis, more than one every two weeks. Each story, headline and all, was approved in advance by McDuffie. The response was even better than the

Foundation had hoped. Each story reached an audience of as many as 25 million people. Other media would follow the *Enquirer*'s lead and call the Foundation to ask if the stories were accurate. When told "yes," the Foundation got *more* coverage, from TV stations and newspapers around the country.

On most stories we'd tell readers they could get more information from their local chapter of the Arthritis Foundation. Immediately, the chapters were swamped with calls. On a few occasions, Mathon or McDuffie asked us to delay a story for a couple of weeks so they could prepare their local chapters for the onslaught.

After working together for less than a year, the Arthritis Foundation gave the *Enquirer* its Distinguished Service Award for 1982. Articles editor Dan Schwartz, our editor on arthritis stories, accompanied me to Atlanta to receive the award at the Foundation's annual meeting.

I'd been asked to give a speech, and I was nervous as hell. There'd be nearly a thousand top doctors and health professionals staring up at me. I knew Mathon loved us, but what sort reception would I get from everyone else?

I needn't have worried. When Schwartz and I were introduced on the dais, the audience went wild, cheering and applauding. I felt like a pop star. Later, dozens of doctors made a point of telling us how much they appreciated the *Enquirer* coverage.

Several years later, in a speech to the Public Relations Society of America, Mathon recounted the story of our strange "marriage" and concluded, "Everyone loves to hate the *Enquirer*, but we consider them a friend and an ally."

Within a couple of years, we made the same arrangements with the American Cancer Society and the Heart Association. They got approval on stories and headlines, we got some terrific exclusives, plus access to the greatest researchers around the world. It was a win/win situation. The biggest winners were our readers.

The only complaints we ever heard came from the mainstream press. The same writers who formerly panned us for running inaccurate stories now criticized us for allowing medical experts to approve medical articles. "You're making it difficult for other journalists," one journalist told me. "Only editors should make final decisions on stories."

I would just shrug, thinking: "How many copies does *your* paper sell?"

The *Enquirer* received hundreds of thousands of letters from readers, an amazing number written by grateful people who thanked us for providing the latest medical information, information that changed their lives for the better. Those were the letters I treasured most.

THE 1970S— TO THE TOP

Early in June '73, my internal office telephone rang. Picking up, I heard the familiar "Got a sec?"—the summons from Mr. Pope.

Almost as soon as I sat down in front of his big desk, he said, "I have good news, Iain. I want you to be my executive editor."

Everything after that was surreal, as if I were in a dream. I barely remember his compliments about my work and the faith he had in me, about the big raise to come, plus the company car.

Of course, I was feeling a mixture of elation, happiness, excitement, and some trepidation. But I also felt an intense disbelief and disorientation. I, a boy from a tiny Scottish mining town, had just been asked to run the whole news- and photo-gathering operation of a major American publication. It didn't seem real.

But it was. And I knew I couldn't behave in front of GP as if I were floating on a cocaine cloud. I imagine I gave the requisite responses—and then thought of my friend Bill Dick.

Mr. Pope, prepared for that question, said, "Bill will be disappointed. I don't want to lose him. Please tell him the news, and if you want to give him a raise, then do it. He works for you now."

I left Gene's office in a daze. Bill had been my colleague and best friend for years. I wondered what I would do if the situation were reversed, and I believe I could have accepted it.

When I told Bill he was shocked, disappointed, angry. He told me, "I can work for you, but Mr. Pope should have had the courtesy to tell me himself. I have to resign."

This was awful. But I devised a compromise. I got permission from GP to create a job, director of promotion (essentially public relations officer), and Bill accepted the position with a raise. I figured out I could get him back into editorial when his ego had recovered. (Bill did soon return to editorial, and became one of the legends of the *Enquirer*. I always knew he had it in him.)

Mr. Pope held an editorial meeting to announce the changes, and I officially became number-three in his pecking order, under editor Nat Chrzan and managing editor Carl Grothmann. Within days, however, it became clear that—in running the news, writing, and photo operations—I was Gene's principal editorial executive.

As executive editor, I knew my new domain would be the key to the success of the *Enquirer*. I was now totally responsible for:

- Production of the raw ideas that would become stories or photos.
- Running the articles department, which would make assignments to reporters, then submit completed files.
- Supervising the rewrite team that would turn the files into snappy, readable copy.
- Overseeing the photo department, whose job was to obtain dramatic pictures.

Only when stories were ready to go, rewritten and complete with photos, would we turn them over to the managing editor, whose department would write headlines and design the pages.

My job was the key to success or failure of the *Enquirer*. Weak page-one choices? My fault. Dull stories inside the paper? That would be me. Fuzzy writing? Me again. And rotten photos? That's right, blame Iain Calder. No wonder the executive editor position had been a career graveyard. Over the previous ten years, six good veteran journalists had held the position. All six had bitten the dust.

Just days after the good news, when I was still enjoying promotion euphoria, my friend and *Enquirer* production chief Barney Giambalvo offered some advice: "Start looking for a new job." Barney had been with Pope since about 1960 and had watched all six execs go down in flames. He said, "You'll have a three- or four-month honeymoon. Mr. Pope will love everything you do. Then there'll be three to six months when he'll be in neutral. Then the Boss will start to wonder how he ever thought you could do the job. Soon you'll be gone. It's happened the same way every single time." I knew he was right. Barney wasn't trying to freak me out; he was being a real friend.

But like every other new *Enquirer* executive editor, I believed I was different. Over the next few weeks, I decided to *be* totally different from those other guys. They all had one thing in common: They were afraid of Gene Pope and slavishly followed his lead. They didn't try to shake things up and turn their department into a reflection of themselves.

I was determined to rock'n'roll. And if I failed, the only thing GP could do was fire me. I told my wife, Jane, "He can't kill me or give me cancer."

If I'd thought about it more carefully, I might have realized that I was mistaken. With all his old Mob connections, it's possible GP actually *could* have had me rubbed out. Thank God I didn't think of that.

In previous years, I'd often thought about how the paper could be energized, how much talent was being wasted, and how quite a few staffers did just enough to get by. Now I had the chance to make changes.

We were still working bankers' hours: in at eight or nine in the morning and out at four or five. The office was deserted on Saturdays and Sundays, as if news suddenly stopped for the weekend. In the first couple of weeks, I came in early and stayed late, hoping my example would inspire the others. But it didn't.

Up to now, I'd been one of the guys—friendly with articles editors, writers, photo assignment editors, and layout deskmen. We'd drink after work, hold parties at our different houses, and generally be good pals.

Within a few days of being promoted, I knew I had to decide: be buddies with my editors and reporters, or be their boss. I swallowed hard and chose to be a hard-assed boss.

During my first get-tough meeting with the articles editors, my stomach churned like the sea in a hurricane, but I tried not to show it. I began by saying, "You are not working hard enough."

Friendship was out the window. The room erupted, with insulted editors accusing me of not appreciating the effort they put in.

I calmly made my point: "If you want to keep your jobs, we need better and more stories. If you can do it with magic, then fine. If not, then up the effort."

Slowly the bankers' hours became more like newspaper hours. As we brought in new journalists, we made sure they came with ability *and* a driving work ethic. Within a year I had some editors in the office well before 8 A.M. and others leaving way into the evening. Even voluntary weekends became a way of life for some editors, and certainly for me—I spent five or six hours in the office just about every Saturday and some Sundays.

The result was not just cosmetic. The editorial floor began to buzz with more energy. We were building powerful, dynamic news and photo departments, capable of taking on the challenges that awaited us.

In 1973, these moves were perhaps overkill because we had no real competition. Rupert Murdoch, who would become an American media mogul with his News Corporation, had just put his toe into the American market with an *Enquirer* competitor, the *National Star*; and the *Midnight Globe* was a small would-be rival. We were able to lock up the *Enquirer* on a Friday night, print on the weekends, ship to markets the following week, and finally go on sale ten days later.

Nothing—except for my career—was pushing us into supercharge mode. But this situation was about to change as magazines and TV followed our success, and competition slowly forced us to break and publish stories more quickly.

As executive editor, my whole life seemed to be consumed in a whirlwind of work—even more than before. I'd be in the office six days a week and bring work home for Sundays. Gene would approve every lead or idea before it could be assigned, but before they reached him, I would read each one and filter the best for his possible approval. Apart from saving him time, this system also showed me which editors had the best ideas and the best stringer networks.

Time with my family suffered. In 1972, we had a second son, Glen—named after Glen Campbell, whom we'd met in Vegas at the supermarket convention celebrity party. My wife was born to be a mother, and she made up for my consistent lack of family time by raising two sons who have become fine young men.

I kept coming up with ideas for new editorial concepts and ways to streamline and improve our editorial system. For instance, I was certain that to get the best exclusives we needed two bureaus—one in Los Angeles to make Hollywood contacts and break celebrity stories, and one in London to cover Europe.

Gene was like the tide. When it came in, he'd let me open a bureau; when it went out, he'd make me close it. He liked his most important editors close at hand. He wanted control, control and, most of all, *control*. When he could call an editor into his office and look him or her in the eye, he felt more secure. A bureau chief in L.A. or London was a *very* senior editor, thousands of miles away—and that made GP uncomfortable.

Luckily, reason won out. Most of the time, at least. In 1974 Gene finally agreed to open a Los Angeles bureau. My choice for the first L.A. bureau chief was my old friend Al Coombes.

Since he'd left the *Enquirer* nine years earlier, Al had worked for a number of other publications, gone to law school, and passed the California bar. He agreed to open and staff the bureau for me, and it was an instant success. We broke lots of good stories, in part because Al brought an intensity to the operation.

I kept coming up with more and more ideas to improve the *Enquirer*, and since I was junior in rank to both editor Nat Chrzan and managing editor Carl Grothmann, I proposed many of my ideas through them. Both were old-style GP survivors and their philosophy was, Keep your head down and just do what the Boss says. Whenever I made a suggestion, they'd always say, "Good idea. Why don't *you* mention it to GP?"

So I did—time and again. Soon I was spending much more time with the Boss than they were.

At one point, when I said, "Yes, Mr. Pope," he grunted, "You gotta stop using that 'Mr. Pope.' Call me Gene, Boss, or anything else you want."

How do you suddenly call God by his first name? I went, "Yes, Mist . . . okay"—and walked out.

It took me about two weeks to say the word "Gene," and I worried that a bolt of lightning would strike me dead for blasphemy. But when my editors heard me call GP by his first name in one of his meetings, my reputation took another leap.

That year passed in a flash. Then, in September 1974, I got another historic "Iain, got a sec?" phone call. As I sat down, Gene complimented me on a great year's work.

Then he continued, "I want you to be my number-one editor. You're going to run the whole editorial department for me. And I'm making you a company vice president."

It was like a strange dream, listening through fog as he said he'd pay me more than $200,000 a year. (That was 500 times more than the $8 per week I'd made in my first job eighteen years earlier.) Plus I was to dump my company Ford and get *any* car I wanted.

Gene, however, would not name me editor. I was now to be senior to Chrzan and Grothmann, but GP liked Nat so much he refused to take away his editor title. "Outside of that," he said, "we'll call you anything you want."

I looked though titles in a dozen magazines and hit on "editorial director." It was kind of meaningless, but, wow, this was Iain Calder from Slamannan making zillions of dollars and running the whole show for GP. If I wasn't careful, I'd wake up.

The big question—what car should I choose? The safe choice was a Cadillac. Our executive vice president had a Caddie, so did our vice president of sales. They cost a *fortune*—close to $12,000.

When I told Jane the news, we danced around the kitchen whooping with glee before we got down to the business of selecting a car. Jane asked, "What do you really want . . . really, *really* want?" A good question, but a dangerous answer. The car of my dreams was the top-of-the-line Mercedes 450 SEL, a car so expensive that only moguls and movie stars could afford them.

"What the heck," said Jane. "Mr. Pope said *any* car, didn't he? Go for it."

Still, I was afraid that GP would think I was grabby and extortionate. I didn't make up my mind until the next morning in GP's office. When he asked if I'd decided on a car, I blurted out, "Yes—the Mercedes 450 SEL." Gene asked what it cost, and when I said $20,000, he nearly choked. While he was gasping, I quickly offered, "I'll pay for half of it from my new raise."

But the Boss replied, "I said any car, and we'll get you your Mercedes." About a week later, I was driving the most magnificent silver auto I'd ever seen. I felt I could die happy.

My decision was a stroke of luck for Lois Pope. She had wanted a Mercedes for years, but Gene had resisted, saying they were overpriced and a crummy car. Within a year, Lois had a Mercedes of her own—thanks to Jane.

Then, within about two weeks, I thought my dream job as editorial director had ended before it really began.

★ ★ ★

Not long after my promotion, Gene invited Jane and me to dinner with Lois and him at his favorite Italian restaurant, Paoletti's. Joining us would be the Popes' close friends Jim Johnston, administrator of John F. Kennedy Memorial Hospital, and his wife, also named Jane.

My Jane and I were really nervous. It had been two weeks since I had been made editorial director, and it was the first time we'd been invited to dinner with Gene and Lois. We had socialized with GP and Lois at functions but never at a private, social dinner, so I had no idea how the evening would go. With some trepidation, we drove off in my gleaming silver Mercedes to Paoletti's.

The evening began beautifully. Gene was the consummate host, putting us all at ease, and Jim had an easy, humorous charm that kept everyone laughing. The men dominated the conversation—and the drinking. Both Gene and Jim could put away booze like they had hollow legs, and they both outweighed me by fifty pounds or more. They could hold their liquor *much* better than I could.

I didn't know it at the time, but Gene's rule as host was: No glass shall *ever* be empty. Since his tips qualified him for Diner of the Year, *every* year, the waiters followed his orders to the letter.

Throughout our lively conversation, I'd take swigs from my glass

of fine Scotch. That's all I'd ordered, one glass. But without my notic-
ing, the refills kept coming, and that one glass never emptied. I was
slowly draining a small swimming pool of whisky.

Since I did have a tiny bit of training in Scotch-imbibing, I was
able to hold my own during the fine meal. But after dinner, Gene
moved us all to the bar, which was kept open even after all the other
patrons had left.

All I remember of the next couple of hours is an immense amount
of laughter—everyone seemed funnier than Bob Hope and Johnny
Carson combined. I do recall Gene saying he wasn't a strict boss but
just a pussycat, which had me rolling around the floor, screaming in
laughter.

I was having a *wonderful* time. My wife was aghast that her just-
promoted husband was making an ass of himself in front of the Boss
and the Boss's wife. Jane could see the nice big salary, the nice new
Mercedes, and all the other nice things that belonged to the promised American Dream slowly slipping into the Atlantic Ocean.

When it was finally time to go, I stepped off the bar stool and
slowly sank into a kneeling position—and stayed there. My legs
didn't work. Gene took one arm, Jane the other. They helped me stag-
ger outside and poured me into the passenger side of my new car.
Jane got behind the wheel, and we drove off.

Within a few hundred yards, as we passed the million-dollar
mansions on the coast road, my head was out the window and I was
upchucking all that expensive Scotch all over my beautiful car.

I don't remember that, or anything else. When I awoke at noon
the next day, I had a hangover that made medieval torture seem a
blessing by comparison.

Jane greeted me with the words, "So you've finally woken up. Do
you know what you did last night?" Her tone suggested it had been
very, *very* bad.

Continued Jane, "I'll *tell* you what you did last night. If I were Mr.
Pope, I would fire you. You got so drunk you embarrassed me *and*
Mr. Pope. Lois was obviously astonished that someone like you
could be her husband's top man." She began to recount details. I
begged for her to stop, at least until I felt a little better. But I got the
full story.

That was a bad Sunday, and Monday morning wasn't much better. I walked into the office expecting my promising career to come to an end.

Gene didn't say a word.

Years later I heard him say, "I don't trust a man who doesn't drink."

The years 1970 to 1974 were when the *Enquirer* was really *becoming* the *Enquirer*. At the beginning of the decade, we were still finding our focus. We were developing regular series like "Rags to Riches" and going all-out on medical stories. One thing we *weren't* doing was breaking big, exclusive Hollywood exposés. A typical page-one photo and story in '72 or '73 would be a romance for TV's *Rifleman*, Chuck Connors; Jane Fonda in love with husband-to-be Tom Hayden; *Green Acres* star Eva Gabor picking her fifth husband. These were a long way from our later celebrity exclusives exposing affairs, crimes, and various scandals. At that time, still feeling safe, much of Hollywood willingly cooperated with us. One of our features was "Why I Like the *Enquirer*," by the likes of Glenn Ford, Cary Grant, Mae West, George Hamilton, and Oscar winner Ernest Borgnine.

But with widespread distribution in supermarkets across the country, Americans were finding in the *Enquirer* the kind of stories they could get nowhere else. The thirty-two-page package (later to double in size) was—for its time—a groundbreaking, irresistible blend of celebrities, health, self-help, UFOs, predictions, quizzes, cute photos, and—most of all—human interest stories. For 20 cents, in each issue a reader would find a selection of regular features such as "Young Achiever," a young person who'd made it big; "Rags to Riches," someone who became a millionaire despite a poverty-stricken childhood; "Good Samaritan," a big-hearted person who helped others for altruistic reasons; "Escape from the Rat Race," a successful professional man or woman who gave up the big bucks for a simpler, less affluent lifestyle; "Hero Award," a special *Enquirer* honor for someone who risked life and limb to save another.

These weren't just stories. They were an escape from the over-stressed everyday life of the average American. They were *hope*. If a poor boy with no shoes can end up owning a $100 million shoe factory, then just *maybe* . . .

Every week, the *Enquirer* offered useful tips—how to spot a phony salesman, or how to save money at the supermarket. Top psychiatrists gave advice to help fix a rocky marriage, or suggested ways to tame an out-of-control child.

Even if we didn't succeed in transforming our reader's life, we gave her a short interlude of dreams and entertainment. I say "her" because 80 percent of our buyers were women shoppers, and maybe 70 percent of our readers were female.

This formula, later copied by other magazines, was part of Gene Pope's genius. Despite his heritage of wealth and power, Gene had an uncanny feel for the average American's dreams and desires.

At this time, we also began to encourage buyers to feel that they were part of an *Enquirer* family of readers. We ran contests such as our "Reader's Photo of the Week," in which we paid for the best photo. Literally thousands of photographs arrived each week. We ran polls for readers to give their opinions and votes on the hottest subjects of the day. Eventually we got so much mail—ten times more mail than the rest of the town put together—that the Lantana post office insisted we get our own zip code (33464). One of our amazingly successful columns, "Marsha May's Tales of True Courage," elicited thousands of letters that would bring a hardened reporter to tears. Like the mother who wrote about her little girl who knew she was dying of cancer. The daughter asked, "Mommy, do they have windows in heaven, 'cos when I get there I want to look down and see you." Stories like these really jump-started our readers' emotions.

Some years ago, a reporter asked what success at the *Enquirer* meant to me. My answer: "I see a working wife and mother at the end of a difficult day, her children finally in bed and her husband watching football on TV. She has thirty minutes of free time and decides to spend it reading the *Enquirer*. We bring her entertainment, useful information to help improve her health and her life, plus emotional involvement with people less fortunate. We let her laugh at our jokes and cartoons and get angry at politicians or tricksters who cheat ordinary people. We give her glimpses into the lives of the rich and famous, who often have worse problems than she does—and we bring her a whole host of surprises page after page. If we have brought a little bit of happiness into her difficult life, then that's the mark of success for me."

In the early '70s, before our commando squad of great reporters had begun to shake up the news business, we still hadn't quite achieved that goal I described. But we were on our way . . . with a vengeance.

By the mid-seventies the *Enquirer* was covering Hollywood the way the *Washington Post* covered Congress. With the L.A. bureau up and running, we developed contacts who knew what was going on in movies, on TV, and with individual stars. We infiltrated the unions and the business-affairs offices of major networks, studios, and agents. How did that help us get stories? They had all the paperwork on contracts, payments, and other deep financial secrets.

Our job was to find out what our readers wanted to know. Is the average person interested in the financial affairs of their co-workers, friends, neighbors? Are you kidding? They're *dying* to know. So we revealed to *Enquirer* readers the paychecks of the TV superstars of the time. Who makes the most—your favorite star or mine?

In our August 5, 1975, issue we reported that the top money-earner on TV was—no surprise—Johnny Carson, with a whopping $3 million annually. Peter Falk as Columbo rated $825,000, about $100,000 more per year than *The Rockford Files*' Jim Garner, but less than Carroll O'Connor, who drew down $880,000 annually as Archie Bunker.

Mary Tyler Moore was the queen of the big bucks with an annual take of $1 million for her show, while Richard Thomas—John Boy on *The Waltons*—had to get by on $310,000, and poor Sherman Hemsley, star of *The Jeffersons*, was practically starving on a paltry $200,000.

Readers loved this stuff, and they could get it only in the *Enquirer*. Hollywood hated it—but they could never figure out how we uncovered their secrets.

The following week we revealed more info good enough to talk about at the office water cooler. How much did the top shows cost to make? *Happy Days* was the most expensive half-hour sitcom at $140,000 per episode, with *All in the Family* and *M*A*S*H* coming in at $130,000 each. *The Bob Newhart Show* was in third place, at $120,000 per episode. One-hour dramas were obviously more expensive. Even the slumping *Marcus Welby, M.D.* cost the network $305,000 per episode.

These bucks were huge for the mid-seventies, but they hardly compare with today's figures, with NBC shelling out a whopping $13 million for each and every episode of *ER*. That same network paid each cast member of *Friends* a $1 million fee per show, plus a share of the syndication profits, which added up to about $20 million a year. Kelsey Grammer reportedly had a contract for $1.6 million for each *Frasier* show, a deal that netted him $76 million through 2004 and cost his network more than $5 million per episode.

That same year, 1975, we "outed" the paychecks of TV's top news anchors. Walter Cronkite of CBS led the way with an annual $750,000, with Barbara Walters taking home a surprising $700,000 a year. NBC's John Chancellor was the only other TV journalist even close, with $600,000. That would hardly be lunch money for today's TV newshounds, who jockey for salaries of $7 to $10 million and maybe more.

Today, you can find stories like this in every business section of a newspaper or weekly magazine. Back then, *no one* reported any info about stars and their money.

Why did we spend countless months digging up this kind of material? It gave our readers something that non-*Enquirer* readers didn't get: gossipy information to share with others. Even if they didn't consciously recognize it, through the *Enquirer* readers felt connected, as if they were in on the stars' secrets and part of a community larger than themselves.

Our sources weren't limited to the business offices of the stars. If you were a major star who made news in Hollywood, the *Enquirer* would have a circle of contacts around you who were on our payroll—all eager to make a buck with a story idea or details on an article already in the works.

Without your having any clue, we might have your hairdresser, your manicurist, an aide in your lawyer's office, someone in the offices of your publicist and your agent, several workers on the TV or movie set, your best friend or his/her spouse, your sister, your aunt, your real estate agent, your travel agent, your doctor's assistant, your answering service, or your bodyguard. We might even have the top studio executives who wanted their TV show or movie on our cover—at the expense of their star. The list would be endless on the celebrities who were front-page news.

Many of these contacts were already rich. They didn't spill the beans for the money (though they took it), but for the thrill and the power of seeing a page-one *Enquirer* story and knowing they were the secret source. Quite often, the secret sources were the stars themselves, who swore us to secrecy. When their faces shone out on our supermarket covers, they could have it both ways—they got the publicity they wanted but could say to their Hollywood friends: How do these creeps get their information?

We paid these sources only on publication. Many tips, when checked out, were phony, so no money passed hands. Only when our normal reporting found the story accurate would we print it and pay the source.

Sometimes the source would tell the whole story to a friend— and not even know they were spilling the beans to the *Enquirer*.

Like the ob/gyn of one very famous movie star. She and her TV heartthrob husband had just celebrated the birth of their daughter when reporter Cindy Solomon was asked to get full details. Cindy, who worked on our gossip column, had sources all around Tinseltown.

One *Enquirer* friend was a wealthy woman who went to the same obstetrician as the movie-star mom. She told Cindy that the doc was a pal and she was sure she could get him to talk.

Cindy said: Go get a checkup.

With her feet in the medical stirrups, our undercover patient heard the whole story of the star's delivery. Without revealing any confidential medical details, the doctor regaled her with everything that had gone on. He had no idea he was, in effect, talking with the *National Enquirer.*

Then he dropped the gee-whiz news. The baby had been born with a minor, but fixable, deformity of the hand.

Bingo. Cindy had a great story.

The celebrity mom and dad must have wondered where the heck the *Enquirer* got all this amazing information. Hundreds, even thousands of stars felt the same way over the years. Seldom did they realize: the person they were bitching to might have been the actual source.

Why don't I name the parents now since we identified them at the time? To protect the innocent doctor, who had done nothing wrong but who might feel some embarrassment, years later.

Sometimes our sources amazed even me.

When George Peppard died in Los Angeles, a hospital contact called to break the news to Cindy.

Cindy: "You're sure he's dead?"

Contact: "I'm *very* sure."

Cindy: "How can you be that certain?"

Contact: "Right now, I'm putting his body into a body bag. I stopped for a second to let you know."

Our sources were certain about their priorities. Call the *Enquirer*, then finish your work.

As our celebrity coverage expanded, we quickly discovered that our readers *never* got tired of reading about Jacqueline Bouvier Kennedy. In the mid-sixties, she was known worldwide as the beautiful, tragic widow of America's assassinated president. Then, in October 1968, came the bombshell: America's beloved Jackie marries Greek shipping super-millionaire Ari Onassis.

Her story was a gold mine. Everybody wanted to read about why Mrs. Kennedy would "besmirch" the Kennedy family's Camelot legacy by marrying this homely, ethics-challenged tycoon—even if he was probably the wealthiest man in the world.

The list of stories we ran was almost endless, and our readers lapped them up, boosting our already spiking circulation. After the first year of Jackie O. coverage, we got pretty good at it. We infiltrated Ari's people in Europe and had some peripheral Kennedy and Bouvier people on our payroll. But even with all our contacts, getting those stories wasn't easy. It took some scrambling, and a little ingenuity.

In the spring of 1973, several years after the wedding on the Greek isle of Skorpios, Ari and Jackie finally traveled back to the United States on their super-yacht *Christina*, named after Ari's only daughter. He brought his glorious ship and his glorious bride to—believe it or not—Palm Beach . . . *right on our doorstep.*

Gene Pope called an immediate meeting of his articles editors—including me, since that was before my promotion. "Ari and Jackie are right here on our doorstep. If we can't get an exclusive, then we're not worth a damn." Those were his actual words, but all the editors knew what he really meant was, "If we can't get an exclusive, then all of *you* are not worth a damn."

So here you have a dozen editors who love their Florida lifestyle and desperately want to keep their salaries, which are three times what they could earn anywhere else. They are sitting around Gene Pope's big desk in his big office and the Big Chief is saying, "So who wants to handle this?"

The question was, Which editor wanted to take on breaking a story on one of the world's richest men, with millions to spend to protect the privacy of himself and his new, world-class trophy wife, a woman who would be furious if anyone broke his security? Who wanted to be the lemon in the squeeze press between Ari Onassis and Generoso Pope, Jr. Volunteers anyone?

For a few seconds that seemed like eternity, no one spoke. We all knew *someone* had to break the silence or Gene would know we were all cowards at heart. *That* would definitely mean some heads rolling.

Suddenly, chief articles editor Selig Adler spoke up. Selig had been the managing editor of the now-defunct New York *Daily Mirror*. Gene loved having a former major league editor on his staff and listened to him.

"Gene . . ." he began. I and all the other editors began to sigh with relief. Selig had volunteered. We were safe.

Selig continued: "Gene, I believe the best person to handle this is . . . *Iain.*"

I gulped. I froze. Every other editor was nodding vigorously. *Brilliant, Selig! What a good idea. Iain, the very man for the job.*

Gene said: "Okay, Iain. You want the job?"

What do you say when the guillotine is whistling down toward your neck? You might as well pretend to be brave. "Sure, Mr. Pope . . ." were the words I heard coming out of my mouth.

"Then stay, Iain," said the Boss as the other editors cravenly filed out of Pope's office, trying not to run. "We'll work out a plan together."

Gene's plan was very simple. We had about fourteen reporters on staff in Lantana, and Gene wanted to use all of them on the story. All fourteen, at one time.

The *Christina,* too large to dock in Palm Beach, was anchored in the middle of the Intracoastal Waterway, midway between Palm Beach and West Palm Beach, a few hundred yards from both. Gene's order was to put seven reporters on one side of the Intracoastal and seven reporters on the other side.

I've always said Gene was a genius. He knew what readers wanted, he knew great stories and layouts when he saw them, he was brilliant at distribution and marketing. He could get more out of people than anyone I ever met.

But he had no idea how to get a story.

His plan was *nuts.* The reporters would be falling over each other, so obvious that the Onassis security guards would spot them easily.

Telling Gene he was wrong was like handling weeping gelignite. And if you don't know how dangerous that is, just take my word for it.

"Mr. Pope," I ventured. "I think fourteen reporters might be overkill. I could probably handle it with *fewer* . . ."

You've heard the song, "Whatever Lola wants . . ." Well, Mr. Pope rewrote the lyrics and inserted his own name. "Iain, I want *all* our reporters on this. *All.* Get it?"

Yes, sir!

I summoned all our reporters and told them to go after the inside story of Ari and Jackie on the *Christina.* I wanted to know *everything* that had happened on that yacht. The gossip, the new couple's activities, what people said, what they wore. Everything—including any pictures taken by employees or crew. Jackie and Ari were the hottest couple in the world, America wanted details, and it was our job to get it for them.

It was a rousing speech, a great, inspiring send-off for the fourteen reporters. But the result was exactly what I expected—nothing. Day after day, our seven reporters on the east bank would get the same as the seven on the west. Nothing.

Luckily, I had a secret weapon, unknown even to me—a newly hired reporter named Jim McCandlish, a veteran world traveler who'd worked in five countries on three continents before he was twenty-five years old. In those first frustrating days, I discovered that the one taking charge of this group of tough, experienced, battle-hardened reporters was the newest and youngest—McCandlish. He was the one on the phone to me, telling me what was going on and what they had planned, giving me editorial suggestions.

Finally, after about four days of nothing, Gene let me handle the story my way. I freed twelve of the reporters and gave the assignment to McCandlish and one other guy. The idea was to stay away from the ship and practically move into the nearby bars and make friends with the ship's crew members.

Hallelujah! The plan worked, and we scooped the world with a great story, but the *New York Times* might not have approved of our methods. Jim helped persuade one of the crew to jump ship, and we paid for his trip back to Greece.

Vasilios Vlachos was a young sailor on the *Christina*, and Jim befriended him in one of the bars. After a few nights, they started to like each other, and Vasilios began to tell Jim his problems. He was lonesome and lovesick. He had a beautiful girl back home who loved him and had promised to marry him—months ago.

McCandlish would gently ask what was worrying him. Were there other handsome men in his hometown, who might try to lure his love away? Yes. Was he sure she would remain true? No.

As the bar friendship progressed, Vasilios became more and more depressed. The *Christina* would not return to Greece for many months.

Jim, a helpful guy, was willing to ask his boss (me) if we'd fund Vasilios's flight home. Jim would never, *ever* encourage him to leave the ship. That would be wrong. But if Vasilios did decide, on his own, to leave the ship, the *Enquirer* might be generous and fly him home. We might even throw in $500 or so in expenses, so he could impress his ladylove when he returned.

But in return, we needed a little something. For the next few days, Vasilios would have to talk to everyone he knew on the ship, get all the information he could about Ari and Jackie. And by the way, here's a little Instamatic camera to shoot some photographs on board.

The deal was done. Every night Jim debriefed Vasilios and assigned him more questions. And when our Greek friend left the ship for good, he sat down with Jim and some writers and emptied his mind and his heart.

By the time our presses were rolling out the exclusive story and pictures, Vasilios had deplaned in Greece and reunited with his love. Presumably, they lived happily ever after.

It makes you feel good to help young people in love.

McCandlish went on to cover hundreds, if not thousands, of stories for the *Enquirer*, and he's still a valued freelance contributor. But I was never more grateful to him than the time he saved my bacon on the story of Ari, Jackie—and Vasilios.

In the next five years, nothing could match our series of scoops involving yet more stories about Ari and Jackie O. Since Jackie was the most famous woman in the world, it really boosted circulation.

It was no secret in Greece that Ari and Jackie were married in name only. She spent his money faster than a U.S. congressman on a pork-barrel binge, and he was seeing old flame Maria Callas, plus any other cuties he fancied.

The Onassis family and business executives were beginning to hate the former Mrs. Kennedy. This was fertile ground for one of our brilliant reporters, David Burk, a Briton who'd been based in Greece for much of his stellar journalistic career.

Burk made great contacts at high levels within the Onassis empire, who often told him what was really happening. We knew they might be using us for anti-Jackie stories, but we were careful. As a result, we were usually ahead of the field with Ari-Jackie stories.

The jackpot came in September 1974 when a photographer shot Ari with drooping eyelids, kept open with strips of adhesive tape. He looked awful. When we checked with medical experts—and insiders within the Onassis empire—the terrible truth came out. Onassis had been diagnosed with myasthenia gravis, a fatal, paralyzing disease, and had maybe a year or so to live—at most.

Jackie would soon be a widow again.

Our cover was an international sensation. And just five months later, Onassis, perhaps recognizing that we were functionally the paper of record on his marriage, picked the *Enquirer* out of all the world's media and gave us two exclusive face-to-face interviews.

On January 14, 1975, he told us he was offering a reward of $1 million for anyone who could track down the killer of his only son. Alexander Onassis had died two years earlier when a plane he was flying crashed. Ari was convinced someone had murdered him by tampering with the aircraft. (In the end, no one claimed the reward, and Alexander's death remains officially an accident.)

Onassis must have been pleased with our coverage, because a few days later he sat down with us in his New York headquarters and talked about his disease in public for the first time ever. In our February 4 issue, he admitted his doctors at Manhattan's Memorial Sloan-Kettering Cancer Center had originally diagnosed myasthenia gravis. They were mistaken, he claimed. The problem had been his thymus gland, and he was now cured.

The sixty-eight-year-old billionaire blinked his eyelids to show our reporter the problem had gone.

He was lying, of course. It was his last interview.

Within days, Ari was admitted to the American Hospital of Paris, and we ran amazing paparazzi pictures taken through his hospital-room windows. Soon he was in a coma; then he died.

Ari's funeral, held on the private Onassis-owned Greek island of Skorpios, where his son Alexander was buried, was quite strange.

While Ari was deathly ill in Paris, Jackie was still enjoying the high life. She was not at his bedside when he died. This behavior sparked a deadly feud between Jackie and the family, especially Christina, Ari's only surviving child and heir to the Onassis fortune.

At the funeral, the *Enquirer* was ready for whatever amazing drama was about to ensue.

Only minutes after news of Onassis's death flashed around the world, we sprang into action. I asked my old pal Bill Dick, now an associate editor, to fly from Florida to Paris with one reporter and two photographers. Another veteran staffer, Lee Harrison, took a direct flight from Houston to Paris, and our Washington, D.C., reporter, Bill Cole, caught a flight from there. Noel Botham and another reporter from our London bureau rushed to France, where they were joined by our key Onassis staffer, David Burk. Bill Dick was now running a commando squad of nine staffers, soon joined by another twelve European freelancers—a total of twenty-one reporters. We were *serious*.

Lee Harrison recalls, "In Houston I had great medical contacts at Baylor Hospital, and they put me in touch with a nurse at American Hospital of Paris. She had nursed Ari through his last days and gave me all the details, including the surprising fact that Jackie had not visited her husband on his deathbed."

This was great stuff, and Bill Dick made sure we got every detail from Paris before he headed his team toward Greece and the funeral. Our Onassis sources came up trumps. We received permission to have a special, *Enquirer*-filled limo in the funeral cortège. And, by special permission from the Onassis family and the Greek government, we covered the funeral by helicopter and boat as well. No other newspaper—even those from Greece—was granted that access. Our contacts, after years of working with the Onassis family, were *very* good.

On our April 8, 1975, cover we ran:

EXCLUSIVE PHOTOS & STORIES ON ONASSIS DEATH
JACKIE VS. CHRISTINA: A BITTER FEUD

The stories were amazing. The photos were even more amazing. From the time Jackie arrived in Paris from New York to view Ari's body for the first time, she was smiling. In hundreds of pictures in France, in Greece, before the funeral, during the funeral, and after the funeral, Jackie had this smile on her face. Sometimes it was a small flickering grin, sometimes it was her trademark wide, radiant smile.

We ran two contrasting cover photos. "After JFK's Death" showed a deeply distressed widow's face etched with grief. "After Ari's Death" showed Jackie with a broad smile and sparkling eyes, looking like someone having a ball.

The inside photos were just as startling. Under the headline JACKIE'S BIZARRE BEHAVIOR BEFORE AND AFTER ARI'S DEATH, our readers saw the widow cold-shouldered by Christina and Ari's family. The widow—traditionally up front, just behind the casket—was trailing behind at least ten people.

And in picture after picture, surrounded by tearful, grim-faced mourners, Jackie stands out with that big smile.

Some people might charitably have attributed Jackie's smiles to the terrible shock of being widowed a second time. If so, our following week's issue might have changed their minds.

Just seventy-two hours after the funeral, Jackie was in the south of France for a fun-filled vacation with friends, and we had more laughing pictures of the merry widow, this time on her way to a bull-fight—all totally exclusive, of course.

About a month later Christina denied to the world's press that there was any rift; indeed, she and Jackie shared "friendship and respect." Two days later, both women attended a special religious memorial service for Ari on the isle of Skorpios.

The only reporters allowed at the service were David Burk and colleague John Checkley, from our London bureau. Nobody from *Time* magazine, from the *New York Times*, or even from the Greek press was permitted to attend.

Once again—just for *Enquirer* readers—our guys saw "friendship and respect" go out the window. Jackie was totally snubbed.

She was not allowed to kiss her husband's tomb first—a hallowed tradition. Instead daughter Christina appropriated that right. Christina refused to say hello to or even look at Jackie. At the lunch after the ceremony, Jackie was not at the table of honor, but instead relegated to a small table off to the side.

The following day Jackie was in the VIP lounge at the Athens airport, waiting for a flight back to the United States. Her companion noticed Archbishop Iakavos, head of the Greek Orthodox Church in North America, waiting for the same flight and walked over to him. She asked, "Do you see who your fellow passenger is?"

The Archbishop replied, "Yes. Ask her to please stay in her seat. I don't want to talk with her."

★ ★ ★

I liked and admired Mrs. Onassis (even if we outed her as the Merry Widow). Besides being beautiful and intelligent, she seemed to retain her regal poise and sweetness even in the face of the sweaty, unruly paparazzi who pursued her. She sold many *Enquirers* for us, and in later years her handsome son, John, interviewed me extensively, wrote a kind story, and highlighted the multi-page feature on the cover of his magazine *George*.

Belatedly, I must say I'm sorry that I helped create a monster who, more than any other journalist, made her life miserable. His name was Ron Galella.

When I first met Galella, he was just another freelance photographer trying to scrape out a living. He was a big, burly, untidy-looking guy who didn't impress me as likely to become one of America's most famous photographers. But he had one blazing asset—an unmatched, bulldog determination to *get the picture*. Like the first ones he took for us, in the 1960s, of Elizabeth Taylor and Richard Burton.

The couple had traveled to London with four pet dogs. British authorities wouldn't allow the dogs into the country without the mandatory six-month rabies quarantine. La Liz was upset, so the British government let the dogs stay on a luxury barge on the Thames River. The mooring was in a bad area, surrounded by old, broken-down warehouses, but with good security on board, Liz and Dick were willing to put up with the inconvenience for the sake of their pets.

It was the opportunity of a lifetime for a possessed photographer like Galella. I had told him that we'd buy any exclusive pictures for big bucks, so he spent his own money to get to London, where he crept into a filthy, abandoned warehouse overlooking the barge. For five days, twenty-four hours a day, he ate, drank, and did everything else that comes with a stakeout, not moving from the warehouse, just waiting for Taylor and Burton to show on deck. Then, using a powerful telescopic lens, he shot photo after photo from his lookout point above.

During those five days, he had the company of his own pets— dozens of hungry rats, scurrying around and trying to snatch pieces of his sandwiches.

When Ron returned to the United States with a sackful of great photos, I published an interview with him on his quite harrowing story of the stakeout. Ron's pictures made page one, and we created America's first famous paparazzo with name recognition.

Ron worked for the *Enquirer* for many years (we paid the most for photos), but over time his bulldog personality became more extreme, and he began to think of himself as a celebrity, giving personal interviews to magazines and TV programs. We began using his services less frequently.

Then he started to stake out and photograph Jackie quite aggressively, moving very close to her and her children. Jackie was upset enough to go to court and get a restraining order against Ron Galella that prevented him from coming too near her.

I believe most editors were on Mrs. Onassis's side. I certainly felt that Ron, a great photographer, had crossed the line and begun to believe his own public relations stories. His search for the limelight had become as important as his pictures —not something most editors appreciate.

After Mrs. Onassis succeeded in court, Ron's celebrity status began to wane. He had had his fifteen minutes of fame, and I'm just sorry it was purchased by invading the personal space of Jackie and her kids.

THE MYSTERIOUS
MR. POPE

What is Gene Pope really, really like?" I was asked that question constantly.

He was complicated. To many who were fired, sometimes on a whim, he was a cruel, arbitrary tyrant. To the charities he supported and to the employees he helped when they were in trouble, Gene was a caring benefactor. To most of us, he was a genius who knew what America wanted to read and who unleashed an uncanny ability to achieve anything he wanted.

GP was always tough, never satisfied. He used his immense IQ to manipulate everyone around him.

He was also a quirky eccentric, someone who always remained unpredictable.

GP often dismissed a story idea as too mundane by saying, "It happens every day."

An articles editor once sent in a story lead about a modern-day sect in South America that made annual sacrifices to a volcano. Each year, they tied up a terrified young virgin, dragged her to the edge of the volcano, and threw her into the fiery cauldron to appease their gods. This wasn't history—it was still happening.

We had a reputable American university professor backing up the story, and a trip to South America could have brought us the dramatic details.

GP considered the lead, then returned it to the articles editor, who began laughing like crazy. When colleagues asked why, he showed them his rejected idea sheet. On it, in the familiar red-ink scrawl, was GP's reaction: "Happens every day."

Gene loved presenting himself as a regular guy. He was always telling people he was proud to wear shirts and pants from Sears, and he just adored his Chevy—a well-traveled Impala he'd had for years. His senior executives drove new company Cadillacs, and as editorial director I had a top-of-the-line Mercedes. Gene used to sneer at us for not wanting the best—a big Chevy.

When he finally turned in his Impala for a new Chevrolet Caprice, he was disappointed with it, but, not surprisingly, he kept his feelings secret from me and his other executives.

To the guys in office services, the car was a nightmare.

"Don't like the way it rides," he told them. "Too damn soft. Fix it."

"Don't like this new automatic transmission," he said. "Fix it."

Yessir, said manager Joe Chin and his deputy, Bruce Hull. The new model had five-speed transmission, so they had a mechanic install a three-speed transmission from an earlier model. Hallelujah! Gene was happy with the new, old transmission.

The soft ride was something else, however. They tried everything. They installed heavy-duty springs for a harder ride. "No good," said Gene. Then they tried *really* heavy truck springs. "Still no damn good," said Gene.

This went on for weeks while the Chevy dealer and local mechanics were running out of ideas. Pope was getting impatient.

The brilliant solution was born out of frustration—a fairly common event at the *Enquirer*. Chin and Hull started driving around town looking for an old Chevrolet Impala, the model Gene had driven before the Caprice. They spotted one in the Kmart parking lot. Not in good shape, but the right model.

When the owner returned, he must have thought Christmas had

come early. Two strangers jumped out of their car and told him, "We want to borrow your old car, take out the springs and shocks, put new ones in—and we'll upgrade anything else you want. Free." The owner thought about it, then asked for new air-conditioning and a couple of other things. The two guys just nodded.

The deal done, Chin and Hull ran the driver home and took his car away. Hull told me later, "I can't believe the guy trusted us. But our mechanic switched out the shocks and springs, installed new air-conditioning, and then we returned the car. The owner still had no idea what was going on, but he was one happy fella."

Gene now had his new car, complete with old transmission and *really* old springs. But he was happy—and that was what counted. Even if his Chevy finally cost him almost as much as a Mercedes.

One day, executive editor Tom Kuncl, chief writer Mike Walker, and I were all in Gene's office when he started telling us about That Car.

"I just got a great paint job on my car. It cost me just thirty-nine dollars," boasted Gene. "Want to see it?" From GP, that wasn't a question—it was a command.

We walked out to observe the perfection that GP customarily demanded. But when we spotted the car, Kuncl, Walker, and I couldn't make eye contact with each other: We would have burst out laughing and lost our jobs. The paint job was bumpy, smeared, and blotchy, as if the painter needed a white cane and a German shepherd guide dog to get around.

Years later Kuncl and I would both laugh when we recalled the ensuing conversation. "Looks good," said one of us. "Looks very good," said another. "Looks really, *really* great," said the third. We practically wrote a symphony right there in the parking lot, singing the praises of this paint job. According to us, the painter had to be related to Michelangelo.

The Boss glowed with pride. We'd made him happy. And, as the old Ford commercial said, that was our Job One.

★★★

If GP wanted something a certain way, he got it.

Bob Young, our English photo editor, was a snappy dresser. Everyone in our office wore casual clothes, and I was probably the only man to wear a long-sleeved shirt. Bob, however, liked to come to the office with a jacket and tie. When the coat came off, the tie stayed on.

The rest of us wore casual clothes because Gene Pope wore casual clothes. He'd tell New York visitors, from bankers to advertising executives, that casual was the dress for Lantana. Just about everyone got the message.

Bob Young didn't. First, Gene ribbed him about his ties. Bob kept wearing them. One day, Gene told Bob that wearing ties in Florida was pretty dumb. That should have been enough, but the next day Bob wore a tie. It was like waving a red cape at a bull.

Gene stomped out to the photo desk and asked Bob, "Can I see your tie?"

Bob, thinking he'd finally won over the Boss, proudly held it out. Gene produced a pair of scissors and cut the tie in half.

Young never again wore a tie in the office.

GP always got his way, but not always by demanding or threatening.

At one point, in the days before computers, Gene grew annoyed because his writers wouldn't use proper margins when typing up their stories. Different margins meant there was no standard number of words on a page (wider margins mean fewer words per page; narrow margins, more), making it difficult for GP to figure out how many column inches a four- or five-page story would take up.

He complained endlessly, but the writers still wouldn't use the right margins.

One morning, the writers began complaining in unison about their typewriters. Something was jammed on every single one.

During the night, after all the writers had left, Gene had had a typewriter mechanic come in and actually weld the margins solidly in place. They were set at the GP-mandated width and nobody could move them.

Once again, Mr. Pope got his way.

★ ★ ★

GP could be ruthless, even cruel, when it came to firing people. But he was also incredibly generous to loyal employees when they were in trouble, especially medical trouble.

There are literally too many examples to record, but here are a few highlights:

An employee's handicapped daughter received a state-of-the-art wheelchair, delivered to her front door, which gave the little girl mobility she'd never dreamed of.

One editor's wife began showing signs of bipolar disorder (manic-depression). Her local doctors were baffled. Just one day after Gene found out about the problem, she was being evaluated at the world-renowned Johns Hopkins medical facility in Baltimore by some of the world's greatest specialists. The problem turned out to be a drug she'd been prescribed.

After four months, she came home, restored to health. But the bill for her treatment was $50,000 over the insurance coverage—more than the editor could imagine paying. He wrote a note to GP, hoping to arrange an advance on his salary, or a short-term loan, or something. The Boss read the note and paid the whole bill. The editor told me, "After that incident there is literally nothing I wouldn't have done for Mr. Pope."

Then there was our layout editor Joe Dean, a short, 300-pound-plus, roly-poly guy who had the slowest feet and the fastest mind in the place.

Joe was not only twice his fighting weight, but he also had heart problems and suffered from diabetes that was slowly clouding his vision.

But when Joe decided to retire, GP's generosity, and his fondness for Joe, kicked in. The Boss called me into his office to meet with him and Joe. Gene announced, "Joe wants to retire, and we need to find a replacement."

GP continued, "Joe, we'll keep you on full salary. Just go home and relax."

Joe: "No, Boss, I can't accept that. Just give me half salary."

GP: "Joe, I said full salary."

Joe: "Boss, that's too much. Just half."

This went on as my head swiveled back and forth like at a tennis match.

Finally GP gave in. "Joe, we'll split the difference and make it three-quarters salary," he said. "Not another word." And he ordered me to tell the salary clerk.

Guy Galiardo, our treasurer, remembers a clerk at the printing plant who needed an operation for a life-threatening heart condition, and we found the best surgeon was in Boston. The lady didn't want to go to Boston; she wanted to be in Atlanta, close to her daughter. Guy recounts, "Gene said okay. We paid the doctor in Boston to fly to Atlanta for the operation. We also kept the lady on our payroll for more than a year.

"When it came to health," said Guy, "Mr. Pope had the biggest heart. I know. I signed the checks."

Over the years, Mr. Pope came up with some strange ideas. I like to think they were his way of getting his editors all to think "outside the box" and come up with story ideas that were totally original. Whatever they were, the job of trying to turn GP's brainstorms into reality often fell to me, especially after I became editorial director.

With his engineer's mind and training, Gene often dreamed up mechanical stunts, such as building tiny robot helicopters with built-in cameras to buzz over celebrity homes and take exclusive photos. That idea was technically feasible, but it crashed when I pointed out that the wee photo-copters would be considered an invasion of privacy, and we'd be sued for millions.

That didn't stop Gene's search for innovative reporting gadgets. He kept saying, "Find a way to use a submarine on a story." When I failed at this task, GP held a special editors' meeting and demanded that *they* come up with ideas. No luck.

Then it seemed we might have our submarine opportunity after all. Our stop-at-nothing photographer Jim Leggett couldn't get pictures of Caroline Kennedy, who was yachting in the Caribbean with a boyfriend. Jim followed in a small boat, but every time he got close enough to take long-lens pictures, Caroline's Secret Service agents warned her to stay hidden.

Frustrated, Leggett suddenly thought: "submarine." He figured he could work out a way to take pictures through a periscope and now claims he got prices to buy or rent more than one sub. Jim thought we could put a *National Enquirer* logo on the conning tower, so our celebrity targets could see it when the sub surfaced.

Gene nixed the whole idea. According to Jim, "GP decided that with the Secret Service protecting Caroline, they might call in a war plane to depth-charge us."

That was the end of the submarine saga, but GP just moved his plan of attack from the sea to the air.

When President Nixon was in office, we were in the middle of a national energy shortage. Nixon went on TV asking folks to cut back on air-conditioning and pool heating. Good citizens were conserving wherever possible.

Gene Pope ordered his staff to monitor electricity use at work and at home. He told everyone he'd even turned down the thermostat on his heated pool, and this gave him an idea.

Nixon often vacationed at the "winter White House," the luxury home of his good friend multi-millionaire Bebe Rebozo, in Key Biscayne, Florida. Wondered GP, did Nixon waste energy by keeping the pool heated to 85 or 90 degrees?

How to find out? By chance, Al Coombes, by now the *Enquirer*'s L.A. bureau chief, was visiting Lantana and was chatting with GP when the idea struck.

Al says, "GP suddenly thought of a plan to find the water temperature in the Rebozo pool. Get a U2 spy plane, fit it with a temperature-sensing, infrared camera, and fly it over Key Biscayne. Then we'd know if the president was swimming in energy-wasting overheated pool water."

Coombes was assigned the job of arranging the U2 spy plane and the special camera. Coombes had a well-deserved reputation as a hard-charging, get-it-done journalist who'd broken a myriad of great exclusives, but even he couldn't persuade the U.S. Air Force to turn over one of its multi-million-dollar spy planes to the *National Enquirer*. Especially when we couldn't reveal that the real purpose was to spy on the U.S. president and commander in chief.

After a few weeks of no results, Gene tried a new tack. He found heat-sensing cameras through a civilian company, then got reporter

Lee Harrison to hire a helicopter and fly the camera over Rebozo's house.

Recalls Harrison: "Photographer Vince Eckersley and I told the chopper pilot we were real-estate guys and we wanted to fly over the area to snap photos. But when we came near the Florida White House he refused to fly over, saying it was a restricted zone. He said no, just wouldn't do it—not even for big bucks. 'We'll get shot down by Air Force jets,' he whined." Big baby.

Harrison and Eckersely then tried the land route. They donned the ugliest Hawaiian shirts they could find, rented a bicycle for two, and began pedaling around Key Biscayne. Just obviously harmless tourists —armed with thermometers in their pockets.

Since Nixon was in Washington, they thought they might be allowed to look around the pool area. No way. They were stopped cold by Secret Service agents, who were on duty all the time. Finally, the story was dead.

I didn't believe GP really cared about getting this story, so I let our guys try all these crazy stunts. If it had *really* been a major story, I'm almost certain I could have bribed Bebe Robozo's pool-maintenance people to get us the pool temperature. But I reserved this kind of delicate move for genuine circulation-boosting stories.

Like most publishers, GP craved circulation, influence, and power. But in typical GP fashion, he took things a few steps further than most.

One day at a weekly lunch meeting of senior executives, out of the blue he came out with his bombshell. Wouldn't it be great to have our own country, perhaps an island, where we could all live and work together, rule ourselves, and even print our own stamps and money?

Well, no. Everyone would quit rather than live in a community populated exclusively by *Enquirer* employees and their families. But who would step up and tell the Boss his idea stank? No one.

Gene waxed on, oblivious to the frozen smiles of his senior staff. We could have stores, movie theaters, churches in a Caribbean paradise, where it would be heaven to work and play. And we could call it Enquirerland!

Hoping Gene was just ribbing us, we tried to ignore his enthusiasm. But after lunch, he ordered me to find someplace where he could establish his new country.

That night, I told Jane about my new assignment. "What, are you kidding?" was her response. "You'll be going alone." I suspect all our top executives got the same reaction from their spouses.

However, being the ever-loyal number two, I gave the assignment to several good reporters. Bill Burt had just the man for the job. One of his freelancers was none other than explorer and adventurer writer Lester Hemingway, younger brother of legendary author Ernest Hemingway.

Recalls Burt, "I chuckled when I first outlined the mission to Lester. But Lester, a prodigious boozer like his late brother, didn't blink an eye. He whooped, 'What a great idea. I'm on it right away.'"

A few days later, visiting Lester at his Miami home, Burt found the tables and floors covered with maps. Lester had decided the ideal location would be an island in the Bahamas chain—and he had a few possibilities. While Lester was poring over his maps, I had another reporter visiting the United Nations to learn how to turn an island into a bona fide country.

Over the following weeks, Lester visited my office several times. The problem, he announced, was that all the habitable islands in the Bahamas chain were, in fact (and not surprisingly) already owned by the government of the Bahamas. However, through his extensive contacts, he believed the right place could be had . . . for a price.

At first GP asked me about our new country almost every day, then he suddenly stopped and never mentioned the idea again. The whole project just died a quiet death. My pet theory is, the Boss mentioned it to his wife, and Lois shot him down instantly. Plus, he must have realized he'd miss his favorite Italian restaurant.

Lester, a happy-go-lucky sort, accepted the decision—plus a few thousand dollars for his work. And we were saved from a move to Enquirerland.

BUILDING THE TEAM

One of my top priorities throughout the '70s was putting together the best news-gathering team possible. That meant getting rid of the weakest links, replacing them with great editors and reporters, then setting up a system that would push them to the max.

During the early days in Florida, recruiting established American journalists was very difficult. (And I can't imagine how much more difficult it would have been if we were trying to get people to settle in Enquirerland!) We paid huge salaries, were located in a dream location with no state income tax, and offered an opportunity to tackle the biggest stories all over the world. We should have been irresistible. The downside was our old reputation for gore and the tacky word "tabloid." We were, however, able to recruit young Americans and train them to be brilliant journalists.

But to get already-trained, eager, and hungry recruits, we had to go to Britain. At least once a year I traveled to London, Manchester, and Glasgow, the main news centers in the United Kingdom, where I interviewed dozens of young men and women who were mesmerized by stories of colleagues who had gone across the Atlantic for adventure with the *Enquirer*.

The rule was that the potential editors and reporters I selected had to take four weeks of vacation and come to Florida for a "tryout." If they flamed out quickly, they might be gone in a week. If they survived all four weeks, we usually offered them a job.

The ones who failed invariably lied and told friends back home they had turned down an offer. But their stories of travel and big expenses, plus the palm trees and sunshine, made the *Enquirer* famous in Britain, and my recruiting trips were *very* successful. Many of the dozens who signed on then are still with the *Enquirer* or have moved on to important positions with other American media. Very few ever went back home.

Some friction developed in the office between the Americans and the cocky newcomers. It would be exaggerating only slightly to describe the situation as the new journalistic War of Independence. In the early days, the Brits seemed to be winning, capturing many of the top editorial slots. As with the original war, however—as we were able to hire more and more outstanding American journalists—ultimate victory went to the Yanks.

Gene pretty much gave me *carte blanche* on hiring and firing. Of course, my mistakes would be pointed out with a comment like "Who could have hired this total idiot?" He seldom made me fire anyone, but if I heard constant criticism about an editor, week after week, clearly I had to rehabilitate this person in Gene's eyes, or let the victim go.

GP often told me, "Half a loaf is *not* better than no loaf at all." That is, never settle for someone who's just okay. If you fire him, it'll force you to find someone great.

Which is why in the 1970s and into the mid-eighties, our lineup of fired employees would have filled Carnegie Hall. Maybe Yankee Stadium.

As for those who left on their own, the list is just as long and far more illustrious. Gene Pope's expectations made us push the envelope and learn ways to achieve results that might have seemed impossible to other news organizations. The result was an editorial training school that helped many of our alumni go on to great accomplishments with other media companies.

To name just a few: Our photo editor Brian Hitchen returned to London, where he became editor of two major newspapers—*The Star* and the *Sunday Express*—and was named a Commander of the

Order of the British Empire, the top award under a knighthood; Mike Hoy, our executive editor, also went to London and became managing editor of the *Times* of London, Britain's most prestigious daily; articles editor Jan Goodwin became executive editor of *Ladies' Home Journal*; reporter Dennis Neeld left us to be the founding editor of *Woman's World* magazine and later went to Germany as a senior executive with one of the world's largest magazine publishers; reporter Steven Chao went on to be president of TV's USA Network; photo editor Nils Paulsen returned to Hamburg to found the very successful woman's newspaper *Bild Der Frau* for Germany's top newspaper company; reporter and editor Judith Regan became a cable TV host and multi-millionaire book publisher; editor Shelley Ross became the most successful-ever executive producer of ABC's *Good Morning America.*

The list goes on—and most ex-*Enquirer* successes credit their Pope-inspired training with helping shape their careers.

If newspapers were bottles of champagne, then 1975 was a vintage year at the *Enquirer*—it was one amazing story after another. One of the best featured Henry Kissinger's garbage. This was one story of ours the other media couldn't, and didn't, ignore.

The brilliant Dr. Kissinger was perhaps the most charismatic and interesting secretary of state in the history of the United States. He wielded great influence on Nixon's foreign policy, was a perennial "must" on the guest list of any social event in D.C., and was a major babe magnet. He had relationships with quite a few dazzling women and famously boasted that "power is the ultimate aphrodisiac." Since he was a man given to deliberate and precise phrasing, it can be assumed he was speaking directly from experience.

All of which put him directly into the crosshairs of the *Enquirer*. Normally, our readers would snort if we wrote about a secretary of state. Imagine our covering Kissinger's predecessor, William Rogers, or his successor, Cyrus Vance. *Who?*

Henry was different. Because of his splashy lifestyle and his PR-fueled media presence, *this* secretary of state had wandered onto *our* field of battle. But how should the *Enquirer* cover the man engineering foreign relations with countries like China and Russia?

One editor floated a balloon: "What does Mr. Kissinger's garbage tell us about him?" It was a good idea—a small story that might be interesting. I never imagined that small story would put us in the pages of the *Washington Post* and on TV newscasts all over the country.

The reporter assigned to the task was Jay Gourley, an inspired choice. Thirty minutes after midnight on July 1, 1975, Gourley made his move on Dumbarton Street in the Georgetown area of Washington, D.C., where dozens of neatly tied plastic garbage bags lined the curb, waiting for pickup some hours later.

A Secret Service agent was posted on the porch of the Kissinger house, but that didn't stop Jay. Quickly, he grabbed the first of five green garbage bags and loaded it into his car. The bodyguard, suddenly spotting Jay, raced down the steps shouting, "Stop!"

Gourley calmly kept loading trash bags into his car. The bewildered agent didn't physically restrain Gourley but did keep telling him to stop. Soon all the bags were in the car. So the agent then ordered, "Don't leave."

Within minutes, more Secret Service agents and assorted other cops had arrived. The senior officer told Jay, "If you don't put these bags back, you go to jail."

Gourley, having done his homework on his legal rights, simply replied, "Okay, jail it is. But first, you really ought to check with your superiors."

That stopped them. The puzzled law-enforcement officers demanded identification, and Gourley showed them his White House credentials, obtained a year or so earlier. The Secret Service questioned him for about an hour, then threw up their hands and let him keep the garbage.

Gourley took the bags home and did what no journalism school had ever trained anyone to do. He went through the garbage, bit by yucky bit.

A *Washington Post* reporter, Ron Shaffer, had been tipped off about the garbage raid and turned up at Gourley's door. Being a good guy, Jay let him look through the stuff. The *Post* ran Shaffer's story about how the *Enquirer*'s antics had been a bust. Dr. K's trash had turned up a coat hanger, an empty vichyssoise can, an unopened package of moldy, uneaten English muffins, soda cans, etc. In other words, it was just a load of garbage.

Right. Of course, Gourley had pre-sorted the material and kept the good stuff for the *Enquirer* before letting Shaffer see the rejects.

Gourley's *Enquirer* story was a revelation. It began: "Secretary of State Henry Kissinger's household garbage contained hundreds of Secret Service documents which would be of vital interest to a potential assassin. . . ."

Jay discovered one document showing that the Secret Service was testing a new light code system for all its limousines. Another described the number and type of weapons kept in the limos. Other papers listed the numbers and names of agents guarding Kissinger, plus schedules for his travel and even his confidential Secret Service identity code. A number of supposedly secret memos from senior agents at the Secret Service were also in the trash.

We printed a list of the embarrassing documents—along with the benign empty soup cans, etc.—*without* any details that could assist an enemy of the United States.

Kissinger's State Department went ballistic and attacked the *Enquirer*. State Department officials didn't reveal if Kissinger had now invested in a home document shredder, but off the record we learned that their boss's private remarks were not publishable.

All over the country, the media joined in the attack. With a few exceptions they excoriated us for "trash-napping," while regaling their readers with *all* the juicy details of what we dug up. This is a classic hypocritical technique of journalism that may never go out of style. (One columnist sniffed that a search of his own trash showed he used copies of the *Enquirer* to house-train his puppy. According to Gourley, Kissinger used the *Washington Post* to house-train *his* dog.)

Later in 1975, in a piece for *Washington Monthly* magazine, Gourley quoted Ohio columnist Robert Popp from the *East Liverpool Review*. Popp told his readers: "Gutter journalism still is restricted to the very, very few who pander to a certain small audience."

Jay's response: "Small? I don't know about the *East Liverpool Review* . . . but the circulation of the *National Enquirer* is more than four million copies."

My response: Just keep spelling the name right.

There's a postscript to the Kissinger garbage saga. You'd think the Secretary of State would be so embarrassed at being caught throwing confidential documents in the public trash that he'd never, ever compromise state secrets again. You'd be wrong.

Just a few months later, in our October 7 issue, we ran a headline: KISSINGER CARELESSLY LETS SECRET DOCUMENTS BE PHOTOGRAPHED.

At a security conference in Finland, Kissinger was reading documents marked "top secret"—while foreign photographers in a balcony above him snapped away. After obtaining the photos, we contacted the CIA, and as a result, CIA director William Colby sent a top agent to our Lantana offices to view them.

The CIA asked us—and we agreed—to blur portions of the photos before we published them. No wonder. The photos showed the names of CIA agents in the Far East; a draft of a sensitive cable to Jordan's King Hussein; instructions from President Ford regarding delicate international security negotiations; reports on explosive situations in the Middle East.

These photos had been shot by an Italian, but cameramen from communist East Germany and the Soviet Union were all in position to take the same shots.

Behind the scenes, and off the record, officials and former officials told us they were shocked at and disturbed by Kissinger's "gross irresponsibility."

If Henry the K was embarrassed, he never showed any sign of it. And his pals in the Washington press corps didn't make him suffer. Later I wondered, If this is one of the most brilliant men in the world, maybe the material was fake and he *wanted* the commies to get it.

And if you believe that, there's a bridge in Brooklyn I can get for you at a cut rate.

Celebrities in California, already nervous about their secrets ending up in our pages, persuaded the Beverly Hills city fathers to pass a local ordinance making it a crime for anyone other than official garbagemen to pick up the trash.

In Lantana, trash-napping was still legal, so our local newspaper, the *Palm Beach Post*, "stole" some *Enquirer* trash from the Dumpsters outside the office. Not much in there—but it was a cute stunt, and the story was picked up on national TV.

★ ★ ★

The *Enquirer* wasn't all light reading. Mostly, but not entirely. We'd run stories on government waste and opened our pages to prominent U.S. senators and congressmen for messages on important current events. From the '70s onward, every nominated Democratic and Republican candidate for president wrote byline pieces for our readers on why he should be president.

In retrospect—and in view of the September 11 outrage, when Middle East terrorists destroyed the World Trade Center—perhaps our most significant serious story was on March 25, 1975, when a major headline warned America:

U.S. IS ARMING & TRAINING ARABS WITH WEAPONS THAT
ONE DAY COULD BE USED AGAINST US

With Desert Storm and the war against terrorism still years away, our story was strangely prophetic.

It began: "Are our leaders insane?" We described how the United States was sending billions of dollars worth of planes, missiles, and guns to Middle Eastern countries—and flying an army of specialists over to teach the Arabs how to use them.

U.S. senators, including Hubert Humphrey, Vance Hartke, and William Proxmire, told us that some of the most modern weapons were being shipped to Arab countries even *before* U.S. forces were fully equipped. The newest F-14 fighter was being sold before it was fully in service with the U.S. Navy.

One senator told us that 10,000 American experts were in Arab countries, training their forces for war.

The main beneficiary? Iran, which would be taken over by the Ayatollah Khomeini, an avowed enemy of the United States and architect of the 1979 hostage crisis. Today, leaders of that country still spout hate against us—and have been linked to known terrorists.

That's what made us different. For 30 cents, our readers got, in that one issue: an exclusive interview with Cher on her new rockstar love; the secrets of psychic research in Russia; Ann Landers's advice to top celebrities—and a prescient story about Mideast geopolitics. Plus another fifty or sixty stories and photos.

★ ★ ★

The biggest story of 1975 was broken by Henry Gris, the man who masterminded our earlier supermarket celebrity parties. He claimed he was born in Lithuania; he definitely had a European flair. Henry, perhaps the most urbane reporter in Hollywood, counted among his friends Cary Grant, Kirk Douglas, and Fred Astaire, as well as Rhonda Fleming, Audrey Hepburn, and Sophia Loren.

Henry could get interviews with most of the Hollywood A-list. The problem was, he had so much old-fashioned courtesy that he wouldn't ask the tough questions. He once spoke with Princess Grace about how the press hounded her family. Henry asked his gentle questions with such refined chivalry that Her Highness did not have the heart to point out that his own publication, the *Enquirer*, probably had the most aggressive hounds. So to get the story, we sometimes had to double-team Henry with a younger, more aggressive partner.

But this aristocratic gentleman broke a red-hot political story that had America's major media—including the *New York Times*, the *Los Angeles Times*, and the three TV networks—scrambling for our crumbs.

The story began in the Soviet Union during World War II. Near the end of the war, a handsome young U.S. naval officer named Jackson Tate, based in Moscow, had an affair with one of the USSR's most beautiful movie stars, Zoya Fyodorova.

Tate was recalled to America, never knowing that Zoya was pregnant and that she gave birth to his daughter, Victoria, in 1945. Zoya was arrested—at least in part because of her affair with an American—and sent to a work camp for eight years. When Stalin died, Zoya was released and reunited with her daughter. Over the years, Zoya told young Victoria everything she could remember about Tate, but they had no way of getting any information about him. They didn't even know if he was still alive.

In 1959, Zoya chanced to meet an American visiting Russia, a young woman named Irina Kirk. Zoya told her the story, and Ms. Kirk was fascinated. She promised to try to track down the American officer, and once back in the States, she spent years keeping her word.

After many false leads in America and numerous meetings in Moscow with Victoria and her mother, Irina fulfilled her promise. In 1974, she met with Jackson Tate, by then a seventy-six-year-old retired admiral living in Orange Park, Florida, to tell him he had a grown daughter he hadn't known existed. Victoria, now a very beautiful woman, was an actress and model in Russia. She had told Irina that she wanted to meet her father—and Admiral Tate wanted to meet her.

In 1974 the Cold War was still raging hot and heavy. A former prisoner like Zoya had no chance to leave the country. A visa for Victoria might prove impossible, too, so Victoria decided her best shot was to make her story public. She met with the Moscow correspondents of the *New York Times* and the *Los Angeles Times* and gave them all the dramatic details.

This was a dream story for the American press. It had sex, politics, a distinguished American admiral, a beautiful Russian daughter who wanted to see her dad. The result was a plethora of big headlines all over the United States and the Western world. On January 27, 1975, the *New York Times* story headline was SOVIET CHILD OF WAR WANTS TO VISIT U.S. FATHER. The TV networks also went wild with the story, and so did all the U.S. magazines.

In Lantana, I was thinking, To heck with the rest of the media. The exclusive story, with all the heart-tugging details, the pictures of the teary-eyed first meeting—all of it belonged in the *Enquirer*. I could *see* it. More important, so could Gene Pope.

We contacted Irina Kirk, now a professor at the University of Connecticut, and offered to buy the exclusive. She was friendly but turned us down. She'd spent fifteen years of her life on this project, and she wanted to become a national figure by arranging the historic father-daughter meeting.

Well, we just took the story away from her. In retrospect, I feel bad for Ms. Kirk. She had no idea how tenacious the upstart *National Enquirer* was, how many resources we had. And she couldn't imagine—and neither did we—that we had a secret weapon named Henry Gris.

We didn't know it at the time, but I'm now fairly sure Henry was a KGB agent, or at least an asset of the Soviet secret police. Nothing else explains *how* he did what he did.

Back in early 1973, Henry had suggested a series called "Psychic Secrets Behind the Iron Curtain." He'd visit top Soviet parapsychology scientists and get access to their work and to the top Russian psychics. A series like this would be irresistible to our readers, but it sounded impossible. This was the height of the Cold War, and there were news reports—and vague rumors and dark whisperings—of psychic war weapons being developed by both sides. I didn't see how we could get access to these psychics, but Henry assured us that he had the contacts to get it done.

GP knew that Henry wasn't a hard-nosed reporter and wouldn't get the details necessary for great stories, so he suggested that either Bill Dick or I go to with him. We both desperately wanted the assignment, so we tossed a coin for it. Bill won. Over the next five or six years the Gris-Dick team visited Russia repeatedly and always came back with incredible stories. We knew that Henry spoke Russian, but after the first visit Bill learned that Henry's Russian sounded native—absolutely no accent.

When the *New York Times* broke the Admiral's daughter story, Henry and Bill happened to be in Moscow for the psychics series. I called them: "Drop everything and contact Victoria Fyodorova. We want this one exclusively."

Within forty-eight hours Henry was talking to Zoya and Victoria. They were happy to see him and, like everyone, found him charming. But they didn't want to know about exclusives. They were loyal to Irina Kirk.

When our reporters returned to Florida, we sent Henry to see Admiral Tate. Gris brought along letters and photos of Victoria. Tate was unconvinced about an exclusive, but fortunately they had a friend in common—a famous Hollywood producer. This producer helped broker a deal with the Admiral, and then everything else fell into place. Within a couple of weeks, we'd signed an exclusivity contract with everyone involved. Henry would obtain an exit visa for Victoria, we'd book a first-class flight from Moscow to the United States, we'd provide a luxurious hideout where the Admiral and his daughter could be together, safe from any bad old reporters—and we'd give Victoria $10,000 when she arrived.

I okayed the cash part, which was easy. But the visa? Henry thought it wouldn't be a problem, but he was the only one who thought so. Throughout these tension-filled days of negotiations, Tate said over and over he didn't believe Gris could possibly arrange a visa. The American reporters in Moscow, their editors here, the Fyodorovas themselves—no one believed the Soviets would ever release Victoria.

Henry flew back to Russia. Within two days of his arrival, *hey presto*! The visa was granted. Against all odds, Victoria was about to fly to the United States to see her father for the very first time.

This is where I stepped in. To keep our exclusive, we had to run a military-style operation, and I was the general. In retrospect, the campaign was overkill.

I guessed that, as soon as the Western press knew we had Victoria and she was on her way here, they'd park photographers and TV cameras at every airport. They'd find us and follow us—good-bye, exclusive. We also had to make sure no competitor got anything from Victoria—not one photo, not one quote—during the trans-Atlantic journey. And we needed to keep the rendezvous site a total secret.

Working with Gris in Moscow, a small team of editors developed a precisely organized, meticulous plan to deliver Victoria to her father. Irina Kirk had no idea any of this was going on.

First, we rented two connected cottages at the ritzy private community of John's Island, about ninety minutes north of our office. John's Island had security gates—rare in those days—and was exceptionally private. A few days before Victoria was due, Admiral Tate moved there, along with one of our reporters to handle any visitors or phone calls.

Second, when news of the visa hit Moscow, we asked Victoria to hold a small press conference and announce she was leaving on a particular Sunday. Details of the itinerary were handed out and airline tickets were purchased.

This was a diversionary tactic to fool the media.

The press planned their coverage, and we bought more tickets for Henry and Victoria—leaving *one day earlier*.

Henry bought sunglasses and a blonde wig for the dark-haired Victoria, plus a long, bulky coat to hide her movie-star figure. They'd fly to Brussels, rent a room at the airport hotel, then catch the next Pan Am plane to New York. A domestic flight would take them to Miami, where our guys would pick them up.

With the earlier flight, the changed itinerary, and the disguise, we believed we'd covered all bases, just in case any rival reporter suspected our plans and tried to get to Victoria. Then, at our last meeting, I suddenly realized one flaw in our plans.

When they arrived in New York, Henry would have to go through the immigration line for American passports while Victoria would be in the other line for non-Americans. Henry would lose sight of her for at least a few minutes.

Unacceptable. What if another journalist happened to recognize her while she was out of Henry's sight?

So to cover these few minutes when Victoria was separated from Henry, I had London reporter John Checkley meet the pair in Brussels and fly with them to New York. He'd stand in the immigration line with Victoria and stay with her until he could hand her over to Gris. Then he'd fly home.

That all worked perfectly.

The next danger point was Miami. If some newspaper managed to find out we'd gotten Victoria to the United States, they might follow our cars to John's Island. We had three cars meet the midnight flight. The first would carry Victoria, the other two would spot anyone tailing them. If there was a tail, the lead car would take a specific interstate exit that we knew to be very narrow. Our two following cars would screech to a halt, blocking the exit long enough to let Henry and Victoria escape into the night.

All this turned out to be an expensive waste of time. Our original ruse of leaving one day early had fooled everyone. When the press set up to cover Victoria boarding the plane in Moscow, she was already in Florida.

There was only one small snag. By the time she arrived in the United States, Victoria's hair was a mess, she said, from the wig and the long journey. She refused to meet her father without a hairdo.

Luckily, my wife, Jane, had been a hairdresser in an earlier life. (This was one of the many times I've wondered what I'd ever do without her.) The entourage landed in my home at three that morning, and Jane made Victoria look beautiful. At sunrise (good light for photos), Victoria set off to meet her dad with a full heart and lovely hair.

The operation was an incredible success and earned us worldwide publicity. Once our first issue was off the newsstands, on April

15, 1975, we brought Victoria and Admiral Tate to the *Enquirer* offices for a major press conference. More than forty reporters attended, representing all three networks and publications from all over the country, including the *New York Times*. Irina Kirk stayed away. She must have been heartbroken. She really should have worked with us.

Victoria, of course, did not return to Russia. She married an airline pilot that summer. Admiral Tate died three years later, and in those years he was able to get to know the daughter he never knew he had. In 1979 Victoria wrote a best-seller called *The Admiral's Daughter*; in it, she recounts her father's reaction to Henry. The admiral was sure Henry was connected to the KGB; nothing else could explain his incredible connections in the Soviet Union. Teasing Henry, he once said he feared Henry had "blown his cover" by helping his daughter. Henry just laughed; the next time he saw Admiral Tate, he gave him a black leather desk set, with silver embossing that read, "With love, from the KGB."

Was Henry joking? Was he using a joke to reveal a secret? We'll never know for sure—but I do know Henry was a helluva reporter.

We've always been most famous, or infamous, for our celebrity stories, but our massive circulation was built just as much with medical, human-interest, psychic, and "gee-whiz" stories of ordinary people doing extraordinary things. We'd do just about anything to get a great story for our readers.

In the middle of the Cold War, we once dressed reporter Hal Jacques as a Russian general, and, in full uniform, he made his way unchallenged into the Pentagon. Our champion hoaxer was short, try-anything Australian Brian Hogan, who made a career out of crazy antics. Like dressing in an ape suit and pretending to be a gorilla at a Baltimore zoo. Or boxing against a fighting kangaroo in Las Vegas. Or donning a space-alien-type suit and wandering around the small town of Delphos, Kansas, where a local lady whacked him with an umbrella and a farmer almost blasted him with a shotgun.

Hogan's most successful stunt came during the 1970s oil crisis. At a local fancy dress shop in Washington, D.C., Brian rented a Syrian robe and headdress, then picked up a fancy Cadillac from Hertz.

His chauffer/interpreter was another *Enquirer* reporter, Patrick Wilkins, who drove to the Senate Office Building, where security guards waved them into the official parking area.

Inside the Senate office, Wilkins introduced our Aussie reporter as Sheik Ongha Biran (an anagram of his real name), ruler of the (fictitious) oil-rich state of Halat Al-Bhudi. The Sheik could not, of course, speak English but Wilkins interpreted his mumbo jumbo.

One by one, four senators fell for it. Hogan recalls: "The aides and PR men were scrambling to be super-friendly. Not one person asked for ID. It was hard to keep a straight face, but it really wasn't funny. Security for the Senate was obviously non-existent."

Senator John C. Danforth (R-MO) fell over himself to greet the sheik. He was outdone by Senator Henry Bellmon (R-OK) and Senator Gaylord Nelson (D-WI). Senator James Abourezk (D-SD), who was of Arab descent, enthusiastically welcomed our make-believe sheik. But when Senator Abourezk began speaking in Arabic, our guys beat a hasty retreat before they were uncovered.

All four senators posed for pictures, which they surely regretted when our story ran. Even worse for them, Washington's most famous columnist, Jack Anderson, reported the scam a few days later, calling it a "classic hoax."

I don't know what these angry senators said to their security people, but it had some effect. A year later we tried the scam again. This time they wanted to see passports and other identification.

We never did get an official thank-you from the Senate for our security-improving public service.

My final promotion came in August 1975. Like all the others, it was a total surprise.

Gene, as always, ran the whole company. Since my appointment as editorial director, I had put together a major team capable of delivering what Gene wanted. We had recruited numerous great editors and reporters, many from Britain and Australia. I had set up systems to measure performance that were unique in publishing.

I was really proud of our achievements, and Gene obviously liked the results, too.

The other key part of the success equation was circulation—and our supermarket sales force was humming along under Neil Carey and his troops.

The rest of the operation, however, was a real nuisance for Gene. He needed someone to run the finance department, the printing, the telephone system, office services, and all the "boring" components essential to running a business so he wouldn't have to do it himself.

Gene hired a series of executive vice presidents, whose job was to run everything but editorial. They were, essentially, my non-editorial equivalent. Few lasted a year, most less than six months. Some really qualified people came and went in a blur. People like Clay Rohrbach, formerly a successful senior manager at a billion-dollar food company; like Bob Schwartz, an executive with a gold-plated business résumé; like James Linen IV, a distinguished blueblood with an enviable record both in and out of publishing; like Jim Johnson, GP's close friend and administrator of JFK Hospital, who would later break Gene's heart with criminal conduct that landed him in jail; like Saul Herbst, who failed as vice president in the sixties and was brought back for a second failure in the seventies.

These guys were all able executives, but they didn't know how to work for GP. When he gave an order, he expected it to be carried out literally. If he wanted a task accomplished by 10 o'clock the next morning and it took until 11, that was a failure in his eyes. And for all kinds of reasons, they all bit the dust—one by one.

One day he said to me, "Iain, if the next exec doesn't work out, I may have to give you the job."

I was appalled. I loved being Gene's editorial boss. I wanted nothing more—I especially wanted *not* to be in charge of printing, advertising, sales, security, and office services. The idea was a nightmare.

"No, no, no," I responded with a smile that suggested I thought he was kidding.

"Why not?" asked Gene. My answer was simple: "You fire all your executive vice presidents within a year. And I'm really happy in my present job."

It was never mentioned again, even when the next exec was, predictably, sent packing.

That summer I took Jane and the boys on vacation to visit family in Scotland. Not that I could ever get away completely. Gene would always find some reason to call. Once I was in a Glasgow pub, mildly inebriated while celebrating someone's birthday, when Gene tracked me down and called with some Mickey Mouse question. He was just showing he could always reach me.

This trip, we returned to Florida on an August Sunday. About 10 P.M. the phone rang in my home office, and Jane answered.

She shouted, "It's Mr. Pope." My heart sank. He would only call at that hour if something had gone disastrously wrong—and my neck must be on the line.

Gene must have known my trepidation for his first words were, "Iain, I have important news for you—and I think you'll like it."

Wow. The fear was instantly replaced with an incredible sense of anticipation. I couldn't even imagine what was coming.

Gene kept me waiting through a moment of silence, then he said, "I am giving up my title of company president and becoming chairman of the board. Tomorrow morning I will announce to everyone that you are the new president of the *National Enquirer*."

He also said he would shuffle the editorial executives so I could finally have the title editor, instead of editorial director, and he would make me a director of the company.

I was thirty-six.

The next morning Gene called a meeting, and his office overflowed with executives, editors, senior staff, and anyone above janitor who could squeeze in.

It was like hearing my eulogy without having to die first. I can't remember the exact words, but they proclaimed my stature as equivalent to Winston Churchill, William Randolph Hearst, Gandhi, Mother Teresa, Abraham Lincoln, and Harry Truman. Ridiculous, of course, but I didn't feel it proper to interrupt GP's flow.

My new salary was ridiculous, too, somewhere over $300,000. On the other hand, if I thought I was working long hours before, the load had just doubled.

With all our great stories, other media were forced to start paying attention to this upstart publication. Our numbers proved our success: Within five years we'd gone from obscurity and a declining 700,000

readership to more than 2.5 million circulation, with editorial content that enthralled readers and a dazzling marketing plan that was revolutionizing magazine sales.

Time magazine ran major pieces in February 1973 and two years later in 1975. At first the writer seemed astonished by the mix of stories—from DO DOGS HAVE ESP? and ROD STEIGER TALKS ABOUT HIS FACE LIFT to our story of a deprived little girl who consequently received 70,000 Christmas cards and a personal letter from first lady Pat Nixon.

The second piece was much more laudatory, chronicling our near-4 million circulation and the major exclusives we were now breaking.

Enter *60 Minutes*, the renowned CBS news magazine that changed television as much as we changed print journalism.

Throughout the years I've been interviewed on TV many times, both locally and on the national networks. Even Ted Koppel got his chance during a special edition of *Nightline* focusing on the *Enquirer*. I've been pretty happy with most of the interviews.

But for my first TV interview, my *very* first, I faced no less than the premier attack dog of television, Mike Wallace. It was like the Christians versus the lions. And I wasn't the one with the shaggy mane and razor teeth.

I like and respect Mike. But for whatever reason, he clearly had one mission during his *Enquirer* visit: Get Calder.

He interviewed Gene, he interviewed some of my editors and reporters. Then his crew set up the lights and camera in my office, and he began.

Mike interviewed me for more than four hours. He swung, I ducked; he threw an uppercut and I moved back. I was in a verbal fight with the world champion. I thought I was doing okay until I got the Wallace KO.

On camera, he showed me a front page of the *Enquirer* with a cover picture of Raquel Welch and Freddie Prinze, at the time a major TV star.

"That picture isn't real, is it?" queried Wallace. "You took two separate photos and put them together."

It was true. We had what we thought was a real romance story—but no photo of the couple together. Two separate photos had been retouched to make them seem like one picture showing both Raquel and Freddy.

I had a problem. I had been on holiday the week that story had been published. I had no idea why Gene Pope had ordered the put-together. We had never done it before.

If I publicly put the blame on Gene, that would take me off the hook. But telling millions of CBS viewers that your boss is guilty is not a recommended career move. In front of the camera, I sweated for a couple of seconds that seemed like ten minutes.

But I knew I had to fall on my sword.

I said, "We made a mistake. It was wrong. We'll never do it again."

And did I look like an idiot!

To make matters worse, Mike finally stopped the interview and had the cameraman turn the camera on him. Now that he knew what my answers were, he asked the same questions again, but phrased differently. Where he had earlier asked gently: "Iain, so tell me about this photo," it was now more like: "Mr. Calder, what's your explanation for this phony picture?" His gestures, originally soft and friendly, were now fierce and accusatory.

Mike was rigging the tape so that viewers would see him ask the staged tough questions and me give the hesitant genuine answers. In reality, I had answered the question first and he had—with important differences—asked the rephrased question later.

If I'd had any experience being interviewed, I would never have allowed this cheating. *60 Minutes* was at least as deceitful as they accused us of being. The hypocritical practice Mike used has long since been banned at CBS, but it was routine in the '70s.

Luckily, the piece in general was fair and quite positive. But for years, I couldn't watch *60 Minutes* without praying: Don't do a repeat of the *Enquirer* show.

More than twenty-five years later, Jane and I had dinner with Mike Wallace at an event in Palm Beach. We were all very friendly and kept the table laughing as we swapped reporting stories. He told me, "I remember that piece well. I knew you'd get me later in the *Enquirer*. You did run several stories over the years that were not flattering."

I never "got" Mike. We didn't do that with celebrities. The only criterion for a celebrity story—or any story, for that matter—was: Will it interest our readers?

But I was always happy when anyone thought we had an "enemies list" and a "friends list." It translated into the power to get better stories.

But then there were the times when we ended up on someone *else's* enemies list . . .

I'll never forget the threat from Charles Manson. We had just published a story about the infamous mastermind behind the Sharon Tate killings. He obviously didn't like what we wrote because one of his women acolytes soon wrote to the *Enquirer* from behind her prison bars: They would "get" the two top people at the *Enquirer*.

The two top people obviously included Gene as number one. As editor, mine was the first name on the *Enquirer* masthead, and I was also president of the company. I had to assume this qualified me in the assassin's mind as number two.

Our security chief advised me to consider the letter a death threat, so, after alerting GP, we called the local FBI office. After reading the letter, one of the agents gravely pronounced it a legitimate threat to our lives and said that the Manson cult was believed to have members still at large.

Then came the chilling part. About two months ago, an attorney in California had received a similar letter. A few weeks later, as the lawyer left his office, a scruffy-looking man walked up to him and shot him dead. That was two weeks before my letter arrived, and authorities still had no idea who the killer was.

That *really* got my attention.

I asked the FBI agent what he was going to do. His nice, reassuring answer: Nothing. The letter-writer was already in prison for a gazillion years, and the FBI was not in the business of protecting private citizens.

His advice: "Be careful!"

After indulging in some uncharitable thoughts about J. Edgar Hoover and his G-men, my next step was to call home. I told Jane to start packing immediately—she and our sons, Douglas and Glen, were leaving for Scotland the next day. I told her that I couldn't leave, but I wasn't taking any chances with my family.

Jane firmly replied, "We're not going. If you're in danger, then we'll *all* be in danger."

What? She must have just read the script of some B-grade thriller, the scene where the wife says, "I'll die with you, darling."

I didn't want to listen. How could I do my job while worrying about some maniac shooting my whole family? Jane and the boys had to go to Scotland and stay with relatives for a while.

I went to GP and told him the situation. Gene was less concerned than I was. (*He* lived in an oceanfront estate with iron gates and twenty-four-hour security provided by off-duty cops.) Nonetheless, he said, "We'll provide you with round-the-clock protection for as long as you want."

So Jane and the boys stayed, and security was handled by a senior law-enforcement officer at one of the local townships, Captain Ed Dalton of the Boynton Beach police; he hired a team of off-duty cops who took eight-hour shifts—8 A.M., 4 P.M., and midnight—at our house.

We had to tell our neighbors about the letter in case they wanted to keep their children away from our house. Instead, more kids than usual came over to play in our front yard. They loved being guarded by big tough cops who showed off all kinds of guns and bullets.

We were also advised to buy a gun and learn how to shoot it. So an arms instructor for the Delray Beach police, Sergeant Neal Rawls (later to become *Enquirer* head of security) helped us choose a handgun and took Jane and me onto the firing range. Neither of us had ever fired a gun in our lives, but we did learn, especially the safety tips, which we drummed into both our boys.

Our house also had one secret defense weapon—our German Shepherd, Duchess, the best dog anyone ever had. She was the sweetest, gentlest animal when around our family, but she was also fiercely protective of us and our well-being. We knew she was capable of transforming herself into a lethal 90-pound attack machine. She was also really smart.

Our master bedroom was upstairs, and the kids slept downstairs in separate bedrooms. At night Duchess was always on guard downstairs and could wander anywhere on the lower level. One morning the cop on night shift said: "Do you know what your dog does every night? She sleeps on the carpet by the front door, but every two hours she gets up, wanders down the hallway and into one boy's bedroom. She walks around his bed, then goes back into the hallway. She then goes into the second boy's bedroom and walks around. When your dog is satisfied everything is okay, she goes back to the front door and sleeps. Until two hours later—when it all happens again."

The cop added: "When I first saw this, I found it hard to believe. But she does this routine every single night."

Now, if there's a heaven and I ever qualify, there are a lot of people I hope to meet up with. But I really, *really* hope Duchess is there to greet me. She was some friend.

All this security made me feel very calm, but there was a downside for Jane. She's the poster girl for mothering and a great cook besides. She couldn't let these poor cops come off or go on duty without a meal, which meant a lot of cooking. At 8 A.M. there was breakfast for the incoming cop and breakfast for the outgoing cop. At 4 P.M. there was late lunch or early dinner, and at midnight more food for the goers and comers.

She was shopping and cooking, cooking and shopping. She kept notes of what she prepared so she wouldn't give the guards the same meal two days in a row. After five weeks, one of the precinct captains called her and said, "Please stop feeding my men." The officers were all putting on weight, eating first at home and then at the Calder house.

Jane couldn't bring herself to let them go hungry. One week later, however, she announced to me: "I can't take it any more. I'm so tired, I'd rather face Manson."

So we stopped the security operation at our house, although local cops still patrolled our street about ten times more often than normal.

We remained friendly with many of these young policemen. Some went on to become senior officers and a couple made police chief. (One even became an *Enquirer* reporter.) Even twenty-five years later, many of those guys remember Jane and her food!

One footnote: The evening after we stopped the security, Jane bent over and strained her back so badly she was immobilized. I was out playing racketball, so a friend had to summon an ambulance for her. As the stretcher took her away and the ambulance pulled out from the house, some neighbors were whispering: "Oh my, Manson got her!"

Funny . . . but only because it wasn't true.

Years later, I had another, much closer, brush with death, one I knew nothing about until the danger had passed.

It was 1989, and the *Enquirer* was in a state of transition. Gene Pope had died just a few months earlier, the company was being sold, and I was juggling the regular duties of chief executive officer while dealing with seven separate media groups about to bid for the *Enquirer*. Uncertain about their future, our employees were in a state of nervous tension, and I was working up to eighteen hours a day, seven days a week.

I thought that nothing could possibly distract me from the day-to-day madness whirling around me. Boy, was I wrong.

Neal Rawls, our security chief, called on the intercom and said: "Iain, I need to see you right now." His voice betrayed an edge of tension, the last thing you'd expect from Neal. Small, wiry, tough, dedicated, and totally focused, Neal is the kind of cop you want around if bullets are flying and people wanted to hurt you. When you think of Rawls, *Dirty Harry* comes to mind.

I told him to come to my office right away. The story he told still gives me chills.

Some good friends of Rawls at the Palm Beach County Sheriff's Office had just called. A dead man had been found inside a car, a bullet hole in his head. His name was Leonard Sandler, and several years ago he'd been a writer for the *Enquirer*, until the chief writer upgraded the department and Sandler was fired. In Sandler's car were several guns, hundreds of bullets, and a suicide note.

In it Sandler wrote that he was going to kill his girlfriend, go to the *National Enquirer* office and murder Iain Calder, then gun down as many employees as possible, before taking his own life.

Luckily, he had just done it in the wrong order!

The suicide note shook me up. I *knew* Sandler, and it was not hard to envision him walking into my office blasting away. Neal Rawls had a suggestion: Let him buy me a .357 Magnum handgun, load it with anti-personnel bullets, and lock it in a drawer of my desk. I was not convinced. People from Britain, where even cops don't carry guns, are not comfortable with firearms.

Rawls argued, "What if someone comes in shooting at employees and our security guys are in another building? Who will protect our people?" I couldn't exactly see myself as Wyatt Earp, but I gave in to the logic.

So from 1989 until I finally left the *Enquirer* in '98, my bottom right-hand drawer held a Smith and Wesson .357 Magnum. Nobody except Security ever knew. And that gun was never once fired, not even in practice.

By 1977 the *Enquirer* was a must-read for millions of Americans. Mainstream journalists couldn't understand this, but they had to acknowledge the circulation figures, audited by the official Audit Bureau of Circulations (ABC). Late in 1970 we were selling 1.9 million copies per week; in '73 it was 2.9 million; by '75 it was 4.1 million. And by the end of 1976 we were selling an average of 4.7 million copies each and every week. We had done the impossible—surpassed venerable *Time* magazine.

Another magic milestone fell in the first six months of 1977. We averaged more than 5 million copies per week. Then on September 6 of that year, the issue picturing Elvis in his coffin was a 6.7 million total sellout, our highest-ever sale.

If you think we were congratulating ourselves at that point, you'd be wrong. The more successful we were, the harder GP pushed. The editorial staff and I likewise pushed ourselves to the limit. I was coming in at 8 A.M. every weekday and leaving twelve or thirteen hours later, eating lunch at my desk. I was in the office almost every Saturday and taking work home on Sundays. We were making publishing history, but we were all too busy or tired to notice.

We all recognized, however, that we knew which buttons to push to induce Americans to buy our paper. Celebrities dying unexpectedly were always good on the cover. And when we found something new, we ran with it again, again, and again—until everyone was fed up with it.

Take the smash hit TV series of all time: the 1977 *Roots*, Alex Haley's story of a young African brought to America as a slave. Every magazine did stories on *Roots*. Our first cover sold an *extra* half-million copies over regular sales, so we kept going. We dined on that story, gorged on it, devoured it, and kept feeding it back to our readers—with great success for years after. I okayed all kinds of leads on the making of the series, on the celebrities who starred in it, and on the impact of the series on the American public.

We also sent a tape of the series with a TV set to show to Kunta Kinte's original tribe in Africa. One minor problem was the lack of electricity to make the TV work, but we finally overcame that problem with batteries.

When it looked like all the *Roots* stories had been done, we started to uncover the roots of famous celebrities. I directed editors to hire the best genealogy experts in America, and they turned up some amazing material.

I was really excited to learn that Elvis Presley's folks had come from Europe 200 years earlier. They included a blacksmith who fought against the British and knew George Washington. Another Elvis ancestor fought in the Civil War, deserted twice, and became a bigamist with two wives and two families.

Bing Crosby's roots went back to 1635, when a Puritan hit our shores and fathered a son, Thomas Crosby II, who graduated from Harvard in 1653. Bing's ancestor became a minister who preached abstinence on Sundays and sold liquor during the week. *Flexible thinking!*

You just couldn't get this stuff anywhere else.

We did dozens of these roots stories over the next few years, until our readers had had enough and the stories stopped being big sellers.

Another series that lasted almost forever was weight loss. When we ran the Boston Police Diet on the cover, I had no idea it would spawn a publishing industry for the next few decades. We were excerpting a book describing how a diet had helped hundreds of Boston cops lose thousands of pounds. Our message was: You can do it, too.

It was a surprise blockbuster. Strange as it seems now, women's magazines were not front-paging diets back then. We got started running weight-loss story after weight-loss story, everything from the No-

Diet Way to Lose Weight and the Never-Go-Hungry Diet to the World's Greatest Weight Loss Plan and the Superstar Diet, which showed how celebrities like Burt Reynolds, Barbra Streisand, William Holden, and Dinah Shore shed pounds. Every few weeks, we had a new one.

They all worked. Maybe not in making readers slimmer, but certainly in selling papers.

We even started a regular feature: "Slimmer of the Month," where a reader would send before-and-after photos and tell us how she lost the equivalent of three or four bowling balls in weight. We'd send the winner a cash prize and give our other readers a real-life role model.

I used to joke to my editors: Don't ever find a diet that actually works for everyone, or we'll never be able to run another weight-loss program.

For years a clever weight-loss cover *always* sold for us. We were still selling dreams and hopes. Then every other magazine started putting diets on their covers, and the subject lost its magnetism. One thing we always insisted on: Any diet we ran had to be approved as safe and healthy by reputable medical authorities and by our tough-as-nails, in-house medical researchers. I never ceased to be amazed at how many real M.D.s would put their names on quack diets that would clearly be a potential danger to dieters.

I shouldn't have been surprised. Let's face it—by definition, one-quarter of all doctors graduated in the bottom 25 percent of their class in medical school.

At the *Enquirer*, our project planning resembled war-strategy sessions, and damn the expense. I'm sure no journalism professors teach the technique, and many might sneer at the enormous effort expended just to keep a story exclusive. But at the *Enquirer*, we would do almost anything to please our readers and let them feel as if they were in on a secret.

Gene used to contend that journalism school stunted the careers of many potentially great journalists, a philosophy I could easily buy into, since I hadn't attended journalism school, or even college for that matter. If he felt that way, my job was safer.

He also liked to shake up his editors and reporters constantly to keep them from becoming too complacent.

When I suggested that we recruit reporters directly from Ivy League schools, he was enthusiastic. "Just remember, no journalism students," he warned. I wanted to offer $20,000 a year, a huge salary for a beginner. "No," said Gene, "give 'em the same as experienced reporters." That was $31,000 a year—an eye-popping offer for kids in 1978.

The recruiting assignment went to Haydon Cameron, a brilliant Australian editor. I always said that Cameron had missed his calling in life. With his gift for making people, especially women, like and trust him, he should have started his own religion and become a zillionaire cult guru. Instead, after learning his journalistic craft at home in Australia and then in London, he joined the *Enquirer* as a reporter around 1974. I promoted him to assistant executive editor to impress the bureaucrats at the elite universities, and off he went as our recruiter.

Hayden told me later that the recruiting offices thought he was mad, a phony, or a practical joker. Here he was hiring kids as journalists, at starting salaries higher than what some professors were paid. Even stranger, he did *not* want journalism students. Once they realized he was on the level, however, they put out the word—and applications poured in. We had our choice of chemists, economists, historians, English majors—top students from just about every discipline.

After some weeks, Hayden sent me a dozen or so résumés, and we flew half the applicants to Lantana.

I was knocked out by the dazzling intellects of these kids. Individually, they were all smarter than me and my whole editorial department put together, but with my classy office, big desk, and two secretaries, I hid my inferiority quite well.

Some of them, of course, were just "book smart." Others, I felt, could instantly succeed in almost any business. I made offers to four; three passed the customary four-week tryout, and two turned into such major successes that they're now famous in the media world.

The first young star was wiry twenty-one-year-old Steven Chao, just graduated from Harvard, with a degree in the riveting subjects of Latin and Greek and a fellowship in a Ph.D. program at Yale. He was a brash young man with a do-anything attitude and the kind of commonsense intelligence I thought would work well at the *Enquirer*. He loved adventure and had traveled all over South America on almost no money.

What really impressed me was his Chinese laundry story. He said that he needed money at Harvard and figured that other students might know the common wisdom that the best laundries are Chinese. So he, a Chinese-American, hired some kids to pick up laundry, take it to regular non-Chinese local laundries where he'd negotiated a deal, then deliver the clean clothes to Chao's customers.

"I guess perception is reality," he said. He told me he'd made a lot of money, and on leaving Harvard, he had sold the franchise.

I had no idea if this was true or not, but even if he'd made it up, it was a great story. I offered him a job, and he dumped his Yale Ph.D. to come aboard.

Twenty-three years later, Steve told me, "I never had a laundry, and I don't recall the story. But if you remember it . . ."

Not only do I remember the story, I've told it many times over the years.

Chao was an instant success. He was the first reporter to break the O. J. Simpson and Nicole Brown romance. He remembers, "I had cultivated lots of contacts in a really hot club called Daisy on Rodeo Drive in Beverly Hills. It was the hangout for celebrity staff like chauffeurs, hairdressers, and agents. I learned that O.J., who was separated from his wife, was going out with a beautiful blonde white girl.

"Through my contacts I found out where they would be and had a photographer take pictures. Then I called O.J.'s people for a comment."

That's when the twenty-one-year-old learned how far he was from the sheltered halls of Harvard. He began getting threatening calls at home.

Said Chao, "Three different guys who sounded like thugs kept calling and warning me that if I wrote the O.J. story, 'bad things' would happen to me. I even agreed to meet one of them. He was a mean white guy with an open shirt and all kinds of gold jewelry. His message was clear—I could get hurt if we ran the story."

We ran the story. Nothing happened to Chao.

Said Chao years later, "This whole thing was like a dream for me. I'd never imagined being a reporter, certainly not for the *National Enquirer*, but when the Harvard career office told me the paper was offering adventure and thirty-one thousand a year, I couldn't resist. All the other jobs on the list were for seven or eight thousand dollars.

"Within two days of starting work, I was given three credit cards, the first I'd ever owned, and shipped off to Los Angeles to cover the breakup of Barbra Streisand and Jon Peters. They put me up in the ultra-exclusive Beverly Wilshire hotel. The whole thing just blew my mind—I was bursting with happiness."

Chao was even happier to be sent to Brazil to interview Lee Majors, who was making a movie in a little town 300 miles from Rio. It was rumored that Lee and his wife, *Charlie's Angels'* Farrah Fawcett, the hottest TV star in America, were planning a baby.

Majors wouldn't cooperate. Chao went to the location and kept asking, asking, asking for an interview—no luck. Chao wouldn't give up. After more than a week of dogging the star, Chao followed Majors to Rio, where he was staying in a big hotel.

That's where his persistence paid off. Chao always had a freelance photographer with him, just in case. One night he actually had *two* cameramen in the hotel bar waiting for Majors to return from shooting some scenes.

Hallelujah. Majors walks in with two girls, one on each arm. The photographers start flashing off shots, and Majors's bodyguards pounce. They rough up both cameramen, smash their cameras, causing thousands of dollars in damage, and throw the two freelancers out.

Once outside the hotel, the puzzled photographers tell Chao, "These guys are really dumb. They broke our cameras, but they left the film. It should be fine."

The developed film had great pictures of Majors and the two bimbos. Chao called Majors's room the next day. Usually Lee would hang up, but this time he didn't. He knew his choice was either to give Chao an exclusive positive interview about how he and Farrah were trying for a baby . . . or let the *Enquirer* run a photo story with the two girls.

Recalled Chao: "Majors talked his head off, I wrote a really nice, warm story, and we had the Farrah cover we wanted. I even gave him the picture negatives. The whole episode showed me, even at twenty-one, that you never, never, *never* give up."

The *Enquirer* couldn't hold on to someone like Chao, but he credits his training with us for much of his meteoric success. After two years with us, he went back to Harvard for an MBA degree.

Later he applied to Rupert Murdoch for an executive position at Fox. When Murdoch saw "Harvard MBA" on his résumé he was only mildly impressed; when he saw Latin and Greek, his eyes lit up; and when he saw *National Enquirer*, that clinched the deal. Murdoch hired him as vice president of acquisitions.

Not long after he came on, Chao became president of Fox Television, where he helped establish such pioneering and extremely successful series as *America's Most Wanted* and *Cops*. That job suddenly vanished in 1992, when Steven hired a male stripper to perform at a management conference with several VIPs, including Mr. and Mrs. Dick Cheney and Mr. and Mrs. Rupert Murdoch, in attendance. It was meant to prove a point about censorship, according to Chao, but Murdoch canned him. That temporary career blip hasn't stopped the TV industry from regarding Chao as one of the most innovative programming chiefs alive. In 2000 he became the president of USA Cable.

The second "shooting star" recruit was Judith Regan, who went on to become the multi-millionaire president of Regan Books, an imprint of HarperCollins with an outstanding record of best-sellers. She also has her own talk show on the Fox network and has produced several network television specials. Judith has never made it a secret that her four years with the *Enquirer* helped make her a success.

In 1978, when she interviewed with me for her first job, she was a very pretty, dark-haired twenty-one-year-old, maybe 5'4" and 115 pounds. She looked more like naïve teenager than a potential *National Enquirer* reporter.

But I didn't help build one of the greatest news teams in history without being able to spot talent. As she recounted her life history and her struggles to get an education, I could sense the steel behind this ingénue exterior.

A product of Sicilian-Irish bloodlines, Judith was raised in her grandparents' farmhouse in Massachusetts. They spoke only Italian, and Judith remembers as a young child teaching her grandma a few words of English. There was no TV on the farm, and Judith's mother taught her children how to read by the age of three.

When she came to the *Enquirer* interview, she had just graduated from Vassar after writing her final thesis on William Shakespeare. "I intended to attend the Kennedy School of Government at Harvard, but I was down to my last ten dollars and wanted to get some menial job to help me survive the summer." She had gone to the Harvard employment office in Cambridge, where a clerk asked her, "Would you like to work for the *National Enquirer*?" Judith knew almost nothing about the paper, but she thought, What the hell.

One Haydon Cameron interview later, she was invited to fly to Florida for lunch with the editor . . . me. She recalls, "I was dazzled at the prospect of flying all the way to Florida just for lunch."

I almost never went out for lunch, but I did meet with Judith in my office. She told me later, "As I sat there the first thing you said was, 'I don't care where you came from, what your background is, or who you are. I just want to know if you can do the job. If green monkeys could do the job, I'd hire green monkeys.'"

To be honest, I don't remember saying anything this hokey, but apparently it worked on Judith. She told me later that her thoughts were, "I love this man. I just love challenges like this, and I want to work here."

Judith says the money was secondary, even though it was huge. She just wanted to be a part of our organization, with its troupe of freewheeling characters, most of whom had also survived hard times. She fit in really well.

She was attached to the team run by Charles Parmiter, an experienced, crusty editor who'd handled many major stories. He gave her a quick briefing on tight writing, accuracy, and never failing. Then, twenty-four hours after joining up, Judith went out to get her first story.

We gave her an American Express card, a phone card, a Hertz credit card, some cash, and a ticket to Las Vegas, where a big cancer conference was taking place. One of the attendees was a top cancer doctor who'd made an amazing medical breakthrough. He didn't agree to many press interviews, but Judith was given a list of questions and the assignment to get the interview—or else.

Our newest reporter rented a luxury car, stood at the airport gate where the doctor's plane was arriving, and held up a big sign saying "Dr. Smith" or whatever his name was. Thinking someone had ordered a limo for him, he followed Judith to the car, and they headed for the hotel.

A few minutes into the drive, Judith revealed she was an *Enquirer* reporter, and the doc, amused that such a pretty little thing could be so devious, laughed and answered every single question. She had her exclusive interview. Now, what journalism school could have taught her this?

Judith remembers her reporting technique quite well: "I would cheat, make up stories, or do just about anything to find phone numbers or addresses of people I wanted to track down. But I was always honest and up-front with the people themselves. My innocent face, polite talk, and friendly smile usually won people over. I could make people trust me."

Unlike other *Enquirer* reporters who prided themselves on getting to people "through the toilet bowl," Judith says she found the front-door method worked best for her.

Like the time she was asked to find Mia Farrow to talk about her marriage to Frank Sinatra. Judith knew Mia was at her home on Martha's Vineyard. Despite a winter snowstorm, Judith got a boat to take her there, but when she landed she had no idea where Mia's house was.

Since her press deadline was close, Judith went to the most expensive florist on the island. "I want to send flowers to Miss Mia Farrow," she said, assuming many people sent flowers to Mia. The florist accepted the order and sent the flowers out. Judith just followed the florist's van.

It was still snowing when Judith knocked on Farrow's door. The elfin star was surprised to see this pretty young thing on her doorstep, and Judith's very polite, diffident approach broke through the actress's distrust of the press.

Judith says, "I got the interview, and to this day Mia is still a friend."

Young Ms. Regan spent two years distinguishing herself as a reporter before I promoted her to articles editor at age twenty-three. She spent two more years running her own staff of reporters and having her first baby before leaving us for New York and the fame that awaited her.

I helped make Robin Leach *"Rich and Famous."* I fired him.

Robin had emigrated from England to New York before he was twenty-one and impressed *Enquirer* news executives with his drive and ability as a freelance reporter. Still in his twenties and now an *Enquirer* veteran, Robin returned to London on vacation just as I was beginning my career with the paper. That's where I first met him.

As London Bureau Chief, I arranged a dinner for Robin. There were seven of us: my wife, Jane, my deputy, Bill Dick, and his wife, Margaret, plus my sister, Sandra, who was visiting us from Scotland. The seventh was Robin's date—a Miss Something-or-Other and for years both Bill's wife and mine complained about how their husbands couldn't stop staring at this dazzling woman.

That was Robin's secret. You've seen him on TV; he's not ugly, but he ain't no Robert Redford. Yet there's a mixture of drive, intensity, confidence, and charm that makes him a magnet for beautiful women. Even in his early twenties he had style and a legendary black book full of models' and actresses' phone numbers.

By the time I became president and editor of the *Enquirer* in 1976, Robin had made, and was still making, a small fortune as one of our most trusted and prolific freelancers. He was earning more than even our well-paid staffers, filing exclusive after exclusive.

So when he told us he had a major, exclusive interview with Walter Cronkite, my ears perked up. When he told us the story, we got *really* excited. And on December 14, 1976, on the cover right next to the smaller headline "How to Pick a Christmas Tree," we announced in large banner type:

Walter Cronkite: Why I Believe in UFOs
. . . He reveals startling evidence kept secret by U.S. Govt.

This was major-league stuff. Cronkite had been anchor of the elite *CBS Evening News* for many years and was probably the most trusted man in the United States.

Our story, with Leach's byline, revealed that Walter believed in UFOs because of information given to him by space scientists and high-level government officials. Cronkite talked about specific sightings the government had kept secret.

In our story, Cronkite cited astronauts Neil Armstrong and James McDivitt as believers. He also mentioned Senator Barry Goldwater and President Ford and President-elect Carter. All in all, it was a very impressive piece, and we all congratulated Robin on another brilliant job.

Then came a call to Mr. Pope. Secretary Cindy Solomon, who later became one of our gossip columnists, answered the phone and heard, "This is Walter Cronkite. Let me speak to Mr. Pope."

Recalls Cindy, who was just out of her teens, "I nearly jumped out of my skin. Anybody would recognize Walter Cronkite's voice."

She buzzed GP to let him know who was on the line. GP said to Cindy, "What does he want?"

It was obvious why Cronkite was calling; GP was just buying time. Cindy was forced to ask her hero, "Mr. Cronkite, can you tell me what this is about?"

Cronkite: "He'll know."

When Cindy buzzed GP again, the Boss just growled, "Pass him over to Iain."

So I had my first—and last—conversation with Walter Cronkite, America's greatest journalist. He was not happy with the story, didn't recognize any of the quotes, and had no idea who Robin Leach was. He didn't actually say he did *not* believe in UFOs, and you can be damn sure I didn't ask him.

I was sweating bullets as I walked into Gene's office to give him the bad news. GP asked, "Do you believe him?"

It was kind of like asking, "Do you believe God?" I replied that, much as I trusted Leach, it was inconceivable that Walter Cronkite would lie. I added that Cronkite wanted to speak to Mr. Pope personally and it might be a good idea to return his call.

GP did call Walter and quickly agreed with my assessment. We immediately postmortemed the story.

The story had been approved only after Leach assured the editor he had the interview on tape. In those early days we didn't require tapes to be transcribed before publication, so now we asked Leach to send his tape to us. The "interview" tape turned out to be a very brief recording of Cronkite in an elevator with a NASA astronaut, talking about UFO sightings. Nothing on it indicated Cronkite believed in them—and Leach got the recording by chance because he happened to be in the elevator with the two men.

My next move was to tell Robin to fly to Florida immediately, if not sooner.

Robin entered my office with all the confidence of a journalist who was hurt and mystified that I could believe he had made anything up. I began to question him about the story and his interview—line by line, move by move, moment by moment. How had he set up the interview, where had it been done, how long had it lasted?

I really wanted to believe Robin, but he began to do an intellectual tap dance with me, sidestepping some questions, partially answering others, and changing the subject abruptly. I told him, "Don't tap dance with a tap dancer." Tap dancer—hell, I was the company choreographer!

I believe Robin taped the brief exchange on the elevator, then talked with Cronkite for a couple of minutes as he stepped out of a building one day. But as for a full interview . . .

Robin had been a longtime, valued contributor, and he'd be a real loss to our editorial team. I really believe he was basically an honorable reporter, but I had no choice. Even one mistake of this magnitude is one too many. Robin never worked for us again.

In retrospect, this was the best thing that ever happened to Leach. He made lots of friends in Hollywood, including many beautiful women friends like Suzanne Somers. Those friendships led to various TV shows and business ventures, highlighted by *Lifestyles of the Rich and Famous*. Robin is now a multi-millionaire and a celebrity in his own right.

A year or so after the firing I was a guest in the front row at the taping of the hit TV comedy *Three's Company*—and there on the set was Robin, laughing and joking with star Suzanne Somers. He saw me, came over, and shook my hand. No hard feelings.

I've talked to Robin several times over the years, and we've done quite a few stories about him. He's always been friendly.

On the other hand, I have never again had the honor to chat with Walter. I still don't really know if he believes in UFOs. If he wants to tell me, I'd love to get a call.

At the *Enquirer*, each articles editor (AE) was like a mini city editor on a daily newspaper. The AE had an editorial assistant, a team of staff reporters, and a self-generated list of freelance journalists (stringers) all over the world. Each team was responsible for developing story ideas and then, if these were approved, preparing the final story for publication. Even though the system made for lots of internal competition, every once in a while, a team would get lazy. Their ideas would be less exciting, the freelance list would begin to dissipate, and the net result was fewer good stories.

To keep the editorial department crackling with electricity, excitement, and tension, I dreamed up a contest inspired by my days as a young reporter in Scotland. The *Daily Record*, where I had worked, was a national newspaper based in Glasgow. In four or five other cities, the *Record* stationed staff reporters to cover local news there.

When a local reporter went on annual vacation, a Glasgow reporter would take over for a couple of weeks. I vividly remember arriving in the towns of Inverness and Dundee in consecutive years, knowing no one, having no contacts, yet expected to come up with great stories for the national edition.

My bosses knew the lack of local knowledge would just make a young reporter work harder. In a mild panic, I worked day and night—and came up with dozens of great stories that my bosses back in Glasgow loved.

I wasn't the only one to do this. The *Record* editors knew this tactic worked almost every time.

So how could I make this idea work for the *Enquirer*?

I picked two articles-editor teams and two cities, say Atlanta and Boston. I said: "Go there for a month and bring me back great stories, tremendous pictures, and terrific new freelance stringers." The

editors had a few weeks to prepare and then set off with their reporters.

At the end of each foray, I evaluated the quantity and quality of
the results. And—because there were two teams—one would be the
winner. No one wanted to be number two and lose face with their
colleagues in the editorial office, so we usually ended up with a lot
of great stories.

Letting loose our Wild Bunch on these cities at times created a
few problems here and there. But with a combination of skill, intelligence, and luck, they usually came through, without my ever hearing about the glitches.

One such occasion was Balfour vs. Ross in New York City in October 1977. Because New York is so big, I decided to match two
articles-editor teams in the same city.

Malcolm Balfour was—and still is—an ingenious journalist who
can get a story using determination, charm, ingenuity, or a mixture
of all three. He'd honed his skills in Miami before joining us and
knew all the tricks of the trade. He had a strong team that included
Jay Gourley (the infamous garbage thief), Steve Chao, and Jim
McCandlish.

On the other side was Shelley Ross, a young, attractive editor already showing the drive and determination that years after, helped
her become the highly respected executive producer of ABC's *Good
Morning America*. She also had an outstanding team of reporters,
including John Cathcart, the legendary *Enquirer* photo editor who
later got us the pictures of Gary Hart and Donna Rice on the *Monkey
Business*. At this time he was working as a freelancer.

Tiny, dark-haired, and very pretty, Shelley had been enjoying a
mainstream journalistic career writing features for the *Miami Herald* and later the *Fort Lauderdale Sun-Sentinel* when an *Enquirer*
editor read one of her pieces and asked if she'd write a freelance
story for him. Concerned about how that would affect her job, she
consulted her boss, who told her: "Half the people here do work for
the *Enquirer*!"

One freelance story led to another, and eventually I hired her as
a staff reporter ("travel the world at triple the salary" was our sales
pitch) and later promoted her to articles editor to run her own team

of reporters. Then I watched in amusement as my other editors, mostly male and mostly older, struggled to keep up.

The Balfour vs. Ross match looked close on paper. Balfour had the edge in experience and Ross was perhaps more intense. Since each team was looking not only for good stories but also for new reporters and freelancers, it was a great time to be in New York. The city was in the middle of a newspaper strike, and many New York journalists from the *Post* and the *Daily News* were looking for alternative sources of income.

The last few weeks in New York had been a hard grind, but Shelley and her team were feeling good. They'd come up with many good stories, had literally hundreds of other story ideas to take back to Lantana, and they had the names of several promising stringers. Shelley felt her team had won the contest. They were two days from returning to Florida.

Balfour and his rival group had apparently unofficially signed off work and were goofing around in New York, but Shelley insisted that *her* reporters stay on duty. They were typing up last-minute story ideas, and Shelley was interviewing the last group of potential freelancers.

One older lady in this group claimed to have been a famous New York photographer and had albums of her pictures to prove it. Shelley looked through the portfolio quickly. Most of the photos were twenty years old, depicting celebrities long since dead or forgotten.

This lady rated a brush-off, albeit a polite one. Shelley asked for her telephone number. "I don't have a phone," she said, "but I'll give you my address." She jotted down the information on a piece of paper.

"Sure, sure," said Shelley. "We'll write to you if we need anything."

No phone! thought Shelley as she shook hands with the woman and said good-bye. What a total waste of time.

The following day was the last before flying home. Shelley's spies told her that Balfour and his gang had gone off to the racetrack for one last day of fun and booze. Her team was still banging out story ideas.

And that's when the emergency call came in from Lantana. We'd just gotten big news about actor Gig Young. His name may not ring many bells today, but at that time Young was a well-known, well-liked star with a career spanning more than thirty years. He'd won an Oscar for his role as a dance-marathon emcee in *They Shoot Horses, Don't They?* and had a string of unsuccessful marriages, and now came word that he'd shot his wife and then committed suicide in their New York apartment. He was sixty-five, and his wife was thirty-one.

Within seconds, I was phoning Shelley: "We're tearing up the front page, and we want some great stuff on this. It's your story."

Of course, I called Balfour and told him the same thing. It didn't hurt to have two major teams on the same big story.

Shelley remembers being terrified. The *Enquirer* was depending on her to produce a front page in less than forty-eight hours. Her reporters feverishly flung into action. Phones in her hotel suite were ringing off the hook, reporters were shouting at each other, the place was bedlam.

In the middle of this, an assistant comes over to Shelley and says, "The photographer you spoke to yesterday is on a pay phone and really needs to talk with you." Shelley remembers: "I told the assistant: no way. The old woman didn't even have a home telephone. How could she possibly help at a time like this? I just shouted, 'Not now!'"

The old lady was insistent, and the assistant pushed Shelley hard. It was an emergency, and Shelley *had* to talk to her.

Shelley nearly fell off her chair when she heard the woman's first words. "I have some pictures." They were the official wedding photos of Gig Young and his wife getting married, three weeks ago. And *exclusive*. If you could kiss someone over phone lines, the lady's face would have been red with Shelley Ross's lipstick.

Recalls Shelley, "That moment was one of my greatest-ever highs."

So Shelley and the *Enquirer* got lucky. *Sure.* In my forty-plus years in journalism, I've noticed a particular phenomenon. The luckiest reporters, photographers, and editors have always been the ones who worked three times harder than those around them. That's why Shelley has been pretty lucky most of her life.

While Shelley was pushing her troops, the Balfour team was taking it easy and enjoying New York. They'd done well and come up with plenty of leads and stringers. But word was out that Ross was a machine, churning out story after story. Balfour wasn't sure his team would come out on top.

Then came my call on Gig Young's murder-suicide. It so happened that Steve Chao had interviewed Gig Young briefly only a few days before. It was probably the actor's *last* interview before he died—a great coup. But Steve wasn't experienced at extracting the best angle from an interview, so Balfour and a couple of the other reporters helped him punch up the piece.

Once that was done, Balfour decided his team could celebrate. The following day, the last day of the trip, they decided to sneak off for an afternoon at Aqueduct Racetrack. One lone reporter was left behind to man the phones in the hotel, in case of emergencies.

And one came up. Me!

I needed the Balfour team to attack a new angle on the Gig Young story immediately. When we called the hotel, the reporter who answered sounded a little panicky, and he couldn't tell us where his colleagues were. It became obvious that they'd gone AWOL, which would *not* endear them to me.

Years later, McCandlish told me what happened. The reporters were enjoying the ponies when suddenly a voice boomed over the loudspeakers: "Will Mr. Malcolm Balfour please report to the Red Cross office."

The message was "Call Iain Calder. *Now.*" They'd been caught playing hooky in the middle of a major story. They knew it was obviously not the kind of thing I would take lightly. In a subsequent article in *National Review*, Jay Gourley described the reaction of Balfour's team: "Calder is Pope's right-hand man, which is to say he's the one who actually fires people. Never having faced a live, blood-hungry shark, I could not personally contribute to the ensuing conversation about Calder's physical resemblance to the inimical beast."

This was long before cell phones, and there are no outside lines at racetracks. The entire team rushed out of Aqueduct and scrambled for the nearest pay phone. When they reached the reporter at the hotel, he moaned, "We've been found out. They needed us for the story, and we weren't there."

Certain they'd all be fired, Balfour decided they might as well go out in style: Let's go out for drinks and dinner on expenses—and to hell with what happens after.

Thank goodness I wasn't there, or the following might never have occurred.

The team walked into the piano bar at the tony Carlyle Hotel. Whom did they see there but Harry Reasoner, the renowned ABC anchor and CBS *60 Minutes* star. And was Harry with his wife? No. He was giggling and cuddling up to a beautiful blonde.

In those days, the *Enquirer* gave all its reporters little Instamatic cameras in case of an emergency. An emergency like this. Balfour told Gourley, "When I yell 'Shoot!' get a flash picture. Then we'll all run out."

Remembers Gourley, "I had the miniature flash mounted on my Minox camera. 'Hey, Harry!' I yelled. He turned. I flashed."

On the flash, five guys rushed out of the Carlyle, leaving Reasoner and the honey rubbing their eyes and the other patrons wondering what the hell had just happened.

But the fearless Gourley wasn't finished. Knowing that several careers might depend on what was on the film, he barged back into the bar. "One more, Harry," he shouted, and when Reasoner turned again, Gourley flashed once more.

The Good Luck Fairy wasn't done with the Balfour team. Flushed with excitement over their unexpected exclusive, they chose an expensive East Side Italian restaurant for an expenses-paid feast— "maybe the condemned man's last meal," joked one of them.

As fate would have it, they were seated at a table right next to Peter Falk, TV's Columbo, and he was hot, hot, hot.

The *Enquirer* had been trying to get an interview with Falk for months. Before *Columbo* (or after the show went off the air), Falk would have been thrilled to be on the cover of the *Enquirer*. But when stars are red-hot, they love playing hard-to-get.

Columbo is now sitting next to one of the *Enquirer*'s most wily editors with half a dozen of his commando-squad reporters. How do they exploit this situation?

They don't have to. Falk, who has been slow to order, can't make up his mind. He turns, looks at McCandlish and then at McCandlish's plate, and growls like Columbo, "What's that you got? Good?"

Talk about an opening! Within minutes McCandlish has him—to

coin a phrase—eating out of his hand. And the group has Columbo chortling and laughing at their jokes and one-liners.

"Pull up your chairs," orders Falk, and just like that they slide the tables together and are chatting like friends.

Someone decides honesty is the best policy—at least as much honesty as won't get them thrown out of the restaurant. We're all journalists from out of town, they tell Falk, without using the hara-kiri word *"Enquirer."*

Can we ask you some questions, asked our hardly-can-believe-it reporters. Sure, says, Falk, enjoying every moment.

The *Enquirer* had a policy of trying to get all celebrity interviews on tape, so each reporter had a small office tape recorder that was to be carried whenever possible. As McCandlish tells it, "When Falk said it was okay to ask questions, six hands went into six pockets in one choreographed moment, and we thought the clicks of the tape recorders being turned on would deafen the other customers."

But the sounds went unnoticed, the interview went on, and the result was two great stories—one about how astrology had helped make him a star, and the other about his new marriage and why it would be a happy one.

When the team returned, flushed with triumph over Reasoner and Falk, I conveniently forgot about the AWOL incident. How can you fire journalists with such great luck?

I have just one problem with this story. It blows holes in my oft-stated axiom that journalistic luck is a by-product of sweat and hard work. Sometimes, I guess, luck can be a by-product of . . . serendipity.

When Elvis Presley died, many inside Graceland tried to revive him, surrounded by the wailing and tears of friends and relatives. That day, August 16, 1977, was a bad one for articles editor Tom Kuncl. He'd worked three months on a great story: attempts on the life of President Jimmy Carter.

Through excellent sources in Washington, D.C., including former Secret Service agents, Tom had put together a riveting story of crazies and would-be assassins who were foiled before reaching the president. One incident was especially great. On Inauguration Day, a man with a harpoon gun had managed to get within range of Carter but was foiled when an extra harpoon fell out of his coat. Seeing this, two bystanders jumped on the guy and held him until he was arrested.

But Tom couldn't get the story into the *Enquirer*. Gene Pope was throwing all kinds of obstacles in the way, so Tom asked for an audience with the great man.

GP tried all kinds of reasons not to run the article. Looking at some typewritten material Kuncl had handed him, he snorted: "Hell, this writer even needs a new typewriter ribbon. It's so faint I can't even read it." He threw the file into his wastebasket. It was over.

Mad as hell, Tom walked out of GP's office. Someone in Washington must have gotten to the old man and asked for a favor, and that's why he wouldn't publish the story. He angrily kicked a wastebasket in the newsroom, then heard a Scottish voice shout: "Tom, over here."

It was me. I had just been told that Elvis had died, and I wanted Kuncl, a bulldog and one of my best big-story operators, to head up a major action team. Within minutes, he was organizing a reporting group.

Elvis had died at Graceland, his famous mansion in Memphis, Tennessee, and we could expect the world press to descend on Memphis like locusts. To help Kuncl be the hungriest locust and snap up the best exclusive stories and photos, I arranged for our finance department to pick up some cash at our local bank. Kuncl flew off in a chartered Learjet with six top reporters—and a bag containing $50,000 in cash. More money and more staff would be sent later. That was just to get the ball rolling.

Right before he left, I put my hand on Tom's shoulder and told him: "We gotta get this one. It's maybe the biggest ever."

Our editorial room in Lantana was in controlled panic. Every editor was working on Elvis. How had he died? What were his last days and hours and minutes like? Was anyone with him? What was the untold story? We wanted it all—first, best, and exclusive.

Our photo desk had one major imperative: Get a photo of Elvis in his coffin.

The whole power of the *Enquirer* was unleashed—and that was some power. Before Kuncl's crew had even landed in Memphis, we had more editors, freelancers, and private detectives on the ground running. Within thirty-six hours, Kuncl commanded an army of twenty-five reporters and freelancers.

Arriving in Memphis, Kuncl asked reporter Eric Mishara to find a headquarters big enough to accommodate his troops. In about five hours, Mishara had worked magic. A Holiday Inn being refurbished wasn't quite ready for guests, but they were willing to lease a whole floor to us. Done. Then Mishara learned there were no telephones anywhere in the entire hotel. He quickly persuaded the local phone company to install phones, several in each room, on the *Enquirer* floor.

By evening, our guerrillas moved in, with communications working perfectly—an amazing feat by a young reporter.

No one in Graceland was talking, but Kuncl sent everyone out to spread the word: The *Enquirer* was in town and had bags of money for big stories. Uncle Vernon, the King's real-life uncle, was posted at the Graceland gate. He got the message, and something for his trouble, and every Elvis contact we knew was bombarded with messages.

Twenty-four hours later, however, we still had very little, and Kuncl says: "We hadn't slept, and everyone was exhausted. I was beginning to panic, so I gathered twenty or so of my guys around me, then I actually got down on my knees and begged them: 'Please, we must have missed something. Go back out and try again. We've got to get the big story.' I felt like Al Jolson in white-face, and it was so funny everybody laughed and it broke the tension. Re-energized, the reporters went back out and hit every contact a second or third time."

By the end of the second day, seeds were beginning to sprout. People eager for the promised cash began to come to the hotel, where Kuncl's room was Command Central. One female hospital worker brought a big bag, out of which she spilled some blood-soaked sheets on the floor, exclaiming: "These are the sheets that covered the body of Elvis. You'll want to pay me some big bucks for these. Right?" *Wrong*. After almost puking, Kuncl told her to pick up her sheets and get lost.

Our first big break was tracking down the two ambulance paramedics who had picked up the body at Graceland and transported it to Baptist Hospital. We waved some money under their noses and brought them to Kuncl's hotel room.

Kuncl says: "There were four telephones in my room ringing constantly. Reporters were constantly running in and out of the room. The only place I could interview witnesses in peace was the bathroom. One at a time I took the medics into the bathroom. While I sat on the side of the bath and they used the lid-down commode, I debriefed them."

They obviously could give a dramatic eyewitness account of events inside Graceland. When Kuncl called me in Florida, I told him to ship both medics and their wives to Lantana, where we could interview them and write their story. I had two reasons for this: First, Kuncl and his team were still under constant, intense pressure, and this would provide a little relief. Second, and more important, the medics at this point had talked with no other media, and in Lantana we'd have them safe and tucked away from all rival reporters.

A nice contract gave the two medics and their wives some money plus an unexpected Florida vacation.

Things were really zinging for Kuncl by now. Elvis's stepmother, Dee Presley, arrived at the Holiday Inn, offering her story for a price. She was clad in the obligatory black dress, but it was slit all the way up one side, making her look like a hostess from Hong Kong. Pretty sexy for a funeral, Kuncl remembers thinking.

Other friends and relatives arrived in such numbers that often three or four interviews were taking place simultaneously in separate bedrooms.

It was known that Elvis regularly saw psychics. After contacting just about every psychic in western Tennessee, we finally found Christine Lilly Williams, who described how Elvis had been receiving eerie messages from his late mother and was sure death was approaching.

I always thought that if Ms. Williams was really a great psychic she would have known we wanted to interview her right away. But I wasn't going to put *that* in the story.

Kuncl was beginning to piece together a terrific story of how Elvis had died, with details, medical facts, and color no other paper had.

Then came wonderful news. One of our reporters, who had been trying to charm Elvis's current live-in girlfriend, Ginger Alden, for months, called to say he had her in the bag. She wanted money—of course—but she was willing to give us her exclusive story.

We'd hit the jackpot. Ginger had spent the night with Elvis, and she had the definitive account of what had happened step by step, moment by moment. There was no one in the world with a better Elvis story.

We headlined it: GIRL ELVIS WAS GOING TO MARRY TELLS HER HEART-BREAKING STORY, *by Ginger Alden.* She also posed for us, broken-hearted and holding a photo of Elvis.

Ginger, a beautiful twenty-year-old, told an enthralling tale. The day Elvis died, they went to bed sometime after 4 A.M. When she awoke, about 2 P.M., she got out of bed and found him slumped in their bathroom. She described the scene as nurses, doctors, friends all tried to revive the fallen superstar. It was a moment-by-moment description, for *Enquirer* readers only.

Along with the paramedics' story and all the medical details of how drugs had killed Elvis, it was a story package we knew was a winner. And it was all *exclusive.*

The world's press had flooded Memphis with their best reporters, but they just had no chance against our *Enquirer* runaway freight train. Jealously, the newspapers and TV stations in Memphis started running nasty stories about how our reporters were "buying up" information. Their critical stories simply increased the flow of visitors to the Holiday Inn. We were very grateful for their unintended help. Say what you want, but spell the name right.

Later we learned that the Memphis police had infiltrated our operation. We'd hired local messengers and assistants to answer telephones. Two were police "plants" to see if we were illegally bribing officials. We were not. We certainly were bribing people—just not illegally.

Their great stories in the bag, Kuncl and his guys were dead on their feet after four days almost without sleep. There had been no time for showers or letting the rooms be cleaned. Said Kuncl later: "We were in a pig sty on top of a loony bin."

I'd sent another bag of $50,000 cash, so we now had a total of $100,000 in this story. Tom said he had kept careful note of what was given to whom, but in the frenzied turmoil the paper was lost. Kuncl was an honest guy and we believed him. Especially since he'd produced a winner.

We needed just one more thing to make Mr. Pope a happy man— a picture of Elvis in his open casket. Tens of thousands of mourners paid their respects to the King lying in state at Graceland, but photos were forbidden and guards were on duty at all times.

While Kuncl's reporters were frenetically gyrating on all angles, photo editor Brian Hitchen was back in Lantana with just one focused, mandated mission: *Get the picture of Elvis in his coffin.* He sent a small group of photographers to Memphis with that single demand branded into their brains.

Several photographers joined the line of mourners passing the open casket. One, Vincent Eckersley, dressed as a priest and hid his camera inside a hollowed-out Bible. His vestments made him invisible, and he was able to walk past guards at Graceland and wander around without arousing suspicion—until he got too close to the coffin. Desperate, the team mapped out a plan to have someone faint near the coffin and, in the confusion, snap a shot of Elvis.

But in the end, the security was too good. They told Hitchen, "If we try something and fail, it will just make them tighten security— and we'll *never* get the picture."

Hitchen, a veteran newspaper executive from London's biggest dailies, turned to Plan B: Find a friend or relative and bribe them to take a pic. Discover the weakest link, he ordered.

Our cameramen had seen family members standing at each corner of the coffin, mourning silently, as the long line of fans passed. New family came in every couple of hours.

So our guys staked out the front of Graceland and waited until they recognized one of the family members walk out the gate. Photographer Jimmy Sutherland followed the young man to a nearby pub and waited until he went into the men's room. Sutherland joined him and made his pitch.

We'd struck gold. The guy was one of Elvis's cousins, and he was definitely interested in huge money. A deal was cut.

Hitchen told me later: "We were worried about metal detectors, so I bought a plastic mini-camera with a flash, set the range to five feet and taped it, so it couldn't be screwed up. Then we sent it to Memphis."

Sutherland met the cousin back in the same bar lavatory and passed over the camera with explicit instructions on how to use it. Off went the cousin to Graceland.

He hid the camera on his person and stood loyally by the coffin as thousands shuffled past. After the viewing was over he stayed on in the house with other relatives, just talking and drinking. In the middle of the night the cousin sneaked into the darkened viewing area and . . . flash, flash, flash, flash. Four times he snapped.

He didn't leave until morning. Sutherland whisked the cousin and an uncle off to a regional airport about 20 miles away, to avoid being recognized by anyone at the Memphis airport. A private jet flew the relatives and the film to the Lantana airport, where the town's police chief was waiting with an *Enquirer* driver, and they were taken straight to our office.

Hitchen told me the film had arrived, but he didn't want to alert Mr. Pope in case it was a bust. I bit my nails as Hitchen went into the darkroom with our lab chief, Santo Buccafucci, to develop the film. A security man stood guard at the door.

Brian says the next few minutes seemed like weeks. There were four frames. Santo, with sweaty and trembling hands, hung the film to dry. Frames in these mini-cameras are so tiny it was hard to tell what we had. So he put them under the enlarger, and both he and Hitchen gazed intently at what was there.

Frame one: The cousin's blurry face. He had pointed the camera at himself.

Frame two: A picture of the chandelier hanging above the coffin. No sign of Elvis.

Frame three: *Bingo*. Elvis, full face, in the coffin. Just like it had been shot by a professional.

Frame four: Who cared after frame three, but it was another good picture, taken from the side of the casket, showing Elvis in profile.

When Hitchen burst back into the main office, his ear-to-ear grin told me everything I needed to know. We called Gene who, of course, was elated.

Hitchen went to the room where he'd actually locked in the Presley relatives. No figure had yet been mentioned, and Hitchen blurted out: "We'll give you $18,000 for total copyright." Brian said later: "I don't know where I dreamed up that number, but the two men were ecstatic."

When I asked Brian how he felt at that moment, he flashed his famous, beaming grin and answered: "Better than sex."

The end result was our historic September 6, 1977, *National Enquirer* with the headline:

EXCLUSIVE . . .
ELVIS
THE UNTOLD STORY

Beneath the headline was our close-up of Elvis in peaceful repose in his casket, with the underline: *The Last Picture.*

This was a blockbuster. Workers at our plant were taking copies home, our delivery drivers were grabbing them—and when the issue went on sale pandemonium erupted in some southern supermarkets. Customers were snatching up two, three, or more copies at one time.

In Tennessee we were sold out in forty-eight hours. Readers were calling our office begging for copies. One lady was so persistent that I agreed to talk to her. Her plea: She was desperate for that Elvis issue, she would treasure it forever, and was there any way I could send her one. She would pay $50, she said. We tried never to disappoint our readers, so we mailed out a copy for free.

That lady probably helped us sell *another* million copies. A few hours later, a reporter from the AP newswire called for an interview. The *Enquirer* is being criticized for running the casket picture of Elvis—what's your response?

That was easy. The mainstream press and TV routinely run casket photos of dead presidents, popes, and monarchs. Why not Elvis, I asked: He was "King" to many Americans.

Then I remembered the lady who had called earlier. I told the reporter that readers were buying multiple copies as souvenirs. "I know that up to $50 is being offered for one copy," I said. "Who knows what they'll be worth in the future as Elvis memorabilia."

Well, that story hummed across the wires, and newspapers all over the country reported *Enquirer* sellouts and offers of up to $50 for a single copy. That created a second rush in areas of the country where Elvis was less of an idol. Who wouldn't spend 35 cents on a paper that might be worth $50 some day?

Brian Hitchen swears he saw a newswire story about two masked men in one southern state who walked into a supermarket waving guns. They ignored cash in the checkout drawers but gathered up armfuls of our Elvis issue and ran out of the store.

I can't personally vouch for that incident, but the result was a sellout . . . the biggest in our history. That Elvis issue sold an amazing 6,700,000 copies, still our greatest sale of all time. And since the photo is our copyright, we've made a nice profit selling it in syndication all over the world, year after year.

In 1978, on the anniversary of Elvis's death, we knew we couldn't top the Last Picture, but we had to come up with something special. Elvis fans knew we were the source of the best photos and stories on the King, and we couldn't let them down.

We had put together a pretty good package of stories, plus a reprinting of the famous last photo, when one of our guys, Stuart Wilk, uncovered a great exclusive.

A priceless ring that Elvis had worn at his last-ever concert—a gold, diamond, and sapphire beauty that the King himself had helped design—was for sale.

The Memphis jeweler who had worked with Presley on the ring design gave it to the star to wear on his final tour. Elvis wore it every night, but a rough spot inside the ring cut into his finger, and the center diamond was loose.

So he returned it to jeweler Lowell J. Hayes to be repaired. It was covered with blood, but Mr. Hayes cleaned it off, took care of the problems, and was about to return the ring when Elvis suddenly died. Since Presley had never got around to paying for it, ownership of the ring reverted to the jeweler.

Mr. Hayes was willing to sell the ring to the *Enquirer*, and we bought it for somewhere close to $30,000. The ring had been appraised at $13,425, but we would have considered it a bargain at $100,000.

The ring might have been a bit gaudy for Prince Charles, but for Elvis fans it was perfect—four black sapphires set in gold, surrounded by forty-seven diamonds. We even had a photo of Elvis at his last concert wearing the ring on his right hand, proving it was authentic.

The beauty part was telling America that some lucky Elvis fan could have this ring for free. All anyone had to do was buy the *Enquirer*, answer some simple questions—about on the $100 level of *Who Wants to Be a Millionaire*—and send in an entry. The winner would be chosen in a random drawing. You could even send in more than one entry, enticing some fans to buy more than one *Enquirer*.

It was a great page one, and when customers in supermarkets saw the cover, the paper jumped off the shelves.

We didn't quite match the Elvis death issue, but we came close. And somebody somewhere has that priceless Elvis ring. Wonder what it's worth now?

Elvis might have been gone, but his ghost returned to haunt the *Enquirer* several years later—metaphorically, of course.

The famous Elvis-in-his-coffin picture was kept in an office safe and released only to trusted editors when we wanted to rerun it or to sell it for syndication. Never in my wildest dreams did I believe it was in danger.

Then one day I received a call from the head of a tiny photo agency in another state. She said she'd gotten a call from an *Enquirer* editor who'd offered her a stolen, black-market copy of our Elvis picture for the sum of $20,000. It was obvious that she had agreed, believing she could make a fortune selling it around the world.

She told me that her attorney had warned her she was risking jail time, and that a call to us would get her off the hook.

I was stunned as she told me the whole story. Three of my staff were involved: a reporter, a photo editor, and one of my most trusted articles editors—a man I thought was totally honest and above reproach.

Surprise turned to cold anger. It takes a lot arouse my deep-seated wrath. This did. These three men, all Brits, were each paid more than $40,000 a year—an *extremely* good salary in the 1970s. They were thieves, and, worse, they were traitors. They would pay.

The woman agreed to help me set a trap. After informing Gene Pope, I hired retired Palm Beach sheriff Bill Heidtman to coordinate a plan with the West Palm Beach police. The syndication woman, at my request, contacted her go-between, my reporter, and said she'd send a messenger to deliver the $20,000 and pick up the photo in a local hotel room.

I quarterbacked every detail of the sting. We arranged for the meeting at a room in the airport hotel. In the next room were the ex-sheriff, a police inspector, a massive, imposing sergeant in plain clothes, and me. I had picked up a thick wad of bills totaling $20,000 at a local bank and, rather nervously, driven to the hotel.

We gave the cash to the big sergeant, then wired him for sound. The receiver was in our room, so we could hear every word. Just before the sergeant went next door to wait for the handover, I said: "I want you to give this guy the biggest fright of his life." The big man just smiled.

At the appointed time, my reporter arrived at the rendezvous room and was ushered in. After a few minutes, the sergeant took out the envelope stuffed with cash and said: "Do you have the Elvis picture?"

When the reporter handed over the photo, the sergeant whipped out his .357. It was only a brief moment before he said: "I'm from the police. You are under arrest." But my treasonous reporter must have had a total fit. This huge messenger was surely about to kill him. It must have been a huge relief when he heard the word "Police!" and felt handcuffs click on his wrists.

As the sergeant pushed his man into our room, the reporter saw me. His body sagged, and he just muttered, "Aw, Iain."

One down. He was on his way to jail. Now we went after the articles editor, who was working in the office. I wanted the cops to walk into our newsroom, handcuff him, and haul him off to the pokey. That they did.

Two uniformed policemen caught up with him as he was walking out to lunch with a couple of colleagues. As he was put under arrest, the editor, whom I would have trusted with the lives of my children, fainted and collapsed in a heap.

The third man, the photo editor, was on vacation, and we didn't catch up with him for several days.

We never figured out why the three did it. The money was almost peanuts to these highly paid journalists. And the first time the photo appeared in a publication, we would have found out. This nutty crime made no sense.

Gene and I finally decided not to prosecute, but the men had to uproot themselves and their families from south Florida. And at first it was tough for them to get good jobs.

Why don't I name them now? It's been nearly a quarter of a century, they've been punished and suffered humiliation. It's enough.

Over the decades, I caught several lower-level staffers trying to cheat or steal from the company. But nothing shattered me like the betrayal of these three.

By the time we rolled out the Elvis campaign, we'd developed a hard-working, never-say-die group of reporters, ready to do whatever it took to get the story. Yes, we used techniques that other publications looked down on. Over the years, we got a lot of flak for paying sources. I do not apologize. We paid—and still do pay—for story ideas, and we will "buy up" a major source for an exclusive on a newsworthy story.

Story ideas first. Mainstream media professionals say it's okay to pay a journalist for a story idea. The *Enquirer* says it's okay to pay *anyone* for a story idea—whether the lead comes from a journalist, a plumber, or a housewife. Everything will be checked out by professional reporters, and we pay only when the story is published. Our paper often requests story ideas for cash directly from our readers, and literally thousands of ordinary people have responded over the years. I'd love to debate the integrity of that with anyone.

Now comes the charge that if we pay for stories or interviews, the subject will make up "facts" just to get cash. True—and just as many make up fantasies for free. It's the job of a professional news organization to check the veracity of what they're told. That's what we do. I won't speak for other publications since I don't have firsthand knowledge, but the *Enquirer*'s record of breaking the big stories—from Gary Hart to O. J. Simpson—proves we're second to none when it comes to verifying stories. I guarantee that over the years we killed many, many more stories than we ran—just because the stories didn't check out. Once I did a count, and I think we killed something like six story assignments for every one that made it into the paper.

One example was a tip that Madonna had been treated for thyroid cancer at Cedars-Sinai hospital in Los Angeles. The lead was confirmed, separately, by two apparently good sources, a CAT-scan operator and an X-ray technician. We checked further, even going through her trash, which revealed only a couple of intimate notes from her boyfriend, who nicknamed her "Sloppy." Days of investigations revealed that Madonna indeed had cancer, but it wasn't the famous singer but a middle-aged woman named Madonna Hernandez. It cost us thousands of dollars to disprove the story—but that's our job.

We paid big bucks for big stories only occasionally: Joan Collins's wedding exclusive, Liberace's gay lover's story, a confession from the female drug dealer who admitted she had inadvertently killed John Belushi, the clerk who sold O.J. a knife that fit the description of the murder weapon. We weren't buying their words—we were buying exclusivity. As a weekly, the *Enquirer* has a longer lead time than daily papers and TV shows—they can steal a story and rush it into print or on the air before we even reach the supermarket rack. Our defense is to sign the key people to contracts and make sure they keep quiet until the issue is no longer on sale.

The next question is: Why do other news organizations refuse to pay for exclusives? Why only the *Enquirer* and other tabloids? Many of the others *do* pay, silly. They just disguise it.

60 Minutes broke a big tobacco story that spawned the major motion picture *The Insider*—and, according to the *Wall Street Jour-*

nal, they paid their main source $12,000. Does that mean they paid their source? "Oh no," they protested, "we were paying him as a *consultant*." Gimme a break.

In August 2002, CNN ran shocking video of Al Qaeda training sessions, showing instruction in bomb-building, ambush, and kidnapping, plus some really grisly footage of what appears to be poison-gas testing on several unfortunate dogs. At first, CNN didn't admit to paying for the tape, but soon CNN chairman Walter Isaacson 'fessed up that, yes, "a reasonable amount, $30,000, was paid to the those individuals who recovered the tapes, which we all know to be standard practice in this business." According to Isaacson's statement, the network paid "no money to Al Qaeda or anyone associated with Al Qaeda." Excuse me, but how the hell does *he* know that? Once the money left CNN's hands, they have no idea where it ended up. Every penny could have gone into Al Qaeda's pockets.

On June 16, 2003, CNN anchorman Aaron Brown was interviewing former NBC *Today* show executive editor Steve Friedman and needling him on the networks paying exclusive interview subjects with inducements other than hard cash.

If top interviewers like Barbara Walters, in order to get a major exclusive, offered to introduce the hot subject to a subsidiary company who would publish their book or to a movie producer who would pay big bucks for a movie of the week, wasn't that the same as just paying for the story, asked Brown.

Friedman, after a little hesitation, admitted that Brown was correct: "It would be cleaner if everyone was paid," he said. Friedman went on to criticize CBS with their "holier than thou" claim of *never* paying for a story or interview. He pointed out that CBS officials were hypocrites. As far back as the Watergate era, CBS' *60 Minutes* paid Nixon aide H. R. Haldeman $25,000 for some home movies. CBS went on to claim they did *not* pay for the exclusive interview that followed. The money, they said, was for the home movies.

These were the high-principled newsmen who criticized the *Enquirer* when we openly paid sources for exclusives. Isn't it mildly reminiscent of the dozens, if not hundreds, of Catholic priests, who for decades called for high morals from the pulpit, while secretly allowing young boys and girls to be molested by their fellow clerics?

We know that the average local newspaper and TV station doesn't pay for breaking news interviews. Neither do we. But *People* has paid many times for big, exclusive stories—when must-see photos are involved. Photos of weddings, newborns, and honeymoons have them reaching for their checkbook. Their worst big-bucks decision was buying the rights to the photos and story of Elvis Presley's first grandchild. We broke *People*'s exclusive by having an *Enquirer* reporter infiltrate their security squad guarding the child. I think our (free) picture was better than theirs.

If celebrities or others write books, it's apparently okay to pay the author for exclusive rights. No one would ever, ever lie in a book just to make more money, goes the theory. *Right.* Actually, it could be argued that publishers deliver *less* integrity when they pay for book rights, because they don't even check the text for accuracy.

Now for TV shows—from the morning shows to the hard-fought battles among the prime-time giants like *20/20* and *Dateline*. Whenever there's a major story, all the news superstars want the big exclusive. Behind the scenes the jostling for the Big One is like what happens when a roast beef is thrown into a pool of piranhas. Do you think the producers and star journalists all just politely make a phone call and wait for an answer?

Definitely not. They throw out all kinds of goodies. If there's an agent, he or she might get an unwritten promise to "look after your clients" in the future—which means some minor star will get airtime in future as a thank-you. Or the network will plug just about anything the agent suggests, including books and movies that might be real dogs but won't be criticized on air. Maybe no money changes hands. But the financial goodies involved make *Enquirer* cash payouts look feeble. A plug for a movie on national TV is *priceless*.

New York Post columnist Cindy Adams knows just about every secret in New York. She wrote a scathing piece about TV journalists in her February 18, 1998, column, describing how TV shows were luring their hottest, most-wanted guests.

At the time, the number-one target for TV interview shows was thirty-five-year-old teacher Mary Kay LeTourneau, who had seduced a thirteen-year-old former pupil and had his baby and would later have another daughter with the teenager.

According to Cindy Adams, as an inducement to clinch the exclusive, one TV news show flew two of LeTourneau's attorneys and their wives to New York, providing first-class limos to and from the airports. Airfare for four, accommodations at a five-star hotel, wining and dining like VIPs, introductions to network news stars, the best seats for *Saturday Night Live*—the attorneys wanted it, they got it.

Cindy said this was now standard operating procedure for TV shows. The attorneys, she revealed, get to control ancillary shows, guaranteed mentions on shows, etc., etc. All of which is worth *cash*.

Wrote Cindy: "Mind, the show's hosts can say with all honesty, 'We do not and have not paid these people to come on air.'"

Cindy's closing comment: "Just letting you know how it's done, kiddies."

I'm not knocking it. But how can these newspeople barter away goodies, then whack the *Enquirer* for paying the honest and upfront way?

Another big lie—all our celebrity stories were fabrications. Nope—not even close.

When we revealed on our cover in August 1989 that Jane Fonda and Ted Turner were secretly dating, the *New York Post* and wire services quoted Jane's press agent, saying our story was all wet. No romance.

Fonda and Turner announced they were serious about each other the following March; it was a prelude to their marriage.

When we published the exclusive story in July 1990 that Tom Cruise was engaged to Nicole Kidman, our all-American hero denied it on *Oprah*. The audience cheered as he said there was no truth to the story.

They married on Christmas Eve of the same year.

Our stories were almost always correct. Mainstream journalism fed Americans the lie that these, and most of our other celebrity stories, were just made up. Our readers knew the real truth. You don't have to expend the largest editorial budget in print journalism if you can invent stories.

Did we ever make a mistake? Yes. We ran many thousands of stories each year, and we did make an occasional error. We've apologized for these and occasionally paid out some money. I've fired staffers and stringers for either lying or being careless, but our record is excellent, and I'm proud of it. Show me the publication that hasn't goofed. The *Washington Post* had to hand back a Pulitzer Prize when their reporter Janet Cooke admitted she concocted a story. The ABC newsmagazine *20/20* ran a photo of U.S. prisoners of war supposedly abandoned in Vietnam to prove their thesis "The Men We Left Behind." Later it came out that the photo actually showed Army guys who had been *freed* from POW camps.

But the biggest lie that's told about the *Enquirer* is that we were sued all the time for inaccurate stories, that we lost many lawsuits due to inaccuracies. Absolutely not true.

We were *threatened* with lawsuits all the time. While I was running the *Enquirer* news machine, literally hundreds of celebrities announced they were going to sue us. Very, very few actually did. There were myriad reasons for these phony threats, including:

- Drumming up publicity.
- Persuading an irate wife that there really was no overnight blonde at the Marriott.
- Showing the Hollywood community they would fight the "evil empire."
- Sending a message, through their attorneys, that they were litigious and we'd better watch out when publishing future stories.

Sometimes the stars would actually file suit to convince the world they were serious, then let the suit quietly drop after gossip columnists and TV celebrity shows had trumpeted their righteous indignation all over America.

I liked to imagine the PR flacks in Hollywood and their star clients chortling at how the *Enquirer* was embarrassed by their scornful attacks, dutifully run by their pet gossip columnists in newspapers and on TV.

How could they know I loved this stuff!?

These publicists helped make the *Enquirer* one of the best-known product names in the United States. Week after week, one star after another would attack us in print and on the tube. The results were *wonderful* for us.

In the 1980s a researcher confided to me that his firm had run a nationwide survey on how recognizable certain top brand names were. The *Enquirer's* name recognition scored just under that of Coca-Cola and the Ford Motor Company, and well ahead of some brands that were spending hundreds of millions of dollars on advertising. I was told, however, that the research company decided to drop the *Enquirer* from the final list. Companies such as Kraft and Campbell Soup would have been unhappy to learn that their brand recognition was lower than the *Enquirer's*! And they never did know that, until now.

About that time, I compared our current libel lawsuits to those at the three networks. We had three or four cases against us, while ABC, NBC, and CBS had more than one hundred *each*. One program alone, *60 Minutes*, was named as a plaintiff in more lawsuits than we were. This was remarkable, since they probably broadcast seventy-five new stories per year while we published, including column items, more than seventy-five per *week*—or close to 4,000 per year. The vast majority of the suits filed against *60 Minutes* were probably unjustified. But so were the ones filed against us.

During all my time in the *Enquirer* editorial department, from 1964 through 1995, we lost only one case—in 1981, to Carol Burnett. At the time, it seemed like a disaster. In hindsight, it was probably one of the best things that happened to us.

THE BURNETT CASE

In 1976 R. Couri Hay was a gossip reporter for us. That meant he was responsible for obtaining items from sources and paid stringers. The actual column was headlined under the name Steve Tinney but was written by chief writer Mike Walker.

Hay was based in New York City, and Walker was in Lantana. When the raw copy arrived in Lantana, Walker would read it for sense, for reader interest, and for his judgment about any extra work needed to check veracity. He often chose the items that he would write, and he was, in effect, the column editor. When Walker was happy with the column, he'd send copies to me and Gene Pope. GP, of course, was the final arbiter.

On March 2, 1976, we ran an item headlined: CAROL BURNETT AND HENRY K. IN ROW. It was all of four sentences: "In a Washington restaurant, a boisterous Carol Burnett had a loud argument with another diner, Henry Kissinger. Then she traipsed around the place offering everyone a bite of her dessert. But Carol really raised eyebrows when she accidentally knocked a glass of wine over one diner and started giggling instead of apologizing. The guy wasn't amused and 'accidentally' spilled a glass of water over Carol's dress."

It seemed fairly tame compared to other types of items we often ran. I suppose a nuclear bomb is also harmless until it explodes.

This item exploded—big time. We wound up being blasted, pounded, and vilified on network TV and in newspapers and magazines all over the country. Mainstream journalists, many of whom were outraged by the phenomenal success of the *Enquirer*, had been waiting for this chance to attack us. Now they took every shot they could.

Carol Burnett's lawyers contacted us to the say the item was false. R. Couri Hay said he had a good eyewitness source in the restaurant, and a second reporter actually called the restaurant's public relations representative, who confirmed some, but not all, of the details.

But as soon as the threat of a lawsuit loomed, the sources would not stand by our copy. Either they froze in fear, or in fact the main thrust of our item really was wrong.

Our attorney, Meyer Kimmel, an old-time lawyer who had been with Gene forever, was a smart old guy, but he did not specialize in libel law. His opinion was that since we could not prove the item, we should run a retraction. It was an easy call: We had to admit we had made a mistake and tell Carol and the world we were sorry.

Following our investigation, we ran the following *mea culpa*: "An item in this column on March 2 erroneously reported that Carol Burnett had an argument with Henry Kissinger at a Washington restaurant and became boisterous, disturbing other guests. We understand these events did not occur, and we are sorry for any embarrassment our report may have caused Miss Burnett."

I was sure that was the end of that. Boy, was I wrong. Carol was on a rampage. She claimed we had implied she was a drunk, and she became the Heroine of Hollywood with her holy war against the *Enquirer*.

It took several years to get us to court. But she did.

By the time we came to trial, we'd hired one of America's most prestigious law firms, Rogers and Wells of New York City. They hired a top gun, William Masterson, to run their Los Angeles office, and his top priority was to win this case.

Bill Masterson had the aura of a movie star. He was tall, handsome, articulate, and intelligent, an accomplished litigator, a wine connoisseur, and a bon vivant. I wish we had never hired him.

His strategy was to know everything about the case but to keep me in the dark. His logic: If you don't know the details, you can't be asked to give them to the other side.

That may have been the upside. The downside was that I didn't know how much Masterson himself was missing in preparing the case.

For example, one cornerstone of the case was the judge's ruling on whether the *Enquirer* was a newspaper or a magazine. Under California statute, a newspaper had the right to issue a retraction on a published story they later learned was false. This meant that the plaintiff had no right to punitive damages, since an apology had been made. Magazines, for some reason, had no such rights.

We said right on our cover: "Biggest Circulation of any Paper in America." We were black and white then, and we didn't have a staple in the centerfold. It was obvious to us that we were a newspaper.

I arrived in Los Angeles on the Friday before the trial was to begin. The first argument on Monday morning would be the newspaper vs. magazine question. Masterson and our other L.A. counsel informed me that Burnett's team had an expert witness, an eminent journalism professor from the University of California, Berkeley, who would say the *Enquirer* was a magazine.

"Who is *our* expert witness?" I asked.

Silence. "We don't have one," confessed the attorneys.

I nearly hit the ceiling. Perhaps I even used language not considered totally proper. We'd had years to prepare the case. Why *didn't* we have an expert witness? I told Masterson to get *somebody*. He protested it was Friday night, and my answer was roughly: "I don't give a hoot. Please get it done." My actual words were probably quite a bit stronger, but my intent was clear.

On Monday we had our "expert"—a lecturer from Long Beach State. It was like putting a high school science teacher up against Einstein.

Of course, the judge ruled with Einstein. And I had this awful sinking feeling that if this was typical of our preparation and strategy, our case was doomed.

The next few days were a nightmare. Each day, the trial was carried on national television. All three networks. If men from Mars had landed, I don't think that news would have pushed us off the air or the front pages of the local papers. Guess who were the good guys and who wore the black hats?

Our witnesses were pretty good, but so was Carol's lawyer, Barry Langberg. Our attorneys did not prepare us well for questioning, and I admit Carol's lawyer had me twisting and turning on the stand. (Years later, when I was prepared by our new law firm, Williams and Connolly, I learned what great pre-questioning preparation can do for a witness.)

Carol Burnett, of course, was brilliant. She had the jury laughing, frowning, sad, happy, and angry—whatever and whenever she wanted. She told them how these few gossip-column lines had devastated her because of a history of alcoholism in her family. One of her anecdotes was especially wonderful. According to Carol, after the item was printed, she was walking in New York City when a passing cabby leaned out of his window and made a nasty crack about her drinking. She was so, *so* upset, and it was these evil *Enquirer* people who had caused all this.

Did our lawyers attack her? Did they point out the inconsistencies in her story? Did they describe her TV show, on which she does skits making fun of people who drink too much? Did they go into her personal life to probe her private habits?

No, no, no—and no.

Our policy, said Mr. Masterson, was to treat Carol kindly and to win on the law.

In his final summing-up, our lead attorney was an orator without peer. Masterson tried to convince the jury that a verdict against the *Enquirer* was a blow to the freedoms of America and an insult to the Constitution and the great men who had drafted our First Amendment protections.

I'm not sure the jury knew what he was talking about. They were just thinking, "How much should we give Carol . . . and how do I get her autograph?"

The verdict finally came in. Burnett was awarded $300,000 in general damages and another $1.3 million in punitive damages—for a total of $1.6 million. It was an astounding figure in those days.

The judge quickly cut it in half. A court of appeals cut it again. Finally we settled for a sum we agreed to keep secret, but which one magazine later reported as $200,000. I'm told Carol didn't care about the money. She just wanted the victory and, in fact, gave most or all of the award to journalism programs at the University of California at Berkeley and the University of Hawaii.

For the *Enquirer*, the aftermath of the L.A. verdict was really depressing. The media trumpeted the victory of good over evil, of Burnett over the Dragon. It was a major story on TV and radio stations all across the country, followed the next day by page-one banner headlines from Seattle to Miami. Pundits from mainstream journalism gleefully forecast our doom.

The reality was quite different. We'd received thousands of letters from readers encouraging us onward into battle, and actually sending us money. And circulation was *up*. The publicity was not hurting the paper.

But psychologically, it was a major loss, especially for a company that just wasn't used to losing. Constant media criticism hurt the morale of our reporters while they were out doing interviews.

Despite the temporary pain, life soon continued on as usual, and Carol Burnett's lawsuit ended up doing us a favor. Maybe we *had* been too cavalier on some stories. Maybe we needed a change.

We, of course, fired Rogers and Wells. They also soon parted company with Bill Masterson, who continued to enjoy a fine career as a litigator and later a judge.

The case was nirvana for Carol Burnett. Already a beloved TV star, she was now rivaling Mother Teresa in Hollywood. She basked in the glow of being the star who had actually beaten the *Enquirer* in court. Thankfully, during my time running the paper, she was the only one.

Sometimes people ask if we "got even" with Burnett in later years with negative stories. It never happened. Neither Gene nor I had any bitterness toward her. She beat us fair and square. If I ever met Carol, I would be honored and happy to say "hello." Whether the feeling is mutual is probably quite another story.

THE 1980S—
STRONGER THAN EVER

We'd thought we were doing a good job on editorial, but after the Burnett experience, we began to focus on improving the accuracy of our stories. Gene had already directed me to form a vigorous research department that would check facts, listen to interview tapes, and set stringent standards for approving stories before publication. Our tough new Truth Squad became a critical element in the *National Enquirer*'s success in the '80s and beyond.

And we retained Williams and Connolly—in my biased opinion, the premier First Amendment law firm in the United States. After that switch, and during my editorial tenure, we never lost another libel case in court.

The principal partner in Williams and Connolly, and the man who ran the show, was a giant among American attorneys. Edward Bennett Williams had an incredible record defending famous clients in trouble. He had saved the necks of such lovable American heroes as Senator Joseph McCarthy, mob boss Frank Costello, Teamster head Jimmy Hoffa, and Congressman Adam Clayton Powell. He also owned the Baltimore Orioles baseball team and was president of the Washington Redskins football franchise. Ed, a huge bear of a man, had been an adviser to a handful of U.S. presidents and, when we hired him, was an important member of the National Security Council.

When Ed flew to Lantana for his first meeting with Gene and me, as he walked into GP's office he radiated power and confidence.

It didn't take long for him to evaluate and solve our potential problems. His plan was to send one or more of his lawyers from D.C. to Lantana two days each week, to read each story and column item and look at every photo. The lawyers would have total access to each story file with the reporter's original copy, and if necessary, they could question any reporter or editor they wanted.

Not one word would appear in the *National Enquirer* until it had been reviewed and approved by Williams and Connolly.

Before long our attorneys were an integral part of our team—as vital as our editors and reporters. Along with our research department, they forced all of us to operate with even higher standards than previously.

Editors began to fax early copy to Washington for advance rulings before the attorneys' weekly visit. They also asked for legal rulings on how to approach stories. For example, we might want to take a photo in a hospital. How could we get the picture without invading someone's privacy? Williams and Connolly would tell us.

Before the '80s were half over, I knew more about libel and invasion of privacy law than 95 percent of all the lawyers in America. But I always remembered that Williams and Connolly knew a lot more than I did.

On occasion, I disagreed with one of our visiting attorneys. I'd call a more senior partner in Washington and ask him to overrule the decision and let me publish the story. Sometimes I won, sometimes I lost.

On very rare occasions, I would disagree with the senior partner and appeal directly to Ed Williams. It was amazing how often he would grunt: "Just go with it."

I remember vividly one touchy Ted Kennedy story I really believed we should run. At every legal level, I was told, "No way." I called Ed, and after he'd listened for a few moments he said: "Go with it. If Ted Kennedy ever threatens to sue, I'll call him and take care of it. I have enough on that guy . . ."

The Williams team was initially headed by one of the most outstanding attorneys you could ever meet. Irving Younger had been a brilliant law professor and lecturer, a judge, and a legal author of national fame, and now he was pre-screening *Enquirer* material.

However, the details, the questioning, the long hours of reading this material really weren't Irving's thing, so Ed replaced him with David Kendall, a youthful-looking, deceptively modest attorney who never mentioned his glittering background. David had been a Rhodes Scholar and a clerk to a Supreme Court justice; he also spent several perilous years in the South during the height of the segregation battles, defending black Americans against brutal racists. Kendall came close to being murdered, and a few of his fellow legal volunteers were shot to death.

A class act and an intellect of distinction, David is now one of America's most brilliant and famous lawyers, having been thrust into the media limelight as counsel to Bill and Hillary Clinton during the turbulent Monica Lewinsky/impeachment days.

David continued to run the *Enquirer* pre-publication review until 2001, when the *Enquirer* was under new ownership. He headed a team of younger associates who traveled each week to Florida. He told me, "From the beginning, this was one job that all the young lawyers wanted. Handling *Enquirer* stories and working with your editors and reporters was considered the most exciting and challenging work in the office."

Ed Williams organized a second group of attorneys to handle any lawsuits against the *Enquirer*. That team was headed by Paul Wolff, a short, stocky, ferocious attack-dog litigator, known to his friends and even his wife as just "Wolf," probably without the extra "f." He's a nice guy off-duty, but in action he consistently proves himself worthy of his carnivorous surname. For years, it always gave me a warm feeling to know that the Strategic Air Command would protect me from Russian missiles and the superb, fearsome Mr. Wolff would defend me from everything else.

When we had a demand for retraction, it was Wolff's job to investigate the file for accuracy and come up with the facts, even if it showed mistakes by one of the other lawyers on Kendall's team. Wolff's team always dragged out the truth—even if it sometimes hurt.

★ ★ ★

While we were fine-tuning our operation in the early '70s, we were attracting direct competition for the first time. Aussie media mogul Rupert Murdoch tried to buy the *Enquirer*. When he was rebuffed, he started up the competing *Star*.

Up to that point, Rupert had dominated every market he entered. First, he took over his father's failing newspaper in Sydney and built it into a powerhouse. Soon, he owned the biggest newspaper empire Down Under. Hunting bigger prey, he descended on Great Britain and within a few years owned the number-one media company there, including London's most prestigious and venerable daily, the *Times*.

Naturally, Murdoch expected he'd steamroll his American cousins with, first, *Star* magazine and later the *New York Post*. He failed on both counts. The *Post* has lost millions of dollars for decades, and *Star* has never been close to overtaking our circulation. Of course, Rupert went on to become a TV and movie mogul, but around 1990, when he suffered a credit crunch, he sold *Star* to the *Enquirer* group for around $400 million.

But while *Star* was out there, the competition did make us work harder. Their editorial never matched ours, but their marketing skills were better. When they went from black and white to color in 1979, we were forced to follow suit—but GP insisted on better newsprint and superior, more expensive reproduction.

In the mid-seventies, I'd tried to persuade Gene to advertise on television. He resisted for a couple of years but finally broke down when *Star* started running a TV ad campaign to boost circulation. GP began his own TV campaign—and ended up outspending them maybe 10 to 1.

Gene knew that to pay for a major, nationwide television campaign, he'd have to raise the *Enquirer's* cover price. We'd kept our price at 40 cents for years, even when we went from black and white to color in 1979. Gene hated the fact that a new price would let our competitors raise their prices to match us. Gene would never have admitted it, but he was looking over his shoulder, watching Rupert

Murdoch's *Star* magazine. *Star* had been first with color, and now they were dabbling in TV ads—and beginning to narrow our circulation lead in the Northeast.

The Boss finally decided to embrace the idea of big-time television advertising and, in the fall of 1981, announced that to pay for a massive television campaign, the *Enquirer* would raise its price by over 60 percent—from 40 cents to 65 cents.

The board was shocked. "You're betting the company," warned board member Henry Bowes, who'd been a longtime company adviser. Gene just smiled and confidently said, "It's *my* company."

What the board didn't know was that for many weeks, I had been working with a brilliant ad agency called Compton (later bought by Saatchi and Saatchi) to create and test a series of TV ads. We'd run a number of spots in cities around the country—and raised our cover price to 65 cents. The results were astonishing. When we ran the spots heavily, our sales rose, even at the higher price.

But Gene loved high drama and didn't immediately inform the board that our research indicated it would all work fine.

The campaign became a marketing blockbuster. The agency came up with an extraordinary creative concept that swept the country: "Enquiring Minds Want to Know."

In each commercial, an announcer described a major story from that week's issue, something like, "Is Burt Reynolds really in love with Loni Anderson? Enquiring minds want to know." Then a woman said, "*I* want to know!" Without rushing, we could feature up to five big stories in the spot, which had to be produced weekly to stay current.

In the first full year of the TV campaign, we spent $30 million, and the budgets were almost as large into the mid-eighties.

Those five words—"Enquiring Minds Want to Know"—became a nationwide catchphrase, part of the language. I'd see it in print and hear it on TV, and, once in a while, I'd come across it in movies.

Compton chairman Bob Jordan later told me, "This was the best TV commercial of the eighties." According to his account executive David Basch: "In advertising, companies often test for six months or a year. You guys tested for six *weeks*—and then went national. It was unprecedented in TV ad history. That was one of the greatest experiences of my career." It was a gutsy decision by Gene—part of his genius.

The campaign made the *Enquirer* a brand name known to just about everyone and took us to a new plateau in pricing. Our new campaign also meant Gene now expected me to become an expert in yet another field: TV advertising and production. Calder was point man in buying TV time and creating a new commercial each week. I certainly had the most exciting, and exhausting, job in Lantana.

I am proud of many stories we broke, but none more than the death of John Belushi. We ended up bringing his killer to justice, and embarrassing the Los Angeles Police Department. One newspaper columnist wrote that if the piece had been published in the *Cincinnati Enquirer* instead of the *National Enquirer*, it would have won a Pulitzer Prize for investigative journalism. I really believe that's true!

It was all the work of Tony Brenna and Larry Haley, a good team. Brenna was quick, innovative, and peripatetic. Haley was more deliberate in action, a broad-shouldered bulldog of a newshound who would walk through fire to get his story. If you were in a firefight, the man you'd want with you in your foxhole was ex–Special Forces soldier Haley.

John Belushi, the coke-snorting, booze-guzzling Blues Brother, was the party animal of party-town Hollywood. Everyone knew this talented, ex–*Saturday Night Live* star was a fiery comet nearing a dramatic crash.

On March 5, 1982, Belushi died at age thirty-three from an overdose of drugs in the famed Chateau Marmont hotel on Hollywood's Sunset Strip. Los Angeles detectives quickly completed their investigation, and the Belushi death was destined to become just another heap of old newspaper clippings. But not if we could help it.

Our Los Angeles bureau learned that Belushi's regular drug supplier was a well-known dealer named Cathy Smith. If she had been providing drugs to Belushi for some time before his death, she must have a terrific story. The LAPD knew about Smith and had interviewed her, but they weren't interested in the case. For them, it was just another drug overdose, one of several in L.A. every single day. They'd let Smith go after brief questioning.

Brenna, working out of our L.A. bureau at that time, was the designated bloodhound. Find Cathy Smith. Sure—no problem. After a client snuffs it, drug dealers usually hang around the area; or if they blow town, they leave a forwarding number.

Brenna finally discovered that Cathy Smith had fled to Toronto, fearful the cops would change their minds and arrest her. As she knows now, it wasn't the cops she had to worry about: It was the *Enquirer* in the form of Brenna and Haley.

Since we had no idea where in Toronto she was—or even if she had moved someplace else—I had Haley join Brenna.

The two spent incredibly long hours in seedy bars and drug dens, trying to get the message to Smith: The *Enquirer* wanted to speak with her, and it could be worth a lot of money. Their work paid off— Smith called our offices in Lantana, and we set her up with Larry and Tony.

We made a deal for $20,000, payable on publication of Smith's exclusive story, provided her quotes were on tape. She and the reporters talked for endless hours, and Brenna and Haley were finding out more and more about Belushi and his drug antics. Smith actually admitted she *had* provided the drugs that ultimately killed him.

Smith really liked Belushi and felt she had been *helping* him. She made sure the drugs she sold him weren't contaminated with poisons, and she tried to limit his use as much as possible. She knew he'd do drugs with or without her, and she wanted to make sure he wouldn't get a bad batch. She came across, strangely, as a woman trying to look out for a friend as best she could. But the fact remained—she had supplied the drugs that killed Belushi.

Both reporters told me later that interviewing Smith was harrowing and often dangerous. Whether in a bar or hotel room, they were usually accompanied by Smith's "bodyguard"—a menacing self-described hit man named "Socks" who threatened to kill the reporters if they didn't treat Cathy right.

Sometimes Smith was sober, sometimes she was drunk or high.

And she expected the *Enquirer* to pick up the bar tabs for her and sometimes a gang of friends. Our guys estimated they'd spent thousands of dollars in Toronto's bars.

One night the project almost ended in tragedy. According to Brenna: "We had to drink with her and her friends to make them feel comfortable. And we tried to stay sober. But one night both Larry and I knew they had spiked our drinks. We started feeling really high, losing touch with reality and, frankly, screwing up our minds."

Luckily, they had enough sense left to get out of there. Now, years later, Brenna is still convinced someone slipped an LSD-like substance into their drinks. That incident would have scared off most reporters, but Brenna and Haley stayed the course.

The whole difficult process lasted more than a week, until our guys felt they had an accurate story on tape from Cathy Smith. They sent their raw copy and tapes to Lantana, where one of our senior writers, Bob Smith, read the material and came into my office.

After rewriting the copious material to the correct length, Bob told me: "This is dynamite."

As I read the copy, I realized it *was* explosive. We had a drug queen, on tape, admitting that she, in effect, had killed John Belushi. Although she never meant to.

I said to Smith: "According to this copy, this woman, time after time, is saying she killed Belushi. But she never uses these actual words. Is she willing to say these actual words on tape?"

Brenna recalls: "She had said she killed Belushi many times and in many ways. But now we had to go back with a tape recorder and get the actual words: 'I killed John Belushi.' It was tough, but we did it."

The story ran on our June 19, 1982, cover with a big picture of Belushi, a photo of Cathy Smith, and her words: "I KILLED JOHN BELUSHI." In our copyrighted story, Smith admitted that Belushi had been injected with drugs at least twenty-four times in the last thirty hours of his life. She also said that she personally supplied the heroin in the deadly heroin-cocaine "speedball" that finished him off.

Newspapers, news agencies, and TV stations all over the country picked up the blockbuster story of how the *Enquirer* had broken a major case that the LAPD had kissed off from the beginning.

The end result was a Los Angeles grand jury investigation. We initially refused to hand over the tapes, since our mission had not been to have Smith arrested, but the grand jury subpoenaed them and began a six-month probe of the case. Both Brenna and Haley testified before the grand jury, which finally handed down an indictment. Deputy District Attorney Michael Montagna admitted that our article was "the catalyst for reopening the investigation into Belushi's death."

Smith, extradited from Canada, pleaded guilty to involuntary manslaughter and several lesser charges. She was sentenced to prison and later paroled.

Breaking the Belushi death case did not make us popular with the L.A. bureaucrats. But what else was new?

Brenna and Haley each received the J. Edgar Hoover memorial gold medal for Distinguished Public Service from the American Police Hall of Fame, a national organization of U.S. police chiefs. If you ask me, it *should* have been the Pulitzer.

A few months after the Belushi sensation, we covered the untimely death of another celebrity—Princess Grace of Monaco, our biggest story of the decade. The October 5, 1982, issue of the *Enquirer* began jumping off the supermarket racks the instant they were delivered, and in a few days we had a virtual sell-out, with 97.4% of all copies sold. The final circulation figure was 6,640,000 copies, our second-highest sale in history.

The Grace saga was a triumph for everyone at the *Enquirer*. Except for the senior editor in charge of editorial, Executive Editor Mike Hoy, who ultimately lost his job because of his weak approach to such a major story.

I seldom went out for lunch, but I did on September 13. When I returned, the office was in a state of semi-panic, the normal, appropriate level of excitement and apprehension when a major story was breaking. A car with Princess Grace and her daughter Stephanie in it had plunged down a cliff in Monaco. First reports were that Grace had been killed, although nothing was certain in the confusion around the accident.

My first questions were: Does GP know? And, how are we covering this?

The answers: GP had been told and had agreed to send a couple of reporters from Europe to Monaco. European stringers had been alerted for possible angles, and editors in Lantana were working the phones.

Furious, I stormed into Gene's office. Actually, you didn't "storm" into Pope's office and expect to survive, but on this day I came very close. I knocked on his door, walked in, and said I needed to see him urgently: "Gene, this is the biggest story of the decade. If Grace is dead, we have to hit it with everything we have. We've started to handle it like an ordinary story and Mike Hoy says you approved."

Gene was taken aback by my vehemence and, I think, a little embarrassed that he had agreed to such a weak attack. He just nodded as I outlined what we had to do: Immediately send a major team from Europe and the U.S. into Monaco, plus dispatch a top senior editor to run it. We'd give the editor $50,000 cash—with more in the wings if needed. In addition, we'd have a second senior editor run the story from Florida. GP nodded okay.

As soon as I took control of the Grace story, I rushed about a dozen top freelance reporters and photographers from London, Paris, and Rome to Monte Carlo, the only city in Monaco. Senior editor Paul Levy left with a team of reporters from Florida to run the on-ground operation, while others caught flights from Los Angeles and New York.

By the time most of our people arrived, the death of Princess Grace was official. Journalists from the greatest newspapers and magazines all over Europe and America rushed into Monte Carlo, but no one had a team close to ours in size or aggressiveness. Levy took over the entire ground floor of one hotel, including the patio area and the swimming pool. Technically, other guests could have used the pool, but with our guys running around in a non-stop frenzy, the site lacked the relaxed mood vacationing tourists expect of the Côte d'Azur. The *Enquirer* team was left alone.

I'd done everything possible to put our editorial juggernaut into action, but I was biting my nails like a nervous dad-to-be. I hadn't exactly told Mr. Pope he'd dropped the ball by not forcing Mike Hoy to hit the story harder, but the implication was clear. If, after all the drama, I didn't produce a great result, I'd look like an idiot and a failure. You couldn't do that at the *Enquirer* too often and survive.

My only comfort, apart from this great investigative team, was our secret weapon: London bureau chief Noel Botham. Noel was a veteran newsman who, at twenty-three, had been London's youngest-ever chief reporter at a daily paper. He had some of the all-time best contacts in France and Monaco, and for years had broken great Rainier and Grace stories. In return, he'd spent a small fortune entertaining his sources in the ultra-expensive restaurants of Monte Carlo. Even by *Enquirer* standards, we allowed Noel wide latitude. Now it was payback time.

Levy was running the show, but everyone knew that Botham was the Man in Monaco. One of his contacts was so high up in the Monaco police force that even now, years after the man's death, Noel won't let me identify him. Just take it from me, the guy knew *everything* going on in the tiny principality. Botham described him as wonderful. "He was the godfather of my best friend, and he told me every detail known by the police. We'd talk on the phone several times a day."

The *Enquirer* attacked on three fronts:

- What caused the car to go over the cliff?
- Why the Princess did not get the best medical care after the crash?
- How could we sign the first witness on the crash scene to an exclusive contract?

Our first victory was the eyewitness. The car had tumbled into the garden of a sixty-two-year-old flower grower, Sesto Lequio. He ran to the wreckage and pulled out a young girl, then saw an older woman who seemed unconscious and possibly dead. He didn't know who they were.

The woman opened her eyes, said a few words to the farmer, then closed her eyes for the last time. It was Grace.

When I learned about Lequio, I knew every journalist in the world would want him. We had to get there first, get his story, then keep him quiet until we hit the newsstands a week or so later. It would take lots of Mr. Pope's money. Levy already had $50,000 in cash, and soon more was on the way.

Monsieur Lequio did not drive a hard bargain. He became an *Enquirer* exclusive for about $15,000. After we got every piece of information from him, I suggested to our guys that we offer him a free two-week vacation anywhere in the world: Hawaii, the South Pacific, Hong Kong, anywhere he wanted. The simple, and by now bewildered, man didn't want to leave his little cottage.

We couldn't leave him alone. Otherwise, some sharp rivals would telephone him, knock on his door, or get to him somehow and break our exclusive. So we provided him with lodgers: our reporters. Over the next ten days or so, his phone would be answered by someone like Paul House, our Rome correspondent; when a journalist came to the door, it would be opened by someone like Ken Potter, one of our best staffers, who happened to be built like a linebacker. Nobody spoke to M. Lequio unless we approved, not even his friends and family.

A few days after we'd printed the farmer's story but before we went on sale, I received a semi-hysterical call from Paul Levy, still in Monaco: "The farmer is going stir-crazy." Lequio was so frustrated by his state of house arrest that one day he got drunk, picked up his shotgun, and shot a hole in his own ceiling.

I told Levy, "Tell our guys it's not serious unless he's shooting at people. Stick with it." That's the kind of problem-solving my reporters are paid for. Of course, they did hang on for the next few days, until the paper was on sale and they could tell the old man he could start spending his new riches—the $15,000 that was probably twice his annual income and a bargain for us.

Not only did the farmer give us his second-by-second eyewitness account as the first person at the scene, but he also told us how Grace regained consciousness for a few moments and blurted out a final message: "Please tell them all I love them . . . my husband . . . Caroline . . . Stephanie . . . Albert. Please take care of my baby Stephanie . . . she is badly hurt." He was also able to quash phony reports in the European press that Stephanie, not Grace, had been at the wheel.

This gripping story was the easiest one to get that week.

The *hardest* was our minute-by-minute description of what happened in the car that fateful day. Botham's amazing secret police contact gave him every detail known to the officials. He also told us about the only eyewitness to see the car go off the cliff, truck driver Yves Philly. We bought up Philly exclusively before other journalists knew he even existed.

It doesn't sound like a problem, but here was our quandary: The official version was that Grace was at the wheel of her British Rover when she had some kind of stroke and lost control of the vehicle. Secretly, however, the police believed it might have been suicide, and the facts we uncovered fit their theory.

Recalls Botham: "I was told that Rainier and Grace had a terrible argument that day. Their marriage was having real problems, and Grace was taking medicine for depression. Whatever happened between them, it ended with Grace leaving the home in tears and running toward her car. Stephanie saw how upset her mom was and ran after her, jumping into the passenger seat."

The family had been staying at a mountaintop villa on the French side of the Monaco border. The drive down from the villa was a steep, snaking, treacherous journey.

The eyewitness trucker told us he saw the car ahead of him weaving crazily from side to side, and thought: "Dear God . . . stop them. It's suicide." Philly blasted his horn, and the car seemed to straighten out as it reached a hairpin bend called "Devil's Curse." The trucker breathed a sigh of relief. Suddenly the vehicle accelerated to more than 50 m.p.h. and never attempted to make the bend— Philly saw no brake lights and heard no squeals of brakes. The car flew off the road like a plane, smashing into the trees below and tumbling down the precipitous slope.

As a huge volume of material came in to our office, much of the evidence seemed to back Botham's police source's theory of possible suicide.

If we implied in any way that Grace might have committed suicide, it would be truly sensational. But very quickly I decided not to go with this angle. First, it was just a theory, even if backed by certain facts. The Palace would deny it, we'd endure terrible criticism, and how would we prove the theory?

Even more persuasive: Princess Grace was beloved worldwide. This was a time of mourning, and any mention of suicide, even as a theory, would be inappropriate. I discussed it with Gene, who agreed, so we just ran the story with all the details, letting readers come to their own conclusion.

Our record-setting October 5 issue was headlined:

EXCLUSIVE

GRACE: The <u>Real</u> Story
SHE DIDN'T HAVE TO DIE—THE ONLY PICTURE OF THE CRASH—
HER LAST WORDS—TO THE ONLY PERSON WHO SAW THE ACCIDENT

We used maybe 10 percent of the material our reporters filed. The last words were from our "captive" gardener, but our best story, by far, was that Grace should not have died from her injuries.

She didn't have to die. It sounds impossible, but Princess Grace did not receive the best-possible medical treatment for her injuries.

Our eight-page special inside the paper led off with the story; its first paragraph was: "Princess Grace didn't have to die! She would have survived—if only she'd only received proper medical treatment for head injuries right away after her September 13 car crash."

This shocking claim was backed up by a top French neurosurgeon who had been in Monaco at the time of the tragedy. The doctor, who was called in on the case after it was too late, told us: "The treatment she received was appalling."

Grace was first taken to the local hospital in Monaco, which, at the time, had a mediocre reputation. Almost as close was a modern medical center in Nice, which had the most up-to-date equipment for treating trauma cases.

The Monaco doctors concentrated on internal injuries and broken bones before considering brain damage. Three hours went by before two neurologists arrived, and it was several more hours before they moved the Princess to a private clinic for a CAT scan of the brain. Amazingly, the Monaco hospital did not have its own CAT-scan machine.

By the time doctors learned the extent of her brain damage, Grace was in an irreversible coma.

Our reporters talked with top neurosurgeons in France and the United States who were familiar with the case. Several were so outraged that in criticizing Grace's care they allowed us to quote them by name. It seemed evident that earlier, expert intervention by competent neurosurgeons might have saved Grace's life.

Even the French police commandant who investigated the crash, Captain Roger Benzce, questioned the decision to take Princess Grace to the Monaco hospital. Accident victims with serious injuries are usually taken to Nice, he told us.

Who made the terrible decision to take Grace to Monaco? Prince Rainier, or some bureaucrat? We were never able to find out.

Says Noel Botham: "I don't know if there was anything to hide, but a few days after the crash, Monaco authorities had the death car crushed into a metal cube, taken out to sea, and dropped into the depths of the Mediterranean. That made sure no one would ever inspect the car again to second-guess the investigators."

Our reporters weren't the only ones wondering what officials were hiding. The following week Princess Grace's relatives in America, sister Peggy Conlan and brother Jack Kelly, voiced suspicions of foul play.

I believe their suspicions were just the grievings of devastated siblings. No evidence ever confirmed their fears. But they had reason to be upset, especially given Rainier's refusal to allow an autopsy and a wall of silence from officials when Grace's relatives tried to get details of what had happened.

Our eight-page special and our follow-ups in later weeks were among the best work we ever did. No other publication in the world came *close* to our exclusives. We printed a little box with the name of each editor, reporter, and researcher who contributed. There were fifty-two in all.

The following year, on May 10, 1983, we did a follow-up revealing the agony Grace's dysfunctional family had caused her before she died. Said Noel Botham recently: "Many facts have come out since her death that make me believe Princess Grace really might have tried to kill herself. Clearly we will never know."

Monaco team leader Paul Levy is now deceased, but Botham, who has worked for many of the top European and British publications, been a war correspondent, and written seventeen books, told me: "The *Enquirer* was able to put out the best investigative team of journalists anybody had seen for a century."

More than seven years later, in January 1990, Grace's mother passed away, not knowing that her own Princess had died years earlier. We published this exclusive family secret: Mrs. Margaret Kelly had been so frail and so mentally impaired that the family felt the tragic news could kill her. A look-alike female relative sometimes pretended to be her daughter Grace.

By the early '80s, the *Enquirer* formula was well established. We were selling gossip, news, hopes, dreams, and, above all, emotion. Until GP died, the *Enquirer* was always less than 50 percent celebrity. Sprinkled through the paper were somewhat corny stories about ordinary people doing extraordinary things.

When we ran adventure stories of a woman fighting off a raging bull and saving her child, our readers enjoyed a vicarious thrill. When we ran a "Hero Award" or an "Honest Person Award," readers felt happy to be part of a wonderful society. Or they might ask their spouses: Would *you* have handed back that $10,000 you found in the backyard?

Our "Rags to Riches" stories, like the boy with no shoes who grew up to own a shoestore empire, gave people hope, however fleeting, that they too could make it. The same with our "Woman at the Top" series. Our "Escape from the Rat Race" stories told of successful people who gave up their illustrious jobs, plus the stress and cash, to live a simpler life, perhaps growing their own food in some remote valley. I knew some readers would be saying, "I'd love to get away from it all like that guy."

When we persuaded readers to adopt children with mental or physical handicaps, the whole readership felt like part of a special, generous family. I still treasure a letter from Peggy Soule, executive director of CAP (Children Awaiting Parents). In July 1995 she wrote to me: "Words cannot express our deep gratitude at CAP for the incredible contribution the *National Enquirer* has made over the last 15 years to the waiting children in America." She said we had featured 853 children, and that 552 had been adopted. The most amazing case was a family of seven children in Arizona chosen for adoption in New York after the would-be parents saw the *Enquirer* feature. "Only because of your widespread circulation could these adoptions take place," added Ms. Soule.

When we caught dozens of deadbeat dads who had run out on their families and refused to pay child support, our readers applauded us and felt proud to be a member of our group.

When we ran "Government Waste" stories and blasted officials for squandering our tax dollars, readers felt that someone cared about them. Like the story we headlined in December 1990: YOU'RE PAYING $120,000 TO GET EYE EXAMS FOR FLIES, which really got them mad.

Many times we'd get our readers angry but give them a chance to change things. Animal cruelty especially horrified me and our readers. Like the annual turkey festival in Yellville, Arkansas, where live turkeys were dropped from planes and usually died, desperately fluttering their more or less non-functional wings to slow their fall to doom. Laughing spectators watched the "fun" as some turkeys survived the fall, only to be set upon by gleeful children who beat them to death.

After our story in 1990, letters protesting the cruelty flooded into that little town from all over the world. The local chamber of commerce announced that the "fuss" had led them to abandon the turkey drop, and the local animal rights group told us: "Thank God for the *Enquirer*."

All this made our readers feel good. Even the ones who didn't write knew they were part of something great.

I always respected GP's editorial sense enormously. On the rare occasions when we disagreed, he almost always turned out to be right—sometimes, even when he was wrong.

GP, like most Americans, loved the TV show *M*A*S*H*. I thought it was okay, but features on the show never brought us big sales. Alan Alda, the main star, had almost all the right qualities to be a number-one *Enquirer* best-seller: He was good-looking, he was immensely popular, he topped the TV charts week after week. But he wasn't controversial. He was too obviously a nice guy, a great family man, and a fine actor. There was no gossip, no dirt, and therefore no interest from our readers.

The Boss knew this. We'd been burned a couple of times on Alda covers that didn't sell well, but GP loved the show so much that once, while I was on vacation in Europe, he tried another *M*A*S*H* star on the cover. I called in from Scotland and nearly dropped the telephone when he told me his cover choice that week: Jamie Farr, who played the cross-dressing Klinger, believed in UFOs.

It was a lousy sale.

When *M*A*S*H* came to an end and the final episode was touted as America's biggest secret, we naturally went out and obtained a copy of the top-secret script. We'd give our readers the chance to know the ending before the show ran—a scoop that *really* endeared us to the CBS network.

The question was: Should it be our main page-one head? I wanted to downplay it with a small mention. Gene wanted to make it the number-one cover story. He compromised and let it share the cover with a couple of other headlines—Tom Selleck's divorce settlement and an exclusive on *Dragnet* star Jack Webb's sudden death.

Thank the heavens Gene followed those genius instincts he possessed. It was a blockbuster issue. And giving away the show's ending certainly didn't reduce the viewership. That TV episode on February 28, 1983, had the highest ratings in history, with 71,200,000 TV households tuning in—60 percent of all viewers. (Compare that to today's hits with 17 or 18 percent of viewers. . . .) The success of the *M*A*S*H* finale story led to a whole new way to cover television in the *Enquirer*.

For several years the prime-time soap opera *Dallas* was a destination show for viewers—and the answer to the prayers of an editor who needed cover stories every week of every year. We ran many stories about the private lives of the actors behind the characters who'd hypnotized America—Larry Hagman, Victoria Principal, Patrick Duffy, and Linda Gray, among others.

The success of *Dallas* spawned the ABC imitator *Dynasty*, starring John Forsythe, Linda Evans, and—a real headline-grabber—Joan Collins. They threw in all kinds of old stars like Charlton Heston and Dale Robertson, plus a gaggle of gorgeous starlets like Tracy Scoggins, Emma Samms, and Catherine Oxenberg. *Dallas* gave Heather Locklear, later on *Spin City*, her first major exposure, to coin a phrase. These prime-time soaps were followed by such lesser entities as *Falcon Crest* and *Knots Landing*.

This was manna from heaven. Viewers loved the stars, and so did we. Their lives, loves, fights, marriages, divorces, victories, and defeats became weekly fare.

These were great stories, but our readers really, *really* wanted to know about the characters on the show. My main challenge was to get advance scripts, so my readers would know the plot of an upcoming episode before it ran—plots like "Who Shot J.R.?" When we could do this, our sales *zoomed*. So, as always, we gave our readers what they wanted.

The executives did everything they could to stop our "Sneak Previews."

Their reaction wasn't logical. Readers who were desperate to read our previews were true fans who'd watch the show even when they knew the plot ahead of time. Readers who didn't want to know the story could just skip that page.

This did not matter. The producers of the soaps did not want us to have the information, period. We needed the information, period. It was war. Who won most of the battles? Modesty forbids me to answer the question.

How did we get the scripts? We infiltrated the production companies that filmed the shows, and the sets where they were filmed. Imagine the number of people with access to scripts. Producers, yes, but also secretaries and aides; actors, and probably their agents and maybe some assistants; dozens of set workers, and many others I won't even mention.

As we broke preview after preview, the top producers became increasingly apoplectic. We were clearly pumping up their viewer numbers, but now it had turned into a matter of principle. They tried feeding us phony scripts through double-agent freelance journalists. They secretly numbered scripts with small changes, so that when we ran a story the changes would identify the sources.

The tougher the security, the harder we worked to meet the challenge. We were spending thousands of dollars on scripts we wanted, especially the season-ending cliffhangers. Luckily, Hollywood is full of sleazy characters and people who spend beyond their means, and they all love *Enquirer* checks. When one source dried up, another opened the door. Sometimes we'd have three identical scripts, as we kept encouraging new sources. You never knew where the next source would come from.

A woman called an *Enquirer* reporter and claimed to have the latest script for one prime-time show. We gave her $200 for the script but didn't publish it, since we couldn't verify its authenticity. Week after week, this woman gave us genuine scripts that unfolded word-for-word when the shows ran. She never revealed how she obtained the material.

Finally, I was convinced enough to publish the next script she provided. It was the real stuff, and we gave her $2,000.

During the following months, whenever we needed a script, this mysterious woman would deliver the goods, and we gave her $2,000.

But she was a puzzle. How was she getting the scripts? The reporter told us she was drop-dead gorgeous but knew little else but her name.

I instituted an investigation. The result was a shock, even for editors who were nearly unshockable. Our beautiful source was the mistress of a top TV executive, an executive on the actual soap opera—and he was leaking his own scripts to us through his mistress. The big *Enquirer* checks were paying for their luxurious love-nest apartment.

Meanwhile, at work he was one of the top guys pounding his desk and demanding that his security people track down the traitors. Of course, he knew his little game wasn't really hurting his show because *Enquirer* covers were giving it free publicity.

That was one way to get our exclusives.

Another emerged a couple of years later. Articles editor Joe Policy, who handled many major celebrity stories for us, had developed an incredible source on *Dynasty*, a pipeline into the executive suite that was pure gold.

Our stories of scripts and occurrences on the set were so accurate they got under the skin of the founding producers Esther Shapiro and Aaron Spelling. They and their closest aides were mad as hell.

Policy would hear stories of the execs' meetings and their vain efforts to stop us. Often, we'd know their plans to foil the *Enquirer* before the plans went into action.

Joe would often come into my office chuckling that Spelling and his executive team hated us. "'Hate' is a strong word," I said one time. Answered Joe: "It's not too strong a word for *Dynasty*. They don't know how we're getting their secrets, and they *hate* us."

A peculiar idea crept into my brain. If the Spelling organization hated us that much, it meant they were frustrated beyond belief. Maybe this was an opportunity to, as they say, make lemonade out of lemons.

"What if we approach Aaron Spelling and ask him to cooperate with us?" I asked Policy. "Tell him, If you can't beat us, join us." Joe told me I was mad, bonkers, and out of my mind. I persisted. If he could arrange a personal meeting for me with Spelling, I would suggest a plan by which *Dynasty* would actually give us their scripts in advance and shoot special photos for us. In return we would send them our copy for approval before publication. If they wanted to keep details or special endings out of the *Enquirer*, we'd cooperate.

Shaking his head, Joe left my office, predicting derision when he called L.A. "On the other hand, it would incredible if it worked," he said.

The miracle happened. A hesitant Aaron Spelling agreed to a meeting with his archenemy. Me.

The outside of the Spelling Productions offices, on a major movie lot in Los Angeles, looked like a run-down, nondescript building, with not a hint that it was home to the company that had launched hit after hit, from *Charlie's Angels* to *Dynasty* to *Love Boat*. Once I went through the door into Spelling's office, however, my jaw dropped. "Big," "luxurious"—those words don't begin to describe it. We could have played tennis in this office, with room for spectators. Mr. Spelling sat behind a desk almost as large as my whole office back in Lantana.

I tried to hide my feeling of intimidation as I walked, walked, and walked over to shake hands with him. By his side was executive producer Douglas S. Cramer, a man renowned as a talented but ruthless operator. All of us gathered on the same couch, which was so long we were still a normal room-length away from each other. Cramer did look tough, almost hostile, but Spelling was clearly the boss. He listened carefully to my proposal, then asked, "How do I know I can trust you?"

The answer was easy. If either of us broke the rules, even once, the other would just cancel the deal. It wasn't a contract, just an understanding.

Within a few minutes Aaron Spelling made a handshake deal with me and suggested I work out the details with Douglas Cramer.

We agreed that Cramer would liaise with Joe Policy. He told me: "I might have some initial problems with our stars, but I can handle it." Looking at this guy, I believed him.

That was the start of a relationship that thrived in secrecy. When Policy received scripts, he would tell Cramer what photos we wanted, and a union photographer on the set would take them. We got dozens of amazing, exclusive front pages, and Spelling Productions got incredible, controlled publicity from the nation's biggest weekly.

One of the best among countless examples came in 1985, when *Dynasty*'s season ended with machine-gun-toting terrorists shooting up a church at the wedding of Catherine Oxenberg's character to a handsome prince.

All summer, millions of *Dynasty* fanatics had wondered: Who lives and who dies? On July 30, 1985, we were able to run a great cover with a picture of the shootout and the headline: IT'S OFFICIAL! WHO DIES IN *DYNASTY* MASSACRE. Inside we had photos and details of the first eight episodes of the season. Even non-*Enquirer* readers who loved *Dynasty* had to buy that issue.

Spelling got an extra-special bonus. In 1985, Joan Collins was engaged to Peter Holm, a man distinctly lacking a towering IQ.

This certified non-genius decided to play Russian roulette with Collins's career, telling *Dynasty* that Joan would not appear in the season's opening episode without a really fat pay raise. Even after Holm was informed that Collins still had a year left on her contract, he wouldn't budge. He warned the producers that Joan just might get sick.

The show refused to give in. They quickly wrote Collins out of the first episode, then fired a warning shot—in the *Enquirer*. We reported that, if necessary, Joan Collins would be replaced by Elizabeth Taylor, who had an agreement with Spelling. And if Liz wasn't able to step in, Sophia Loren was standing by in the wings. A dynamite story—and all approved in advance by *Dynasty* executive Douglas Cramer.

When Joan Collins read our piece, she must have had heart palpitations. Breaking a contract was one thing. Losing the best role she'd ever had in her life was something else. Spelling's message via the *Enquirer* was clear: Show up or else. Joan showed up. (Later, Collins did receive a well-deserved raise that brought her pay closer to what co-stars John Forsythe and Linda Evans earned.)

We also helped Spelling (and ourselves) by promoting his *Dynasty* spin-off, an ill-fated series called *The Colbys*. And when Spelling's show *Love Boat* went on special locations like the Egyptian desert, we ran photos promoting the episode.

I believe only Joe Policy could have kept the *Dynasty* relationship functioning. Cramer, a major TV, movie, and Broadway producer, is a prickly character. One of Policy's strengths is working with and getting what he wants out of difficult people. He also brought some fresh ideas to the show. The *Dynasty* people would deny this, but I believe some of their best scenes actually came from Policy. I remember discussing with Joe how a mud-wrestling scene between Linda Evans and Joan Collins would be a hot cover for us and asking him to suggest it. Several months later, Collins and Evans fought in the mud. It really *was* a hot page one.

Most people want to know things before their neighbors do. Information is power and creates status. If you can tell your pals that the teenager across the street is pregnant, you feel important that you knew first. The same principle holds true with news about a Hollywood star. That was one reason we worked so hard for our celebrity exclusives.

The second reason for our exclusives is that people feel better when they know that the rich and famous don't lead perfect, happy lives. When a mother whose son was on drugs learns that some rich star had the same problem, she feels less alone. "If that rich star, with all the support around her, can't keep her boy off cocaine, then perhaps I'm not such a bad person after all," she might think. This isn't just a hunch on my part, but an observation confirmed by a psychological study of our readers in the '90s.

Critics often ask if publishing stories that made celebrities unhappy ever made *me* unhappy. Not often. Most of these stars were happy only when they could control their own publicity—even when they had punched someone, two-timed their spouse, or gone berserk on drugs.

One media columnist, Lewis Grossberger, made me smile. Mr. Grossberger described his puzzlement that celebrities' lives are always *perfect*, with all problems safely in the past—we never read a media profile "in which the star is a mess *right now*. In most celebrity profiles the star was formerly a mess—his or her life a sordid orgy of booze, dope, unsafe sex, and wanton, savage weight gain—until recently! Then, thanks to God, the Betty Ford Center, a new love, a new personal trainer or the all-fungus diet, he Changed His Life and is now a model citizen, sober, thin, hardworking and kind. Oh, and by the way, he's just finished a wonderful new film. Roll the clip.

"With so many celebrity crack-ups, doesn't it figure that just once we'd get a profile, other than in the *National Enquirer*, of a present-day walking disaster?"

I laughed out loud because Grossberger's observations were so true.

★ ★ ★

By the 1980s, the *Enquirer* could jump-start a young celebrity's career. Not just because an *Enquirer* cover photo was seen by maybe 100 million people shopping in supermarkets, but also because all the other celebrity magazines followed our lead. We had the power to turn just about anybody into a major celebrity.

One night after work, I stopped for a quick drink at a local Lantana bar where our reporters hung out. Five or six of them were watching TV—some game show I'd never heard of—and I thought they'd gone nuts. *Enquirer* reporters talked and argued about sports, women, politics, their jobs. They didn't go to a bar to watch television.

I asked the most hard-bitten guy what was up. He pointed at the blonde in the sparkling dress, turning letters. "Vanna," was his answer. "She's gorgeous."

The next day I asked our research department to check on the national ratings of this game show, *Wheel of Fortune.* To my astonishment, it was a blockbuster. It pulled in more viewers during the five days a week it was broadcast than many famous prime-time shows attracted.

"Get me a story on Vanna," I ordered the articles editors. That week, our second lead article on the cover was a photo of Vanna and her colorful wheel of letters. The issue sold like hotcakes.

We'd found a new star and, even better, a new hunting ground: the syndicated shows. Other magazines picked up on our big sale, and Vanna was soon a regular fixture on many supermarket magazine covers. But Vanna never forgot how she got her start and usually cooperated with us. She even gave us the rights to her wedding to George Santo Pietro in Aspen, Colorado, on New Year's Eve, 1990—an exclusive we nearly lost through bad planning.

Vanna's wedding was perfect *Enquirer* material. A beautiful star on her wedding day and only for our readers—it was a dream. But because the wedding was close to our printing deadline, we had to move fast, and we arranged to have a Learjet standing by to fly the photos from Aspen to Florida.

Veteran John South, one of our all-time great reporters, was entrusted with getting the film from the reception to the plane. One editor suggested getting a local driver, but that idea was nixed because the trip was short and easy.

Big mistake. A huge snowstorm blew into Aspen, and the short drive became a nightmare. South, confused by the whiteout, got lost and went in the wrong direction.

Meanwhile the Learjet is waiting, with conditions deteriorating. I'm calling every five minutes. "Did you find him yet?"

Eventually the pilot tells us, "We have fifteen minutes. The airport is going to be closed . . ." Still no South. The minutes are ticking down and I'm pacing the editorial floor, alternately cursing and praying.

With three minutes to go before the airport shuts down, South arrives. The jet lands in Lantana just in time, and we have a great front page. Our cover on January 15, 1991, was:

ONLY IN THE *ENQUIRER*!
VANNA WEDS
HER PERSONAL WEDDING ALBUM—FABULOUS PHOTOS YOU MUST SEE

Inside we had great pictures by Hollywood photographer Peter Borsari, showing the ceremony, the kisses, the couple sprayed with champagne—everything a reader could want.

It was a world exclusive that sold like crazy. The photos of the wedding reception were too late to make that issue, so we ran a second fabulous spread the following week.

Our coverage of the Vanna wedding was ultimately wonderful, but it was days like these that gave me prematurely gray hair.

The *Enquirer* was such a powerhouse in the entertainment business that our relationships with celebrities followed a predictable pattern. Early in their careers, when they were unknowns, they'd stand on their heads to get into our pages. Once they'd made it big, they didn't want to deal with us anymore. Then, when their careers slid downward, they were back to standing on their heads for us. I saw this pattern repeat itself dozens of times.

Of all the stars of the nighttime soaps, the *Enquirer* was closest to Charlene Tilton, the tiny, bubbly, very pretty actress who played Lucy on *Dallas*. Her agent was her ambitious boyfriend, Jon Mercedes, and in the beginning his instincts were good. He made sure Charlene was at every celebrity event—from movie premieres to star softball games. She was the L.A. photographers' best friend, posing endlessly and cheerfully.

She ended up in the *Enquirer* many times, doing photo shoots and interviews whenever we asked. She and Mercedes were charming, friendly guests at our JFK Hospital charity ball. Once, when Charlene did a concert in south Florida with rock'n'roll great Chubby Checker, she and the "Let's Twist Again" singer were guests for dinner in my home.

Slowly, things began to change, however, as Charlene became more famous. Mercedes became more demanding, saying that Charlene, now a "major star," should be paid for anything she did for us. He was starting to believe his own public relations.

Finally, I called Mercedes and asked what was up. After all, we'd helped Charlene's career when she really needed it. His attitude was: "Maybe we're getting too big for you now." My response was: "Charlene's career is good now, but when she's gone and forgotten, the *Enquirer* will still be around." That made Mercedes angry.

When Charlene married country singer Johnny Lee on Valentine's Day, 1982, Mercedes sold the exclusive rights of the wedding to our rival the *Star*. He thought that would really frost us.

Was he ever wrong!

One of my photo editors dug out a gorgeous old *Dallas* photo of Charlene in a beautiful wedding dress. We ran it big on page one. More important, our reporters discovered the couple's most intimate secret: Charlene was expecting.

Our cover of March 9, 1982, beside the beautiful wedding picture was: *DALLAS* BEAUTY 2 MONTHS PREGNANT AS SHE WEDS.

Star's wedding photo showed Charlene in a dress much less spectacular than the one on our cover. Readers who noticed the difference must have wondered which was the real dress. And, of course, *Star* didn't have the pregnancy angle on their cover. Their story was weak, weak, *weak*. I wanted to be a fly on the wall when the *Star* editors saw their exclusive crumble into dust.

If Mercedes had sold the wedding rights to us, he would never have allowed us to front-page the pregnancy angle. As it turned out, we had a blockbuster hit, outselling *Star* by nearly 1 million copies.

Not long after the wedding, *Dallas* folded and Charlene was history. She never had another major role, and Mercedes eventually stopped managing her.

Many years later, in the late '90s, Charlene actually began to write a gossip column for the *Globe*, the third tabloid in the market. Even that job ended a year or so after the new *Enquirer* owners bought the *Globe* and decided to upgrade their editorial.

I feel sorry for Charlene, who is a genuinely nice person. She just should have traded in her Mercedes a couple of years sooner than she did.

By the mid-eighties, our celebrity coverage included more than just face-lifts and romantic romps. Once AIDS hit the scene, rumors spread about stars who might be suffering from this dreaded, fatal new disease. Weeks before we published their stories, we knew that two of the biggest names in Hollywood were AIDS victims. However, running a story that a celebrity had AIDS, without absolute certainty, was playing Russian roulette. If we were wrong they would sue—and end up owning the *Enquirer*. Not a pleasant prospect for my long-term career.

The first AIDS death story we published was on Rock Hudson, the handsome hunk who had romanced countless beauties on the screen and been the fantasy lover of millions of real-life American women. Almost impossible for movie fans to believe, Rock was gay. He and old cowboy star Randolph Scott had frolicked together back in his first days in Hollywood.

By early 1985, just about everyone in Hollywood knew that Rock was very sick. For months, he'd been losing weight and looking gaunt; it seemed almost certain that he had AIDS.

We learned that Rock had been diagnosed with the disease as early as June 1984 at UCLA Medical Center, but we had no proof. It's not enough for reporters to tell you, "Everyone knows." You need specific witnesses or medical evidence that proves the person has a disease.

As his weight dropped—from 200-plus to 140 pounds—Hudson flew to Paris for treatment at the Pasteur Institute, which specialized in AIDS treatments. Nothing worked. Rock tried to continue normal life and even appeared at a TV press conference with old friend Doris Day in July 1985. Even though I knew the story, I was appalled when I saw that the hunky star was now a shrunken, withered shell of a man.

The concern and shock his appearance produced sent Rock immediately back to Paris, where he collapsed in his hotel and was rushed to the American Hospital. As he lay there, deathly ill, doctors administered an experimental drug, HPA-23, which hadn't been approved in the United States.

At last, European sources confirmed what our Hollywood reporters had been telling us. Rock's illness was a secret no longer.

We now had a package of stories—and went with them. To give some idea of the money and effort the *National Enquirer* would expend on major stories, the team that produced this Hudson package numbered fifty-six: It included three senior editors, twenty-two staff reporters and editors, more than a dozen other editors, and a pack of freelance correspondents. All for one story. That's more than most major magazines use for a whole *issue*. And that's why nobody could match us on breaking exclusive stories.

On August 13, 1985, we went with this cover:

Rock Hudson: The *Real* Story
Shocking Reason He Hid AIDS for a Year

This was the first time the real story had come out.

We also discovered another appalling angle—one retold by TV and magazines ever since. Rock Hudson had been a guest star on *Dynasty*, where we had extraordinary sources. We learned that the year before, Rock and his handlers had all denied the rampant rumors that he had AIDS. Hudson flat-out lied.

In one *Dynasty* episode, producers scripted a love scene between Rock and Linda Evans, who played Krystal. Onscreen, Rock kissed Linda Evans—deeply and passionately, selfishly and callously hiding his infection with a dreadful disease.

When they learned the truth, the cast and crew were shocked, angry, and scared. One executive told us: "From the stars to the prop guy, there's not a single person on the set who can understand why Hudson would purposely expose anyone else to the disease."

In the mid-eighties, nobody knew how the disease spread. We know better now, but at that time it was feared that even *touching* might transmit the disease. Rock certainly didn't know what was safe.

Later we found out that even after his diagnosis, Rock was meeting new "friends" at gay bars in West Hollywood and not telling them he was infected. So it was no surprise that he kept it secret from Linda Evans in their passionate kissing scenes.

Linda was terrified. Doctors told her that exchanges of bodily fluids, including saliva, were probably the main sources of infection. Hudson hadn't kissed her just once. There had been several rehearsals of the kissing scene.

We dug out a tape of that *Dynasty* episode, and three weeks after breaking the Rock Hudson AIDS story, we front-paged a huge photo of the *DYNASTY* KISS, with Rock and Linda in full lip-lock.

Many years later, on February 23, 2002, the TV show *Entertainment Tonight* featured the *Dynasty* kiss as one of the top-ten scandals of all time. Aaron Spelling, the show's creator, stated that, during the crisis, the best medical experts told him you could get AIDS from kissing. "We were all in a panic for Linda," he revealed.

As he lay dying, Rock received calls from a number of friends who expressed anger at his disregard for their safety. Rock was ashamed and apologetic. He even asked that a message be sent to Linda Evans, saying simply: "Forgive me."

Our *DYNASTY* KISS story sent a shock wave through movie and TV sets. One star of a TV show changed her contract so she no longer had to kiss her co-star, who was suspected of being gay. Tina Louise, beautiful star of *Gilligan's Island*, had a new TV series and told us, "It's a terribly scary feel knowing you have to kiss someone and . . . [it] could kill you." Another star bemoaned: "Outside of Pat Boone, who can I trust?"

The panic eventually subsided as common sense—and more medical research—kicked in. But Rock had a lot to answer for. His selfish recklessness was a terrible blemish on the career of a major star who'd been loved and admired.

At 8 A.M. on October 2, 1985, in his Beverly Hills mansion, Rock

Hudson slipped into a coma, and one hour later he was dead. His last words were: "I feel okay. I'm at peace with God."

The story of Rock Hudson's death was major for us. A team of forty-one editors, reporters, researchers, and freelance correspondents helped us put out a package of seven full pages. Every media outlet covered his death, of course, but we had the inside details of his last days, including final visits from celebrity friends like comedienne Martha Raye and actress Nancy Walker, who had played his housekeeper on their hit TV show *McMillan and Wife*. Liz Taylor had earlier comforted him and advised him to consult a faith healer. But the big-name stars who formerly basked in his friendship were nowhere to be seen. He did have a vision in which his dead mother visited him and gave him a message.

Our coverage of his death omitted mention of the scandal because we believed it was a time to reflect on his life and what he had left behind.

Our issue on Rock's death, like those of Elvis, Liberace, Princess Grace, John Lennon, JFK, and Natalie Wood, was close to a sellout. When a celebrity dies in unusual circumstances, people just can't get enough, whether in print or on TV. The *Enquirer* had the most powerful investigative staff in the Western world, so on these occasions we were always able to break exclusive material that made us a must-read for many millions of North Americans.

With Rock gone, I figured our days covering him were over. *Wrong.* Within weeks yet another Rock Hudson scandal erupted. On November 12, Rock's longtime lover, Marc Christian, filed suit against the Hudson estate for $10 million. He claimed he'd been having an affair with Hudson for two years before the star died—and all that time Rock had denied having AIDS.

It was another blockbuster story. I told our editors that only one publication should get it—ours.

Two of my best reporters, Tony Brenna and Jerry George, later promoted to Los Angeles bureau chief, "tied up" Christian for an exclusive interview. Our readers got the only detailed account of Rock's bizarre love life before it came out in court.

Our cover: Rock's Lies about AIDS May Cost Me My Life.

Inside, our story began: "Rock Hudson was the most wonderful man in the world—but he played Russian roulette with my life." Christian claimed that, time after time, Rock denied he had AIDS. His doctors knew, many close aides knew, but they conspired to keep the secret from the young lover.

Christian said he learned about Rock's lies only when it came out in the media. Terrified, he realized that he might now have AIDS lurking in his bloodstream but not know for years to come. "Each day could be the day my death sentence begins," lamented Christian.

It was an engrossing story, full of details of the excitement, fun, and final betrayal of their relationship. Rock Hudson once again sold big numbers of the *Enquirer*.

The jury hearing the case believed the young man and awarded him $21 million—more than twice what he'd asked for. Even after a judge cut the award to $5.5 million, Marc Christian still became wealthy. I do not believe he ever contracted AIDS. If he had, it would have run in the *National Enquirer*.

The second big AIDS death story was that of Liberace, the flouncy, bouncy superstar pianist who made his older lady fans' hearts quiver with his flashy clothes and even flashier personality. Known to his friends as Lee, Mr. Showmanship might have seemed lighter on the testosterone than John Wayne, but throughout his career he consistently denied he was gay. In the late 1950s, he even won a lawsuit in Britain against the *Daily Mirror*'s top columnist, Cassandra (pen name of William Connor), who described him as a "winking, sniggering, snuggling, chromium-plated, scent-impregnated, luminous, quivering, giggling, fruit-flavored, mincing, ice-covered heap of mother love." Cassandra may have been the best writer in Britain, but he lost the case when Liberace claimed it made him sound gay. How the heck could anyone have reached *that* conclusion?

Unlike the *Daily Mirror*, the *Enquirer* unequivocally labeled him gay in 1983 when we ran the exclusive story of his young lover, Scott Thorsen, who was suing Liberace for palimony. Liberace did not, however, sue us.

Wladziu Valentino Liberace had fashioned an incredible musical career over the years and drew packed crowds at Carnegie Hall, Madison Square Garden, the Hollywood Bowl, and Chicago's Soldier Field. In 1955 he became highest-paid Las Vegas performer ever, and in 1978 the *Guinness Book of World Records* named him the world's highest-paid musician.

Not long after he broke all kinds of records at New York City's Radio City Music Hall, Liberace was visibly at the peak of a wonderful career and beloved by his myriad fans. He was also *very* sick.

Our contacts told us it was AIDS. We dispatched two top reporters, Charlie Montgomery and David Wright, to Palm Springs, California, where Liberace had been receiving treatment for a very serious condition. The star's public relations spokesman, commenting on the fact that his client looked pale, yellow, and sickly, told reporters that it was the result of a watermelon diet. Liberace had just eaten too much of the fruit. *Yeah, right!* Local reporters printed his statement, which was duly repeated by the national wire services, but we wondered what the PR person had been ingesting.

Our guys could get nothing from the Liberace camp, nothing from the hospital, and nothing from doctors. Who was left? Lesser hospital staffers and . . . nurses, nurses, nurses. Who knows what goes on in a hospital better than the nurses?

Recalls David Wright: "Montgomery and I latched on to a couple of nurses and took them to lunch. We struck gold. One of the nurses had been in the hospital two weeks earlier and was drawing blood from her patient, Mr. Liberace.

"She said that something went wrong and blood spurted over her. Immediately, the senior medical staff went nuts and pulled her aside. A doctor informed her she needed to take tests."

The nurse really began to get worried when, the next day, a special bulletin went up on the hospital staff board. It said that anyone who had been present during the blood-spattering incident *must* go for special tests.

When the nurse went to have her blood tested, she asked the doctor what was the big deal. The doc replied: "It's Liberace. He has AIDS."

Wright and Montgomery then confirmed the account through other medical personnel.

My editors and I were excited. This was major, world-exclusive material.

Our lawyers said "no." Then, "no, no, *no*, *no*, NO." What if the nurses were lying? What if the doctors had made a mistake? What if this? What if that? There wasn't enough backup. I was willing to take the risk—I just knew the story was accurate. But GP wouldn't go along. Not that I blamed him. A mistake of this size could literally cost him his whole empire.

Our reporters and editors were crushed. So was I, but I had to hide it in taking the side of Mr. Pope and the lawyers.

Then came a break. Hank Greenspun, famed columnist of the respected daily the *Las Vegas Sun*, wrote a "blind" item stating that a beloved unnamed star was dying of AIDS. He appealed to the star to admit his condition and get help.

Wright contacted the paper, and they told him how they knew Liberace had contracted the dread disease.

That was the clincher. The attorneys gave the go-ahead and we ran the story: Liberace was dying of AIDS. About the same time we locked up our issue, the *Sun* told their readers that the AIDS victim was Liberace—but it was our story that shocked the world.

In the February 10, 1987, issue—which hit the streets about eight days before the cover date—our headline was: LIBERACE'S SECRET BATTLE WITH AIDS.

When you work for the *Enquirer* the euphoria from a big story lasts about thirty seconds. You always have to think about next week and then the week after that. So Montgomery and Wright were told: Get an exclusive for next week.

Liberace, very sick, was at his home in Palm Springs, protected by security guards. Nobody was talking except the PR guys, still spouting their watermelon-diet fairy tales. Our guys noticed a vacant lot opposite the Palm Springs house, so they rented a trailer and parked it right across from Liberace's home. That way, they were able to keep watch on everything that happened, around the clock.

Remembers Wright: "Late one evening we heard two young kids in the street, shouting and laughing. I went out and saw them listening to some devices. When I walked over they explained they had 'scanners' that could pick up local radio signals. And they had accidentally locked on the frequency of the guards in the Liberace house."

Wright, who makes no claims to being a gadget guy, was amazed and offered the boys $500 to rent their scanners for a few days. Only later did he learn he could have bought them for $75 each at the local Radio Shack.

The scanners were manna from Heaven. Every word spoken into the security walkie-talkies was now being monitored in the *Enquirer* trailer. All kinds of details that wound up in our stories were jotted down, and it was soon obvious that Liberace was getting progressively sicker. Within a couple of days Wright and the guys heard a guard say, "He's gone. We have to make arrangements." Liberace had finally died. It was February 4, 1987, just a couple of days after our AIDS issue had hit the newsstands. Liberace was sixty-seven.

We thought we would get a photo exclusive if they moved the body that night, since all the other reporters left after about 10 P.M. But the next morning, the usual phalanx of TV and print journalists returned, and our guys had lots of company when following the vehicle carrying the body.

For a star accustomed to ermine furs, jewels, private jets, and Rolls-Royces, Liberace's last journey was a tacky affair. A gurney was rolled to his bed, the body was slipped into a plastic bag, and then Liberace was rolled out to the front of the house. No shiny, dignified hearse awaited him, but a plain old gray station wagon.

A cop car followed the station wagon, with a string of media cars trailing behind. Upon reaching the highway, the police car stopped, waved all the press down, and held them for ten minutes until the station wagon was well on its way.

With our early notice, Montgomery and Wright had been able to charter two helicopters with pilots, and we had both flying overhead with *Enquirer* cameramen. Through special walkie-talkies they were able to communicate with our ground forces, telling them where the hearse was heading.

Montgomery had a decent car and apparently was catching up to the station wagon on the highway, but Wright was cursing a blue streak. He had an underpowered subcompact and was pushing it pedal-down, as fast as it would go.

He recalls: "My adrenaline was pumping like mad as the photographer in the helicopter was telling me where the station wagon was. My car was shuddering and threatening to come apart as I topped 90 m.p.h. in the chase.

"I couldn't believe I hadn't reached the wagon when I told the helicopter the landmarks I was passing. Our guy gasped and shouted: 'You've gone five miles past them.'"

In his excitement, Wright had passed the station wagon as well as Montgomery, who was right on its tail, without seeing them. Montgomery was wondering where the hell his friend was going as his rickety little car flew past at top speed.

Wright waited until the wagon caught up and followed it to California's most famous cemetery, Forest Lawn.

Now was the time for Liberace to be at peace forever. But not so fast. His personal physician, Dr. Ronald Daniels, had listed the causes of death as cardiac arrest and congestive heart failure brought on by a degenerative disease of the brain. No mention of AIDS.

Just after the body was embalmed and arrangements were finalized for burial the next day, authorities from the Department of Public Health of Riverside County—the county where Liberace had died—pounced. They rejected the death certificate and ordered Liberace's body removed for autopsy. Said Riverside coroner Raymond Carrillo: "The decision to autopsy was made because of reports that Liberace had AIDS in the *Las Vegas Sun* and the *National Enquirer*, and because they spirited the body out of our jurisdiction." He even hinted at pressing misdemeanor charges against Liberace's aides.

It wasn't until February 9—five days after the death—that the coroner cleared the body for burial. At a press conference, Carrillo said, "He did die of AIDS . . . in my opinion, there was a cover-up."

I was elated by the story we ran. It had the most minute details of Liberace's deathbed, the panic after he died, and the cover-up that failed. I was really proud of our guys.

Looking back on Liberace, I think he might have enjoyed the spectacle that followed his death. In life, this shining star had covered himself in a blaze of glitz and controversy; in death he went out in a last hurrah of publicity. No one ever ignored the Great Liberace.

Our cover of June 2, 1987, was a story that changed history. The photo showed Senator Gary Hart sitting on the deck of a boat with Donna Rice on his knee. He was wearing a T-shirt imprinted with the words "*Monkey Business* Crew."

Senator Hart, the almost-certain choice as Democratic candidate for president in the 1988 election, was the odds-on favorite to beat the Republican nominee and become the forty-first president of the United States. Our photo derailed him, lightweight Michael Dukakis became the Democratic candidate, and the presidency went to George Herbert Walker Bush. And clearly if Bush, Sr., had not made it to the White House, George W. would never, never, *never* have been considered as a candidate for leader of the free world.

The ironic part of the whole event is that without Hart's arrogance, we'd never have been tempted to publish *anything* about him. A few months earlier, I'd have rejected the Donna Rice photo. Gary Hart just wasn't a celebrity as far as our readers were concerned.

However, Senator Hart changed all that when he virtually challenged the nation's press. Rumors of his girl-chasing abounded in Washington; when asked about the rumors, he told reporters the stories weren't true and cavalierly suggested that reporters "put a tail on" him to see he was telling the truth.

That was the first of three mistakes. The second was taking, on March 28, an overnight trip from Miami to the Bahamas on an 83-foot luxury yacht called the *Monkey Business*. That in itself would have been fine, but he was accompanied by Donna Rice, a lovely blonde who had previously dated Bruce Willis, Don Johnson, and Prince Albert of Monaco. With them went Donna's friend Lynn Armandt and Gary's pal William Broadhurst. Senator Hart's third mistake? Six weeks later, he invited Donna to spend the night with him at his townhouse in Washington, D.C., while his wife was in Denver.

The *Miami Herald* had been tipped off about a possible romance, and two of their reporters tailed Donna to Hart's townhouse. When the story broke it made headlines around the world.

Now, and only now, was Gary Hart a major celebrity, worthy of our attention—and directly in our sights. Unluckily for him.

The Senator, supported by his loyal wife, put a public relations spin on the situation. It was *not* an affair, he said. Donna Rice was just a friend. Many sympathetic reporters in D.C. were willing to buy his shaky story, and it seemed he might be able to wriggle out of the hole and regain his presidential bid.

I held a meeting of all our articles editors and told them to scour the country for leads. "There's a real untold story here," I said, "and we want it."

Articles editor Larry Haley ended up handling the story. Larry was the junior editor on our most prolific page-one editorial team. His boss Dan Schwartz, later to become our executive editor, had gone to Europe on a well-deserved vacation, just in time to miss one of the biggest stories of the decade.

Two of our best reporters, Richard Baker and John South, went to Miami, where the *Monkey Business* was docked, to uncover the truth. Several days passed, and while we dug up some good details, no bombshell emerged.

Then, after nearly a week, came a call from our number-one reporter in Los Angeles, Alan Smith. He had contacted one of his best sources, a woman who recruited beautiful young ladies as party escorts and for magazine glamour shots. She knew Lynn Armandt, the second girl on the *Monkey Business*, and she told Smith she had heard about Hart's trip to the Bahamas. This was a *big* breakthrough.

Haley told me later, "Smith mentioned a huge reward for a major exclusive, and the woman promised to contact Lynn to see if she was interested. All America wanted to know the details of Gary Hart and Donna Rice, especially if they'd been having an affair. And if America wanted to know, it was our job to tell them."

Then came the bombshell. Smith's source told him that a picture existed—an actual posed photograph of Senator Gary Hart with a bikinied Donna Rice sitting on his lap.

It was about 8 P.M. in Florida when an excited Larry Haley got this news from Smith. Larry tracked me down to the local racketball court, and without even showering, I rushed back to the office for a strategy session.

Some things sound believable and some don't. This didn't. We're talking about a highly intelligent United States Senator, married and aiming for the presidency, who knew reporters were looking into any extramarital activities. How could he be stupid enough to pose for a photo with a sexy young blonde on his knee?

On the other hand, the *Enquirer* exists because celebrities do stupid things they later regret, so we passed the information on to reporters Baker and South in Miami. They, in turn, pushed, prodded, and poked at sources, trying to find evidence of any such picture. They dangled promises of big, *big* bucks for the photo. For several days, no luck.

We've always promised not to reveal where we got these photos, so no names—but Smith managed to track down the woman, who had *two* photos of the senator with Donna Rice. Smith actually spoke to her on the phone. Desperate to get our hands on these photos, Haley also talked to her several times . . . cajoling, beseeching, pleading, promising. Sometimes she agreed to let us see the pictures, then she'd change her mind. She never let us visit her face to face.

Recalls Haley, "She had a boyfriend who influenced her. She'd agree to a deal—then call back hours later and say she had changed her mind."

This was hard on my old ticker.

Then, as often happens when you work exceptionally hard on something, a major break appeared.

Our photo editor, John Cathcart, got a phone call from a female lawyer in a prominent Miami law firm. She claimed to represent the woman who had come into possession of photos showing Senator Hart and Donna Rice together. She confirmed that it was not photo, singular, but *photos*, plural. It might be possible, said the lawyer, for us to buy the pictures.

The woman had cracked.

When Cathcart ran in to tell me, I almost jumped up and down with excitement. I asked him to negotiate this deal personally. Unlike many photo editors, he had had years of experience in both news- and picture-gathering. If anyone could get these pictures, it was Cathcart.

The next few days were filled with torture and frustration. The lawyer wouldn't let us visit her office, and on the telephone she was encouraging one minute and then dashed our hopes the next. It seemed the woman with the pictures was still torn between wanting money and honoring some promise.

Finally the attorney invited us to her Miami office, so Cathcart drove down with Richard Baker. Time was of the essence. We were locking up the paper and going to press that night, and we needed these photos—fast.

The lawyer's office was riddled with tension. First, the source wanted a *huge* amount of money. I okayed that immediately over the telephone. Then the source walked into the lawyer's office and said she wasn't sure anymore. Cathcart called to say the deal was probably blown.

Suddenly, when Cathcart was alone with the attorney, she opened a drawer, threw the photos on her desk, and said: "Let's work on the contract." Said John later: "I just couldn't believe my eyes. In the photo, Donna Rice was sitting on Hart's lap, both smiling for the camera, with his arm around her waist. I could hardly breathe . . . I was paralyzed at what I saw."

The only difference from reporter Alan Smith's first tip-off was that Donna was wearing a miniskirt, not a bikini.

The second picture was almost equally mesmerizing. It showed all four in a Bahamas nightclub making music on stage, with a grinning Gary looking very merry and holding maracas in his hand.

We had scooped the world. Cathcart worked the phone, finalizing the contract with our lawyers and the source's attorney. Meanwhile, I was on the phone every ten minutes, frantically reminding John I needed the photos *now* or we'd miss deadline. I thanked the lord when the Miami attorney allowed the pictures to be driven the 60 miles to Lantana before the contract was in fact signed.

The source and her lawyer gave us worldwide copyright for all time. We agreed not to reveal the price or to name the woman who sold the photos. Reports of $70,000 or $80,000 have been published, but even now I still feel constrained from either confirming or denying.

While the photos were in transit, I told Mr. Pope we got them for X dollars. Unbelievably, GP said, "That's a lot of money." I told him, "Gene, these are worth *twice* that." He grudgingly said okay, but it was too late anyway because I had already made the deal.

When I first saw the photos on my light table, the feelings that rushed over me were: This is awesome, this is historic.

When GP saw the photos he just looked at Senator Hart and muttered: "What an idiot."

Baker managed to get a short interview with the photo source, and along with other material gathered earlier, we had a great story to go with the incredible photo of Hart with Rice on his knee.

The headlines:

> DONNA RICE—WHAT REALLY HAPPENED
> GARY HART ASKED ME TO MARRY HIM

We knew this exclusive would be major news and planned for a public relations release. Normally, we'd hold a press conference— newspapers and TV stations would visit Lantana, see our cover page, then ask questions.

I nixed that because most of these guys would be jealous we had scooped them and would clutter the exclusive with questions like, Did we pay for the story? Then the national news would be angled away from our cover.

Instead I conferred with David Kendall, who had handled the photo contract for us at our law firm in Washington, D.C. (An ironic detail—David later became the lead lawyer for President Clinton in his Lewinsky and Whitewater travails.)

David and colleague Bob Burnett, agent for Sam Donaldson, set up separate interviews for me with NBC, CBS, and ABC in Washington so that I could control the situation. The interviewers knew that if they asked the wrong questions I could just walk away, leaving their rivals with better taped pieces. I also gave interviews to the *New York Times* and the *Washington Post*.

All three networks gave prominent airtime to the *Enquirer*'s front page, and the story went round the world. We sold a lot of copies.

For Senator Hart, our story was a death blow to his political career. He left the presidential race before we even hit the checkout racks. Our photos and the detail-filled story proved that his cruise on the *Monkey Business* hadn't been an innocent little trip, as he had been claiming.

The Democratic nomination went to Michael Dukakis, who really didn't stand a chance, against George Bush, Sr. I often wonder who would have been our 2001 president if we hadn't found those photos. Certainly not Dubya.

DEATH OF A GENIUS

GP died on October 2, 1988. We could have run a story headlined:

GENE POPE DIDN'T HAVE TO DIE

Part genius, part visionary, part eccentric, Gene was a figure of strange opposites. Utterly ruthless if an employee didn't measure up to his standards, he was also a caring philanthropist if one of his employees, or their families, had major medical problems. Then he would often get them the best medical care in the country. Many times he picked up thousands of dollars in expenses.

He sent his reporters on jaunts all over the world to get stories from the most remote regions of the globe. Yet the somewhat reclusive press baron was himself afraid of flying.

In his magnificent wood-paneled office, behind his massive desk, he ruled his world like an emperor. He dressed more like the janitor. He prided himself on shirts and trousers from Sears, and he drove a Chevy Impala while his executives drove Mercedes, Jaguars, and Cadillacs. On Saturdays he'd come into the office in swim trunks, a golf shirt, and flip-flop sandals.

The most tragic of his contradictions involved his health. He knew more about the latest medical breakthroughs than many doctors; he was chairman of the local JFK Hospital; he was friendly with major medical greats such as Dr. Michael DeBakey, the legendary heart surgeon, and Dr. William Castelli, the famous cardiology researcher who first alerted the United States to the dangers of cholesterol.

Ironically, when this medical-savvy tycoon suffered the first symptoms of heart disease, he ignored them, waving off pleas from his family, his doctors—and me. He was sixty-one and knew his father had succumbed to a heart attack at age fifty-nine. But he believed he was different from normal people. That's what killed him.

From the time we moved to Florida in 1971, Gene never took a single sick day, unless you count the one time he had a monstrous hangover after drinking with the visiting sales force until 5:30 A.M. He never seemed to have the normal colds, flu, infections, or fevers that afflicted most people. So during the early summer of 1988, when he began complaining of chest pains, it was a total shock.

Gene went to JFK Hospital for tests and when he returned, he looked very healthy. "I'm fine," he announced to everyone, and went back to work. His wife, Lois, his children, his senior employees—we all knew he was probably *not* fine. Lois confided that he would not allow his doctors to conduct the invasive tests they'd recommended.

One morning, I went into his office and spoke to him man to man. "Gene," I said. "If this was me or any of your key employees, you would insist we fly to the best cardiac center in the United States for a full overhaul. You must do the same."

"There's no problem," he assured me. "I've just realized what caused the pains in my chest. I had lifted some heavy suitcases from the bed a few days earlier, and it was some kind of muscle strain."

This, from a man who was perhaps 50 pounds overweight, had a family history of heart attacks, smoked three packs of cigarettes a day, ate food like it was about to be banned by the government, and scoffed at exercise. He used to laugh at my three-times-a-week racketball games that occasionally gave me bumps, scrapes, and sprains. Gene would boast: "The only exercise I get is attending the funerals of my friends who exercise."

Jokes were one thing—chest pains could be serious. When GP blamed the heavy suitcases, I protested: "Come on Gene, it's me. You need the best medical care. Please let me set it up."

His eyes suddenly flashing with anger, he retorted: "Iain, I told you I'm fine. Back off. Forget it."

Gene was my mentor, my friend, someone I admired, and a kind of father-figure to me. But first and foremost, he was the Boss. His tone of voice told me I was in the danger zone—and I left it alone. I remember thinking I would be much more forceful if he mentioned chest pains again.

To some extent I understood why Gene refused to travel to the Mayo Clinic or the best hospitals in New York. First, he was afraid to fly. Second, he had just spearheaded the opening of the DeBakey Heart Institute at JFK Hospital, where he chaired the board. Bypassing his own clinic would be embarrassing.

A few weeks later, on October 2, 1988, the second attack came. That Sunday morning, an ex-*Enquirer* editorial executive named Brian Wells, who was close to the Pope family, called to say that Gene had been taken to JFK Hospital. I told my wife that this time Gene would be forced to get proper treatment.

A few minutes later came the call that changed my life.

Maria Pope, Gene's adopted daughter, was on the line. Her voice breaking in emotion, she said: "Iain, Dad is gone. He's dead. He had a heart attack and an ambulance took him to JFK Hospital. He's gone . . ."

It was inconceivable. Gene Pope had been the center of my life for twenty-five years. He was larger than life. He was *immortal*. I told Maria I would be right over.

At the Pope oceanfront mansion, the family and a very small group of associates and friends were milling around as if in a daze. Lois didn't seem to grasp what was happening. Her lovely face was etched in anguish and sorrow—but she walked from room to room asking people if *they* were all right.

When a famous tycoon dies suddenly, speculation always abounds about what *really* happened. We knew that well at the *Enquirer*. In the case of Gene Pope, the only person present was his wife, Lois. Now for the first time, she is allowing the minute-by-minute details of the tragedy to be revealed publicly, in this book.

★★★

According to Lois, everything seemed normal when she woke up next to her still-sleeping husband that morning. As usual, she had planned to drive her mother to 10:30 Mass at their local church. Running a little late, she was hurriedly dressing when she thought she heard Gene crying out, "Dear . . ." in an unusually faint voice.

Wearing only a skirt and bra, she walked out of her dressing room toward the bed. She asked, "What is it?" He didn't answer. "Gene's eyes were open," she says. "He seemed to be staring at the ceiling. I thought he hadn't heard me. So I asked again."

In that moment Mrs. Pope realized something was terribly wrong. Managing to stay calm, she immediately punched the telephone button that went directly to the ever-present security guard at the house and told him to dial 911 for medical help, then began mouth-to-mouth resuscitation.

The bedroom was quite dark, but enough sunlight came in through the closed drapes to illuminate the scene when the guard, Bill Ellam, a moonlighting Lantana police officer, burst in. He, too, tried to revive Mr. Pope.

Describing what was going through her mind at the time, Lois says: "I don't remember any panic. It was like time was suspended. I was giving Gene mouth-to-mouth, trying to get him to breathe. It was like some slow-motion dream, somehow not quite real."

The draperies were pulled open to let the sunlight flood in. And within three or four minutes, the paramedics arrived. They quickly carried Gene over to the window for light and began working on him frantically, even using electric paddles to restart his heart.

"It was only then," says Lois Pope, "that I realized that I might lose my husband. I tried to go to him, but the paramedics almost pushed me away. They weren't being rude, they just had their job to do and needed the space."

Within moments, Gene was transferred to the ambulance. Mrs. Pope wanted to accompany her husband but was told it would interfere with the ongoing effort to revive him.

Gene was chairman of the board at John F. Kennedy Hospital, where he'd led the effort to start the Michael DeBakey Heart Institute not long before. These Pope-inspired doctors had saved the lives of many local heart attack patients. But they couldn't save Gene.

In a special room at JFK Hospital, Lois waited, along with some other family members, with growing trepidation. When doctors finally told her the grim news, Mrs. Pope began to weep for the first time.

"I lost it then," she recalls. "I screamed. I pounded the walls, I shouted why, why . . . and I said I hated God."

I'm not the only one who believes Gene's death could have been avoided. Mrs. Pope also believes that Gene could have lived several years longer.

When he had his first chest pains in the late summer of '88, heart doctors told Lois and him that he needed an angiogram. Clearly, some risks are associated with any procedure, but it was even more clear that this one was necessary. Gene refused treatment.

By ignoring the warning signals and refusing to see the best cardiologists in America (though he always insisted that his staff see the best—even if they were 1,000 miles away) he succumbed to a heart attack that could have been prevented.

The next day at the office was awful. How could we put out the *Enquirer* without GP? It was unthinkable, and we were all close to tears. But lockup was the next day, and the Boss always said: "The reader comes first."

So we made it. A call from Lois made it a little easier. She said: "Iain, you must carry on. We are all depending on you. We have confidence in you, and if you ever need anything, we are all behind you." That helped.

I held meetings and wrote memos, essentially telling everyone that while nobody could ever replace Gene, his legacy was *us*—all his surviving employees. If we maintained his standards, his drive for excellence, and his constant demand for achieving the impossible, we would keep the *Enquirer* on top.

Gene had always been our beacon of strength. We were a family—admittedly weird at times and occasionally dysfunctional—and he had been the patriarch, always exuding confidence even in the most difficult moments. I had to try to fill that huge void, and the staff rallied around me valiantly.

Gene's death created a blizzard of press clippings from papers and magazines around the country. They ranged from the *New York Times'* respectful obituary, headlined "Generoso Pope, Jr., 61, National Enquirer's Owner," to the *New York Post*, which came up with "National Enquirer Owner Goes to Meet Elvis." Weeks later, an editorial cartoon in our local paper, the *Palm Beach Post*, picked up the same theme. When the company was put up for sale, their cartoonist showed Elvis in a spaceship coming down from the sky to buy the *Enquirer*. The scale of the coverage was a measure of Gene's importance in American publishing and belied some of the snide printed remarks that tried to denigrate Gene's impact on the journalistic landscape.

The Pope funeral was one of most impressive ever held in south Florida. The church in Lantana was filled to overflowing with dignitaries, friends, and associates who flew in from all over America to attend. Former photo editor Brian Hitchen traveled from England just to pay his last respects.

Most impressive of all was the reaction of the Palm Beach sheriff's office and officers from local police and fire departments throughout the county. Not only did many of them show up for the funeral service, they lined many of the streets from the church to the gravesite. Police were at every single street intersection, and the funeral procession was waved through each one—never once stopping.

These men—multiple scores of them—were not paid for this. They showed up as volunteers to pay their respects to a benefactor who'd supported local police and firemen for years. If a department needed bulletproof vests but had no money, one call to GP would take care of the problem. If a policeman or fireman was sick and his family was in financial trouble, a check from Mr. Pope would arrive. This was the officers' payback homage.

★★★

I was astonished when Lois asked me to give Gene's eulogy. It was a great honor, but it scared me to death. Still, it gave me a chance to say a few things to and about Gene, and share them with his friends and colleagues—things I could never have said to him in person.

As I walked to the front of the church, which was standing room only, I was strangely calm. I meant every word I was about to say, and I began with a simple declarative sentence: "Gene Pope was the greatest man I've ever known."

Gene's generous record of philanthropy and helping people in the community was evidenced by the overflow turnout at the service. But, as with any good *Enquirer* story, I highlighted GP's record of caring by telling one tear-inducing story.

Days before, I had assigned reporter Ed Sussman to get the best, true GP anecdote he could. He came up trumps with a story I was able to use when I spoke to the mourners:

"One story I heard just yesterday seems to crystallize and illuminate the essence of Gene. A few years ago the director of a local orphanage was taking a group of his boys to visit the *Enquirer*'s Christmas tree—one of Lantana's holiday highlights. One of the boys somehow believed his father was nearby and became hysterical. Crying and yelling for his daddy, nobody could quiet the distraught youngster, who was inconsolable.

"Then Gene arrived at the scene. The owner of America's biggest newspaper—the publishing tycoon Geneoroso Pope, Junior—went over, bent down, and took the tearful little boy by the hand. Somehow, he quieted him down, dried his tears, and asked him gently if he would like to visit the *Enquirer* offices. The little boy nodded and Gene took him to his own office.

"There, where Gene has entertained VIPs ranging from presidential cabinet members and famous movie stars to Billy Graham, he sat the little orphan boy down and personally got him a Coke. With a few kind words and some jokes, he made the boy smile again, and a few moments later a happy child was back with his friends.

"But that's not the end of the story.

"Some days later, there arrived at the orphanage crates of ice cream, a pool table, a Ping-Pong table. Not long after came a check for $30,000. And since then, gifts have never stopped arriving.

"The director of the home said he was absolutely astonished at

Gene's generosity. I'm not. That's the Gene Pope I knew and came to love after working for him for almost twenty-five years."

As I drew to a close I reminded the mourners that some years before, a TV interviewer asked Gene how he would like to be remembered. He thought for a minute and said: "I would like for them to say I made an awful lot of people happy and gave them relief and escape. Millions and millions of them."

He certainly succeeded.

Then I quoted one of Gene's most famous adages: "Don't bore your audience. Be brief." And I returned to my seat.

THE 1990S—
THE SHOW MUST GO ON

Gene left a will appointing three trustees for the *Enquirer*. The chief was Gene's longtime friend Pete Peterson, a multi-millionaire financial tycoon and former secretary of commerce in the Nixon cabinet. Peterson was joined by attorney Jerry Traum, our longtime outside counsel, and a representative from Citibank. GP had mandated that the company be sold, presumably because he didn't think Lois or any of the children could run the business effectively.

No timetable had been fixed, and according to Peterson, I could continue to run things for a year or two before a sale was necessary. He appointed me chairman of the board, president, and chief executive officer, and asked me to remain as editor. Then Peterson held a meeting to announce that I was in charge and the company was *not* for sale in the near future. We had eighteen months to two years to prove we could be successful without Gene. The staff knew I would probably make changes but not the major cuts a new owner might demand. Though still mourning GP, they were reassured by this news.

Within a few weeks, however, I was hearing whispers that Mrs. Pope was nervous about her future. Without Gene to lean on, she seemed worried and on edge. She began pressing the trustees to sell the paper *now*.

I didn't take it too seriously. Peterson had given his word. The paper was doing really well. In these early weeks and months after Gene's death, the machine continued to work smoothly. Editors and reporters kept bringing in great stories like:

- Liz's New Live-in Love Is a 4-Time Jailbird . . . and she doesn't know it. We revealed to Ms. Taylor—and millions of readers — that her new guy, Larry Fortensky, had been locked up for drug possession and drunk driving . . . plus, an ex-wife had accused him of trying to choke her. Liz didn't care, married him, and lived to regret it.
- Exclusive first photos of Burt Reynolds with new baby Quinton, whose mom was wife Loni Anderson.
- Lisa Marie Presley was two months pregnant when she married Danny Keogh.
- Madonna tells cops that hubby Sean Penn beat her and tied her up in a drunken rage. "Marriage over," she says.
- *E.T.*'s Drew Barrymore was in a cocaine and booze clinic at age thirteen.
- A Raquel Welch exclusive interview telling our readers why she was divorcing husband Andre Weinfeld.

These were really compelling stories and photos, and they kept our sales high. In fact, shortly after Gene died, circulation *increased*. Pope's spirit still animated the company, and we were still cooking.

But Lois was growing even more anxious to sell. Peterson told me he would have to move the sale date up. We discussed how to break this crushing news quickly to the staff. I said we had to announce it to everyone in a straightforward honest manner.

This didn't happen. Unknown to me or my senior executives, Peterson had been talking to some New York financial circles about a possible sale. The *Wall Street Journal* picked up the rumors, and Peterson confirmed their story—without even calling me.

I got a call at home the morning the story ran: "Have you seen the *Wall Street Journal*? They say the *Enquirer* is for sale, and Peterson is quoted." The revelation was a shattering blow. Stunned and angry, I knew I would face a staff of employees who were furious, indignant, and in open revolt.

Pete's excuse was that he couldn't lie to the *Journal*. Of course, the story wouldn't have leaked if he hadn't talked about the sale to his Wall Street cronies before telling the staff.

I told him he'd better get down here fast to calm the troops. In the meantime, I held a meeting of our employees and had to admit that they had been misled.

People were talking about walking out in protest. They were so angry I worried that some embittered employee might vandalize our editorial production computers, wiping out whole pages and bringing us to our knees.

I had to find a way to keep the paper going. My take on it to everyone was that, considering the owners we have now, it might be better for everyone to have new owners. We had to show we could do the job, even given the stress and betrayal.

I didn't blame my people. GP's death had stunned them, they were told everything would be okay, and then they had been lied to. They were worried about their jobs, about a new owner firing everyone, or making it difficult to put out a good paper.

No one blamed Lois for wanting to sell. No one could blame the trustees for acceding to her wish. But they had told the media before they told their employees. That was real trouble.

Peterson, a smart guy, realized the dangers. While he did not come to Lantana immediately to face the troops, he did send one of his best young associates, Austin Beutner. This young man did a brilliant job of helping me turn the tide. Together we instituted a plan that gave loyal employees mini golden parachutes to protect them in case they were fired by new owners. That settled many fears.

According to Austin: "I've dealt with dozens of companies and have never experienced such passion and emotion as at the *Enquirer*. It was like you had all been living in Lantana in isolation with Gene Pope as emperor. It wasn't the real world. *Enquirer* staffers seemed to think of themselves as family." (Gene had created Enquirerland after all!)

Beutner was right. In remote Lantana, we had been a family run by one father figure. That was our strength. We gave more to our family, and we could demand more from them. It made us unique and, as we found out a little later, a very valuable commodity.

During this period of unrest, one colleague really stepped up to help out.

David Galpern had joined us as executive vice president and chief financial officer in December 1985. Gene had still wanted someone to run departments outside of editorial, because he thought all that stuff was "boring."

His EVPs, however, didn't last long. Executives with fine business pedigrees and successful careers seemed to go through our revolving doors with remarkable speed. They didn't seem to understand that working for Gene Pope wasn't like anything they'd ever done before.

David was different. He listened to what GP wanted—and got it done. If in doubt, he would ask my advice and take it. Within a few months it was clear he understood you had to run things the GP way. And before long, he was a trusted executive of Gene's, and a friend and trusted colleague of mine.

Now, as chairman and CEO of a company on the sale block and confronting an embittered staff, I found Galpern a godsend. We went out for a cocktail and I asked him to take responsibility for half a dozen departments, from advertising to personnel and administration. It let me concentrate on editorial, production, and just getting the paper out efficiently. We made a good team and kept the company afloat and prospering.

At one point, Peterson came to Lantana to describe how the sale process would work and said I could expect to be approached by various potential buyers who would make me multi-million dollar offers to join with them in the bid.

He said that this would be bad on two counts: (1) If I threw my hat in with one group, it might deter other bidders, who would not want to deal with a hostile CEO/editor, leading to a lower bid price for the Pope family. (2) If a group other than my own did buy the company, they might not make me an offer to remain.

He asked if I and David Galpern would remain uncommitted during the sale period, as an act of loyalty to Gene Pope. After the sale, we could make a deal with the new owners.

Pete was very persuasive. I agreed to the request and did not ask for a quid pro quo, such as a percentage of the sale price as a bonus. If there's any excuse, I was under terrible stress and working 7-day/100-hour weeks—that, plus ignorance and stupidity.

Things turned out okay in the long run, but blowing a chance to make $4 million or more was really pretty dumb.

★ ★ ★

I was surprised by the worldwide interest in acquiring the company Gene had forged. The *Enquirer* might be a bad word to Hollywood celebrities and mainstream American journalists, but some of the world's biggest media companies wanted to own us.

The chase began with thirty bidders, but very quickly the lineup was cut to seven—four from the United States and one each from France, Germany, and the United Kingdom. Each company made at least one major "due diligence" visit to our offices, on each visit bringing a minimum of fifty experts—people to investigate our sales force, circulation department, editorial, finances, payroll, human resources, legal situation, newsprint buying, printing resources, executive team—and me. I was asked so many questions, so many times, that I felt like I'd been examined by seven business proctologists within just a few weeks.

I took a membership at one of Palm Beach County's most upscale dining clubs so the *Enquirer* could host huge dinner parties with the visiting bidders. In one two-month period we had seven dinners with seventy-plus guests at each. Including our office Christmas party that year, I signed an annual bill for almost $150,000. I believe I was the Governor's Club most valuable guest for 1989.

Then a new problem developed.

Paul Pope, Gene and Lois's only son, had recently turned twenty-one and was now thinking the *Enquirer* was his birthright. Peterson had mandated that no *Enquirer* employee could be involved with any of the bidders without the consent of the trustees. Paul, who was on the payroll, had aligned himself with one group, so I was instructed to send him a letter informing him he needed to take a temporary leave of absence. He was planning moves with some of our staff, and I had to order them to desist.

Paul asked for a private meeting with me. He'd been telling anyone who would listen that his father wanted him to run the company if he died. The young man now told me the same thing in person.

I didn't have the heart to tell Paul he was wrong.

About two months before GP's death, Paul had confided in me that his dad had told him he would very soon be named executive editor, my number two and a slot that was open at the time. I was shocked. First, I couldn't believe GP would make that decision without consulting me, and second, I knew Paul wasn't even close to being able to handle the job.

That same day I confronted the Boss with Paul's words, and GP became angry with me, which he very rarely did. "How could you even imagine I would put Paul into that job? Do you think I'm crazy?" Clearly I had touched some nerve. My guess is that GP had said something to his son, then regretted it. Whatever had happened, Gene made it clear that he did not consider Paul middle-level executive material, and that his son was far less than capable of running the whole place.

I just shrugged and said: "I didn't suggest it. Paul said you did."

At our private meeting, however, Paul insisted his father would have wanted him to be chairman of the company. He said his backers would make him chairman. This was impossible. Financial investors of this kind usually put up 20 percent or so of capital, then tour the world to raise the other 80 percent from lenders. There's no way that Citibank, Deutsche Bank, Credit Lyonnais, or any international bank would sink millions into a company headed by a twenty-one-year-old who had never even run a department.

Paul asked: "If I win the bidding war, would you work for me?"

Me: "Under the right conditions, I will work for whatever group wins."

Paul: "Then you must declare up-front that you want me to win. You must be part of my team."

Me, calmly: "I can't do it. I promised your father's trustees to be neutral until the auction is over. Your mother wants the maximum price for your family."

Paul, angrily: "If you're not with me, you're against me." And he stormed out.

What probably happened was this. Paul's financial backers

thought he could deliver management, including me, to scare off some bidders and thus reduce the winning price. When that failed to happen, their interest in him waned.

This episode ended what had been a very friendly relationship. I had spent many hours chatting with young Paul from his early teens on. I really liked the kid, but from that moment on, Paul indicated his dislike for me, even though my work on selling the paper netted him some $40 million.

In later years, he would bitterly accuse unnamed persons of hiding his father's last will, which allegedly left the paper to Paul, and of engaging in machinations that kept him from obtaining ownership of the *Enquirer*. He even suggested there was some mystery in Gene's death and offered a $1 million reward to bring his dad's killer or killers to justice. His accusations distressed his mother, who, after all, was the only person present when Gene died, and caused a rift in the family.

First in line for an en masse visit was the Boston Ventures and McFadden Group. They were first, I was told, because they were the least likely group to win. "Use them for practice," said Pete Peterson.

The guys who would run the company were Peter Callahan, an Irish-American accountant who owned a small but successful magazine publishing company in New York. His two associates were Mike Boylan, another Irish-American and formerly an editor at the *New York Times* and *Us* magazine, and Manny Rabinowitz, a Harvard-educated attorney.

I loved these guys. They were super-smart, they really knew the publishing business, and they were just regular guys who mostly came from poor backgrounds like mine.

Such a pity they were there just for practice.

Then there were the other contenders: French guys from the publishing company Hachette; Britain's Robert Maxwell; Germany's Bauer Group; a financier named Jim Dunning who'd made a fortune from Yellow Pages; Mike Rosenbloom, who owned the rival tabloid *Globe*; and our own employee stock ownership plan (ESOP), a tax-advantaged bid spearheaded by Prudential Financial, which would have allowed *Enquirer* employees to buy the company.

If Boston Ventures was our favorite group, which one did we fear most? Hands down, it was England's Bad Bob.

Robert Maxwell was a huge man, well over 6 feet tall and at least 300 pounds. But even bigger was his reputation as a greedy, lying, cheating shark. Maxwell had been born in central Europe, and his shadowy past supposedly included fighting for the Allies against the Nazis before settling in Britain. He could be brilliant, charismatic, ruthless to the point of cruelty, duplicitous, bombastic, and charming—all at the same time.

He'd bought up various companies in Britain, including the Mirror Corporation, owner of many venerable large-circulation newspapers, and now he wanted to break into the American market. He coveted the *Enquirer*.

Maxwell never actually visited our offices, but he did send his army of minions and talked to me often on the telephone. He was always charming and effusively complimentary, telling me what a great editor I was.

I was very cautious. Friends had warned me: "When you shake hands with Robert Maxwell, count your fingers afterward. One might be missing." I assumed it was a metaphor, but it made me careful.

One evening, Galpern and I had dinner with him on his opulent yacht, the *Lady Ghislane*, named after his daughter. When we arrived at the dock, our eyes glazed over. The *Lady Ghislane*, massive, gleaming, and beautiful, looked like a cruise liner. At the top of the gangplank, two impeccably uniformed attendants greeted us and asked us to remove our shoes. *What!?* Sheepishly, they pointed inside: The whole floor was covered by the most luxurious, thick-piled, very white carpet.

Standing there shoeless—and fortunately with no holes in our socks—we watched Maxwell approach. Like King Kong. I remember thinking he'd make a great wrecking ball. I quickly got back on track.

In a friendly, booming voice, he apologized for the no-shoes rule: His wife didn't want marks on her white carpets. We knew that was a lie; he kept his wife sheltered in luxury back home near London, while he toured the world attending to business.

He led us to a huge lounge with big sofas, chairs, and cushions. Nearby a table was set up for our dinner. When Maxwell settled back, he resembled some modern pasha with servants running and buzzing around to satisfy every whim. We spent a couple of hours talking, laughing, eating, and drinking while he grilled David and me on every aspect of the *Enquirer.*

As we prepared to leave, an apparently satisfied Maxwell announced in his pompous baritone: "Gentlemen, you are hereby reappointed to your positions." The man hadn't even submitted his bid and he was already acting like he owned the company, and us.

After we left, David and I agreed: "Let's hope this buffoon doesn't have the winning bid."

Not only did Maxwell fail in his *Enquirer* bid, but a couple of years later his empire started to crumble. Authorities in Britain began investigating him for illegal financial schemes and raiding his company's pension funds. In the midst of the scandal, Maxwell died mysteriously. He was found floating in the sea, not far from his beloved yacht. It was assumed he had either fallen off the boat accidentally or jumped off to commit suicide.

Many believe he was murdered, a scenario I think is quite likely. Insiders say that in his early days he'd been bankrolled by the Soviet government, and later he was reputed to have been an agent for Mossad, the Israeli secret service. The theory is that, as his empire was crumbling, he threatened to reveal some secret, and the result was his assassination.

Who knows? I'm just happy we never fell into his evil clutches.

Finally, after all the meetings, the questions, the invasions by armies of experts, the struggle to keep the paper clicking on all cylinders, the exhausting long hours, and the company-wide tension, all the bids were in.

Galpern and I flew to New York to await the decision of the trustees. The night before the final meeting, trustee Jerry Traum took us to dinner.

We knew the rules. Each bidder was allowed one bid. There would be no auction and no second "topping" bid. Each group had been told to make their best offer, and the top price would bag the *Enquirer*.

The tension was monstrous. I had been with the *Enquirer* for twenty-five years, and clearly my future had seven different outcomes, some possibly good, some possibly fair, and several definitely bad. At dinner, Traum asked if we had any strong preferences about the new owner. That was easy. Thumbs up for Boston Ventures and a major thumbs down for Maxwell.

Later we learned that our preference might just have made the difference. Boston Ventures did have the top bid and won fair and square. Maxwell was close and had made it clear he would top any other offer. Should the trustees change the rules?

Peterson was known in the financial world as a standup man of integrity, so it didn't surprise anyone when the trustees announced their decision: The original rules must stand, and Maxwell was defeated.

The price was astonishing. When the *Enquirer* went on the market, the consensus within the company was that $250 million would be fair. As the competition heated up, I was sure we could top $300 million and perhaps hit $350 million.

The final price was $412.5 million. Not bad for a company Gene had bought for $75,000.

Maxwell went ballistic when he heard. His people started calling Peterson to complain, and when Pete didn't return their calls, the messages became angrier and more vituperative. One young female assistant, after listening to language that would have made a longshoreman blush, quit in disgust, saying she wasn't paid enough to take this abuse.

The English tycoon stayed in touch with me from time to time. A few months later, when I was in London, Maxwell invited me to his offices and told me that his financial advisers, Rothschild in New York, had advised him badly. This man's word was so suspect that if he had said, "Good morning," I would have put on my pajamas. So the following story is probably false.

Maxwell told me he had wanted to make an initial bid of $425 million. Rothschild told him to go in lower and then top any higher bid. "Forget the rules," they said. "Nobody will turn down a higher bid from Robert Maxwell." Pete Peterson did. Thank the Lord.

While the $412.5 million seemed high to me, the Boston Ventures guys proved to be as smart as I believed. The biggest-ever annual profit made by the *Enquirer* before the sale was $17 million. Within four-plus years, which included buying our chief rival, *Star*, our annual profit was $120 million.

My new—and very different—life was beginning.

In the spring of 1989 the *Enquirer*'s new owners held a big party when the Boston Ventures consortium with the McFadden Group came to take over.

Things looked good. We had a great team in place. Chairman and CEO was Peter Callahan, who felt an eerie link with the *Enquirer*. A high-powered, handsome man with energy to spare, he gave a speech at the party to inspire our troops. He told us that we had Elvis Presley in common.

While Elvis in his coffin had been the *Enquirer*'s biggest-ever sale, the King had actually saved Peter's company years before. Not long after he bought the small McFadden publishing group, it was teetering on the brink of bankruptcy. Then Elvis died, and Peter quickly printed and distributed the first magazine commemorating the death. It flew off the newsstands, made a big profit, and saved Callahan's company. Without Elvis, he said, he would never have been able to buy the *Enquirer*.

Ironically, Callahan had taken over *Us* magazine from the *New York Times* Company a couple of years earlier—just days after it was offered to Gene and me. The *Times* was giving it away for free, since it was not doing well, but Gene nixed my recommendation to snap it up, saying he did not want a New York–based property.

It was at *Us* magazine that Callahan met Michael Boylan, the publication's top editor. If the *Enquirer* had taken over *Us*, Mike would have worked for me. Now the tables had turned: Mike was named vice chairman of the *Enquirer*—and I worked directly for *him*. Frankly, I was happy to report to Boylan, a talented, gregarious Irishman with a knack for making friends.

The other new vice chairman was Manny Rabinowitz, a brilliant, Harvard-educated lawyer whom I came to respect.

It was a good team, and the new bosses tried to make the transition as easy as possible for our executives and staff. They asked the top eight executives to find as much up-front money as we could afford, then arranged for additional loans to buy shares in the new private company. I ended up with about 40 percent of the executive total, with the other seven execs sharing the remainder equally. I took out a loan of more than $1.5 million to buy my shares, and as a group we borrowed nearly $4 million—a sign to the financial community that we really believed in the future of the new company.

Despite my conscious optimism, I sometimes lay awake at night worrying about my loan, increasing day by day at about 9 percent annual interest. I had already committed a lot of the family savings. On one hand, it was thrilling that the bankers had so much confidence in me. On the other, I couldn't help worrying about the whole venture going belly-up. What if a huge earthquake dumped California into the Pacific and eliminated all these wonderful TV and movie stars who graced our covers each week? Dumb, dumb, dumb. But don't judge me too harshly until *you* have $1.5 million in debt hanging over you.

I was now thrust into a new world. Although Boston Ventures had bought the company, we all had to go out into the business world to raise about $140 million in bonds for part of the purchase price. That meant a small team of our bankers and top executives began flying from city to city and country to country, persuading pension funds and financiers to buy *National Enquirer* bonds. The new guys presented their business plan to make millions in profits. My job was to convince possible investors that we could still churn out major exclusives and run the company more efficiently than ever.

It was one great blur of airplane travel and meeting after meeting. The financial world calls it a "road show." We went to Japan for an eighteen-hour visit, flying twenty-five hours to get there and back. We crisscrossed America, visiting ten cities in three days. We must have been a hit because we raised the money we wanted in just a few weeks.

When the new owners took over, I naturally lost my chairman and CEO titles, but I remained as president and editor of the *Enquirer*, executive vice president of the parent company, and a member of the board of directors. Callahan also generously allowed me to stay in Gene Pope's luxurious old office, where I had moved when he died.

It was clear we would now have to run the *Enquirer* as a profit-making corporation, not the private toy Gene had loved so much. We were obviously overstaffed and had a mass of bureaucratic systems so convoluted they'd make an efficiency expert's head spin.

We'd have to trim the fat, streamline the operation, and still turn out great stories. We had to make money—*lots* of it—to pay interest to the new bondholders who had kicked in hundreds of millions.

My editorial spending for 1988 had been nearly $18 million, a sum I was reliably informed topped even *Time* magazine's budget. In the numbers we'd put together for the bidders, I'd estimated my 1990 editorial bill would top $20 million. Fat chance. It showed how far removed I was from the real world of making money in publishing. From the moment Boston Ventures took over until the present day, the *Enquirer*'s editorial costs never again came close to $18 million.

Where Gene had preferred high sales to high profits, the new owners reversed those values immediately. We cut the millions spent annually on TV advertising. We reduced the number of pages in each edition from 64 to 56, then to 48. We repeatedly raised the price, which Gene had kept artificially low. We knew all this would lower sales, but the extra revenue would make us *very* profitable.

Raising the price was difficult since our biggest competitor, *Star*, might undercut our price to steal some readers. We solved that problem within the next year—by buying *Star* from Rupert Murdoch, who was then strapped for cash. It cost another $400 million, probably too much, but worth it for us, since it gave us the ability to raise prices without fear of any major competition.

Not long after buying *Star*, we went public with an IPO (initial public offering), and by the time I left the company, in 1998, I collected several million dollars in profits from my investment with these guys. I'll always be grateful to them for making a comfortable retirement possible for me.

★★★

But in many ways my experience with Boston Ventures and McFadden was bittersweet. My whole life at the *Enquirer* had been building circulation and damn the profits. Now I had to go along with moves that gave our readers less value but made our bottom line look rosy.

Lots of things had to go. Our readers' service had made sure that every letter written to the *Enquirer*—thousands upon thousands each month—received a personal reply. Too expensive. Many hundreds of freelance journalists around the country found their fees a little less generous once we began to watch expenses.

Most difficult of all for me was ending our "team" system. We had built up a group of talented articles editors, each one operating separate news-gathering operations. Every six months, I received a report telling me how many stories each editor and reporter had contributed to the paper. Clippings of the stories were placed in individual folders, with reports of each staffer's contributions. I then spent hours reading the clips, reviewing the quality of the stories, and marking them A, B, or C.

The number of stories and their difficulty then made it easy to rate the contribution of each editor and each reporter—and whether he or she was forging ahead or slipping. Promotions and firings resulted largely from these reviews, rather than the gut-feel decisions in every other newsroom I have ever known.

I was very proud of the team concept, which kept my troops focused, and it was a highlight of my speeches to bankers when raising investment dollars for the new company. I boasted that it took politics out of the newsroom. "It doesn't help an editor to be a drinking buddy of his boss, if he shows up low on the Page One report," I explained.

If only I'd known that Callahan and Boylan had targeted the "team" method for extinction, to be replaced by conventional news-gathering.

The system was very expensive and in many ways inefficient, I must admit, since it kept editors fighting each other for stringers and story leads. The rivalry was intense, and there was no place to hide, so it was very unpopular with many editorial people. The same rivalry, however, had also fueled the explosive energy that had built the *Enquirer*. With apologies to Winston Churchill, who said the same thing about democracy: It was the worst system except for all the rest.

Over the next few years, I had to replace the competing teams with a more conventional structure in which editors worked together and even shared a pool of reporters. With trims in editorial, the days of fifty staffers running a major story were soon gone.

Under Gene, we had an editor for cartoons alone, even though we ran fewer than a dozen per week. We had an editor for "shorts," twenty or so very brief stories, usually rewritten from other newspapers. We had an editor just for the witty, thoughtful sayings sprinkled throughout the paper, usually words of wisdom from philosophers and humorists. We had a full-time book editor, with a deputy and an assistant, to handle excerpts from books that would interest our readers.

They all had to go.

I'm not criticizing these decisions. Most publications ran much leaner and meaner than even the newly trimmed *Enquirer*. It was just tough for me, coming back into the real world of capitalism at work outside of Lantana, where the guiding principle was: Selling less for more money means greater profit.

Our ability to break the big celebrity stories was not affected. We were still the best. But as our pool of reporters and editors shrank, we had to cut back on such things as sending teams to cover big medical conventions around the world. Also, as we cut back our freelance fees, our wonderful stringer network suffered. The amazing, gee-whiz, non-celebrity stories were still there—they were just not quite as amazing or gee-whiz.

At a time when competition from TV, newspapers, and magazines was increasing, we offered fewer pages, no *Enquirer* television ads, and a rapidly increasing price. The nature of the publication was also changing, perhaps imperceptibly to most readers, but changing nonetheless. The result was inevitable—our sales definitely dipped.

This had been anticipated in the brilliant Boston Ventures business plan. They'd seen all tabloid and large-circulation magazine sales weaken gradually, even while GP was still alive, but that didn't bother them one bit.

Our average sales figures for the last six months of 1988, the year Gene died, had hovered around 4,250,000 copies per week at a cover price of 75 cents. During the next six months, while I was selling the company, sales remained fairly constant at four-and-a-quarter million per week—still at 75 cents.

For the month of April '89, just before the new owners took over, our income was $250,000 higher than the previous year; and our operating profit was up nearly $900,000. Still at 75 cents per copy.

Two years later, in 1991, when I moved to editor-in-chief, our weekly sales were down to 3,750,000, but at 95 cents per copy. And when I finally quit working full-time in 1995, our sales were only 2,750,000—but at a cover price of $1.29. (When we moved to Florida in 1971, our price was 15 cents.)

Do the math. Even with falling sales, we were grossing a *lot* more money. And with our expenses being slashed dramatically, the bottom line was putting smiles on the faces of our investors. In 1989 our operating cash flow (profit before taxes, interest, and depreciation) was $17 million. One year later it was $46.8 million. In 1991 it rose to $89.7 million, and in '92 it had soared to $120 million. Even with our huge interest payments on loans and bonds, by '94 our net profit after everything had been paid was $27.8 million.

So while I was hurting journalistically, the company was doing very well—and my investment was paying off handsomely.

The new ownership changed my life in many ways. Not only did I have to run the *Enquirer* to make money as the primary goal, but I also had to operate as the high-visibility executive of a public company.

Chairman Peter Callahan encouraged me to give interviews and lectures, and to travel to meet with journalists and advertisers. Gene had been the opposite. Shy himself, he seldom wanted any of his editors to talk to the press. And he hated for me to travel, except for my vacations. He'd fly six people to Lantana rather than have me fly to New York.

Now I had the chance to train some of my editors as spokesmen to the media. David Perel and Steve Coz sharpened their skills with local reporters before becoming skilled and confident representatives on national television.

My biggest success was gossip columnist Mike Walker, who was a natural.

I allowed him to be a regular guest on local radio, which led to his own nationally syndicated show and later serving as our host on the *National Enquirer* syndicated television program. By sheer force of personality, ego, charisma, and rapid-fire chatter, Mike has been the media face of the *Enquirer* since the mid-eighties. He's been on literally thousands of radio programs and many hundreds of TV shows, and he single-handedly engineered the syndicated *National Enquirer* TV show. Today he's an every-Friday guest on the gargantuan Howard Stern radio show. Mike is almost certainly the most gifted writer ever to work on the paper, and the last three CEOs of the *Enquirer* believe he is the number-one gossip editor anywhere.

His colleagues will undoubtedly groan when reading this, since the praise is sure to feed the largest ego this side of Barbra Streisand.

But facts are facts.

For me, talking about the *Enquirer* quickly became a lot of fun. For years, the media had been frustrated trying to interview top guys at the Big Bad *Enquirer*, and now they jumped at the chance to get us to talk. I was bombarded with requests from print, radio, and TV journalists, and I found time to give interviews a couple of times a month. After being buried in Lantana for decades, I began to feel like a media VIP—a dangerous feeling, which I quickly squelched. Once you start thinking you're good, your best days are probably past.

One of my favorite invitations came from John F. Kennedy, Jr., who asked to interview me for his magazine, *George*, so he could "turn the tables on me." I happily agreed, and he grilled me for hours. I was genuinely impressed by his intelligence and, of course, the famous Kennedy charisma. The published interview featured page after page of Q and A—and a headline about me on the *George* cover. John asked many tough questions. At one point, he asked if I had trouble sleeping at night. My answer: Of course not.

Taking knocks from people who didn't understand the *Enquirer* or from our readers went with the territory.

Critics would snort: "You may have millions of readers, but they're all blue-haired old ladies." My first response would be that there is nothing wrong with being liked by old ladies—blue-, gray-, black-, or brown-haired. They're probably well-loved moms and grandmas.

But the premise was also wrong. I loved getting that question when speaking to bankers, college professors and students, or businessmen. I'd pick a local upscale community and get our local wholesaler to dig out magazine sales figures.

For example, in ritzy Boca Raton, Florida, where I set an attendance record of 400 for a chamber of commerce breakfast meeting, I revealed the following sales figures for the previous month in that well-off town.

Single-copy sales (not including subscriptions):

Newsweek sold 596 copies.
Time sold 496 copies.
Elle sold 162 copies.
Cosmopolitan sold 1,602 copies.
People sold 5,896 copies.
National Enquirer sold 8,208 copies.

As my audience gasped, I joked: "I don't think they were all bought by your chauffeurs and nannies."

I stole this idea from one of our new owners, Michael Boylan, who'd used it to wonderful effect when raising money from bankers. The presentation worked just as well for Grosse Point, Michigan, as for Westchester County, New York, and Beverly Hills, California. The results were always the same.

At one point we even boasted we had more families with a $50,000 per annum income than *Fortune* magazine. It was true, but only because we had a much bigger circulation. Their readers' average income was obviously quite a bit higher than ours. (This is why statistics are worse than "damned lies.")

Before and after Gene's death, our circulation was breathtaking, and the secret was simple: we found out what our readers wanted and gave it to them. That had been part of Gene's genius: he was always in touch with the mood of the nation.

Republican political guru Lee Atwater, the strategist responsible for the election of George Bush as president in 1988, understood this genius. Not long after Atwater died of cancer, his wife told a Republican meeting that her husband's uncanny ability to stay in touch with the average voter came from a surprising place—what she called "his religious reading of the *National Enquirer*." He considered our supermarket tabloid "the pulse of America."

Even given all this, our power and influence could still surprise me. In one issue, we featured a Korean immigrant, Kwang Kim, who'd worked hard to turn a dump in Jersey City, New Jersey, into a little vegetable garden. He tended his garden for five years until one day, as he picked his own vegetables, local cops pounced—and charged him with theft. In court, a common-sense-challenged prosecutor claimed that since the dump was owned by the county, the vegetables were county property.

We blasted the "Joyzy" bureacrats big time. And when Mr. Kim arrived for trial the *Enquirer* was all over the courtroom, said the defense attorney. "Even the prosecutor had a copy of it on her desk," he said. The charges were dismissed. Said a local reporter: "The *Enquirer* made county bureaucrats a laughingstock. And Mr. Kim is back growing and eating his vegetables."

In 1992, a call came in from a small, prestigious advertising agency called Tatham. When I heard their offer I knew it had to be a joke. They wanted me to star in a TV commercial for Hoover—the vacuum cleaner Hoover.

After laughing until my ribs hurt, I explained to the ad guy that my wife would have a heart attack. The closest I'd ever come to using a vacuum cleaner was to move it out of my way.

My laughter stopped when they told me the fee involved—$125,000 for one day's work.

After reading a preliminary script, and with permission from my chairman, I agreed to make the commercial—and turn the money over to the company. That was only fair since the agency really didn't want me as a person; they wanted the editor of the *National Enquirer*.

I couldn't believe my eyes when I arrived on the set. Although the commercial was to be just a teeny fifteen seconds long, an army of people was waiting for me—a total of fifty-five.

There were sound people, lighting people, camera people, writers, producers, directors, makeup artists and fashion artists, guys to plug things in, guys to move things around, people to help other people, men and women inside the building, men and women outside the building. And, of course, there was a crew to feed all these other people.

Someone powdered my nose every few seconds, and someone else fixed my tie when it didn't need fixing.

After standing around for about two hours, the producers gave me the final script. Memorize it, they said. Memorize it? I'd memorized more words ordering breakfast in a diner.

Minutes later I did the first take. I thought it was perfect. Then I did the second, the third, the fourth.

Suddenly they stopped and one guy shrieked, "That's great." I thought we were finished. No way. He liked some phrase I'd used and wanted to punch it up more, so they were going to rewrite the script.

Minutes went by, as four or five men scrunched themselves over the script, making frenzied suggestions. Finally, I walked over. "Hey, guys, I edit things for a living. Can I help?" They accepted a couple of my suggestions, and I went back in front of the camera.

This time I completed my little acting job, sitting on the corner of a desk in an executive office. The producers loved it. So did I.

It went like this:

Announcer: "Iain Calder on dirt."

A line on the screen said: EDITOR OF THE *NATIONAL ENQUIRER*.

Iain: "At the *National Enquirer*, we uncover more dirt than anyone."

Announcer: "Iain Calder on Hoover."

Iain: "Except possibly this Hoover Cleaner with attached tools and hose. It covers all the angles."

Announcer: "Nobody gets the dirt like Hoover."

Iain: "It may get more dirt than we do."

All stars have to make a few demands, just to prove they're important. I had my chance when the producers wanted to film me actually *pushing* the Hoover vacuum cleaner. "No way," I said. "If my wife sees I can do this, she'll have me using the vacuum at home for real."

They just shrugged—okay, Iain. Another temperamental actor. And when the commercial was aired, there was a close-up of what looked like my hand, pushing the Hoover. They'd found an arm double and dressed him in an identical suit. I might as well have done it myself.

We took about five hours to finish this little piece. The agency guys were thrilled. They said commercials, especially using non-actors, could take a day or more.

On October 30, 1992, the *Wall Street Journal* actually ran a little story plugging my new spot. Days later, I began seeing our commercial on prime-time TV in a big way. Hoover must have bought a multi-million-dollar schedule. The spot was on network comedies, dramas, and even the *Tonight* show.

I'd never been this famous. People began recognizing me in stores, and that had never happened even after I appeared on *60 Minutes* in the early '70s.

Suddenly, after about three weeks, the commercial disappeared. Puzzled, I called the agency to ask why. Embarrassed, the executive in charge tried to tap dance around the subject before I finally nailed him. Hoover is owned by Maytag, and apparently the wife of the Maytag chairman saw the commercial one night and shrieked in horror: How can you have our company tied in with that awful *National Enquirer*? she asked.

One phone call later, my one and only commercial disappeared forever into the ether.

My payback came the following year. My little Hoover piece won an Addy award—a national advertising prize—as one of the best television commercials of the year.

So far, I'm batting a thousand. One acting job; one national award. Take that, Paul Newman.

As I mentioned, one of the changes that came to the *Enquirer* after GP's death was the end of the blank-check era. We could still mount a major campaign on the biggest stories, but no longer did we contemplate hiring submarines for a story. If anyone thought the new, leaner *Enquirer* would miss out on scoops, however, they were soon proved wrong. We had a lot more going for us than Gene's deep pockets.

In early 1989, news broke that Lisa Marie Presley was pregnant. Just another good celebrity story—until you realized this baby would be Elvis Presley's first grandchild.

That made it huge. That made it a first baby picture we just had to have.

The due date was Memorial Day, 1989, and as the end of May approached, we got good news and bad news. The good news was that Lisa Marie and her husband, Danny Keogh, were willing to sell the baby's first photo to the highest bidder. The bad news? They would not even *consider* an offer from the *Enquirer*. Apparently we were not their favorite publication.

This opened up an opportunity for *People* magazine and *Star*, both of which were accustomed to eating our dust as we beat them to the big stories. These two publications got together and made a major joint bid for the first pictures of Elvis's grandchild—$500,000. *People* would run the photos the first week, while *Star* would get the best leftovers and publish them the following week. The *Enquirer* would just have to weep in anguished, photo-less despondency.

It was a good plan, but not good enough.

I admit I was worried at first. Our readers were spoiled by our exclusive stories and photos, and they'd remember the historic Elvis coffin picture. Would they be upset if we didn't have the King's grandchild on our cover? Of course.

But how could we give our readers what they wanted and expected? Our rivals would post tip-top security in the hospital once the baby was born. They would do everything to stop us from sneaking a photo and destroying their exclusive. Well, almost everything.

I had one advantage. We had a big staff of expert reporters and could afford to have someone working on a story for months at a time. So with more than three months to go before the birth, we began our mission.

In Los Angeles, we came across a part-time security guard who was friendly with Lisa Marie's security chief; he'd been told to stand by to join the security team at the hospital when the Presley baby arrived. He told us that Priscilla Presley's boyfriend, Marco Garibaldi, was overseeing the whole security operation. We checked the guard out, and his story was for real.

Neither he nor we knew which hospital had been chosen, and, of course, we had just a rough idea of the date. But with three months' lead time, that was the least of our problems. Our man was *not* an ideal security guard. I probably wouldn't have chosen him to guard a garbage dump in the Ozarks. He liked booze, drugs, parties, strip joints, and hookers—trouble of all kinds. Sometimes he seemed more like someone you'd want a guard to protect you *from*.

But he was all that we had, so we treated him like a king. We gave him money. He spent it on girls. We gave him more money. He spent it on booze. We gave him even more money, and who the heck knows what it went toward. Finally, the articles editor running the story assigned a tough, gruff freelancer named Jim Mitteager to babysit the erstwhile guard. Mitteager, a 6-foot, 210-pound former New York City cop, flew from the Big Apple to L.A., and spent week after week keeping our man happy, under control—and alive.

Jim Mitteager was an inspired choice. He had the guard arrange an interview with the security chief. "I'd like to join your protection detail," said Mitteager. The chief, impressed by the candidate's NYPD background, agreed to check him out.

Within a few days the word came back: Mitteager was in. I was pretty excited to learn that one of the security detail protecting Elvis's first grandchild from the *National Enquirer* would be . . . a reporter from the *National Enquirer*.

The Presley public relations team was putting out phony stories about where and when the baby would be born—from Los Angeles to the Midwest to London.

Mitteager managed to keep our secret-weapon guard alive, but by B-for-Baby-Day, we had invested more than $10,000 in his high-living expenses and had suffered a roller coaster of tension. The guy kept wanting more money and constantly threatened to break the deal. We had to keep him happy, since he could still expose Mitteager, but not give him so much cash he'd overdose.

Finally, our ongoing support of the L.A. nightlife economy began to pay off. Lisa Marie went into St. John's Hospital in Santa Monica, and our man actually was hired on the security team, along with Mitteager. Jim was given the shift nobody else wanted—midnight to 8 A.M. This couldn't have been more perfect for us. He'd be alone with the infant at the quietest time of the day.

We gave Mitteager a foolproof camera and instructions on how to use it.

Elvis's first grandchild, a little girl named Danielle, was born on May 29, 1989. It looked like the finish line was in sight.

But not so fast. Over the next couple of days, a private nurse was with the baby every minute. Mitteager couldn't get a moment alone to take the photo. We were close to our deadline, and if the photo wasn't taken within the next twenty-four hours, it would miss our next edition. *People* magazine would beat us.

We did not get the photo. We missed the issue. I was devastated. We did have a great story about the birth, including the guards being alerted about a kidnapping threat by a bizarre cult. Without the photo, though, it wasn't enough.

Then we got lucky. Lisa Marie wanted to look her best for the photo, so she postponed the *People* shoot for a few days, which delayed their issue for one week. The *People* editors, cocky about their half-million-dollar exclusive, didn't push her. They had no idea their "exclusive" was being guarded by the *National Enquirer*.

So we were still in the game. I told my guys, "We *have* to have that photo. This is our last chance."

Following our attorney's advice on how and where to take the photo, Mitteager, finally alone with the baby, pounced. First, he pulled a fluorescent bulb in the room partway out of its socket. When it began to flicker, Mitteager took two quick shots of the baby.

The nurse saw the flashes and ran toward Mitteager. "Did you take a photo?" she demanded. Mitteager retorted: "Don't be stupid. Can't you see the light flickering?" Relieved, she left.

Moments later, following our predetermined plan, Mitteager said he was going to the bathroom but instead went to the parking garage and found a specific trash can. When he saw a "fat man," he dropped the film into the trash. The fat man, a paid stringer, picked up the film and took it to one of our reporters, who flew it to Lantana.

Our on-duty editor was awakened at his home with the exciting news: We've got the pictures. Even after I got the word, I was still petrified. Months of work, planning, and worry had gone into this. What if the pictures were awful? What if the film was blank? There would be no second chance.

Our people met the plane in Palm Beach and sped the film to our offices, where it was rushed into the lab.

The result? Two beautiful, perfect photos of the lovely Elvis grandchild. David Perel, the story's editor, recalls he just started laughing in happy, hysterical relief.

We had "fly on the wall" details of everything that had happened in the hospital, provided by our guard and the other security personnel who'd given him their reports. *And* we had those fabulous first photos.

Our June 20, 1989, issue was headlined:

ELVIS'S FIRST GRANDCHILD
BLOCKBUSTER PHOTOS —PLUS DRAMATIC STORY OF
BABY DANIELLE'S FIRST DAYS

Obviously, I wasn't present when the editors at *People* discovered we'd burst their exclusivity bubble. They went ahead and published their own pictures, but they must have wondered, "How the *hell* did we lose our exclusive?!" Now they know.

The *Los Angeles Times* ran a story about the *People* vs. *Enquirer* photo face-off. The photos were obtained "by checkbook and by stealth," the *LAT* explained. Surprisingly enough, it was Time Inc. that had the checkbook—and *we* had the stealth.

★ ★ ★

Our best, and most determined, reporters and editors came from all kinds of backgrounds—from journalism schools; from prestigious colleges like Harvard and Vassar; from Pulitzer-Prize-winning newspapers like the *Washington Post* and the *Miami Herald*; from mass-circulation British papers like London's *Daily Mirror*; from the best publications in Australia and Canada. And from the Toyota Motor Corporation credit department.

It sounds like a gee-whiz *Enquirer* story, but one of our super-star reporters, Alan Butterfield, joined us straight from the auto company's finance department in Los Angeles. Alan had a degree in journalism and business, but he'd chosen finance as a career, since it paid better than reporting. In 1989, he was working for the Toyota Motor credit department, going after deadbeats defaulting on their car loans.

One of these deadbeats happened to be an ex-construction worker named Larry Fortensky. While tracking down Fortensky, one of Butterfield's colleagues called a relative who told him a strange story: Larry was currently staying at the Betty Ford Center, trying to kick addictions to booze and pills—and he was having an affair with Elizabeth Taylor. *The* Elizabeth Taylor.

When Alan heard the story, his journalistic instincts kicked in and he called the *Enquirer*, passing the tip on to editor Richard Baker, who said he'd check it out.

That one phone call netted Butterfield $1,500, which added up to about three weeks' pay at Toyota. It led to a long string of Taylor-Fortensky romance and wedding stories for the *Enquirer*. And it changed Butterfield's life. *Enquirer* editor Baker, liking the sound of this tipster on the other end of the line, gave him some simple freelance assignments. He kept his day job at Toyota but started spending his evenings on celebrity stakeouts for *Enquirer* assignments—like Kenny Rogers's romance with *Price Is Right* model Janice Pennington, which he kept secret from Mrs. Kenny Rogers. Or the sad news of *Perry Mason* star Raymond Burr's hidden battle against cancer.

Fluent in Spanish, Butterfield became invaluable making contacts with Hispanic maids and drivers for stars in Beverly Hills. In his first year, he made $22,000 from us, about the same as his Toyota salary.

Recalls Butterfield: "I worked long hours, but it was exciting. When we tried to repossess Fortensky's car, I actually spoke to Liz Taylor on the telephone. She lied about knowing the guy, but she actually talked to me! And we finally got his car back. By this time Larry didn't care, because he was living with Liz, his new meal ticket."

By the time Liz decided to marry Fortensky, Butterfield was actively working on that story for us. He tracked down Fortensky's stepbrother, Mike Lacy, and flew to his home in Modesto, California, to make contact. And he "bought up" Lacy for an exclusive on the wedding.

The ceremony would take place at Neverland Ranch, Michael Jackson's theme-park-style estate. The security would be super-tight; a former Mossad agent was in charge of keeping out the media.

Our plan was to infiltrate the celebration through Lacy, a trusted member of the wedding party. Butterfield bought him a fancy $1,000 tuxedo with a special cummerbund, which contained a small camera with an easy-operating button. Our photo editor, Valerie Virga, planned everything down to the last detail. We'd heard that guests would have to pass through metal detectors, so she obtained a plastic mini-camera and tested it by taking it through the metal detectors at the Palm Beach International Airport. It passed.

The idea was for Lacy to open his tux jacket, point his tummy at the wedding ceremony, and start clicking away. Lacy was told that his exclusive photos might be worth up to $100,000.

There was one thing we hadn't planned for: Abstinence did not run in this family. Like his brother Larry, Mike enjoyed a few drinks. More than a few, actually. Mike got roaring drunk at the wedding, and his attempts at taking photos with his belly-cam were a miserable failure. Lacy was so clumsy one of the security detail busted him and grabbed the camera.

It was a disaster for us, but, says Butterfield: "Lacy didn't seem to mind. He said he had a *great* time at the wedding."

The incident should have sent a message to Liz about her husband's family. After all, her new brother-in-law had tried to sneak photos, against her wishes, on what was supposed to be one of the happiest days (or one of the *eight* happiest days) of her life.

★ ★ ★

There were plenty of Liz and Larry stories that were much easier to report. Take our cover story from March 30, 1993: LIZ'S NEIGHBOR FLEES HOME AFTER LARRY THREATENS TO BREAK HIS LEGS.

It told of a court battle between Liz, Larry, and their Bel-Air neighbor Max Hoshahn. The neighbor claimed that the star couple took down a boundary fence between their luxury homes and erected an ugly new fence that was 20 feet across the property line—on his $5 million property.

Hoshahn's attorney told a judge that his client feared for his safety. According to our story, Fortensky had threatened to break his legs.

Liz and Larry sued. Why, I'll never understand. Most of the story came from court records.

It turned out the *Enquirer,* however, *had* made a couple of mistakes. In a court appeal to decide if the libel suit should proceed, the judges agreed that Fortensky had not, as we wrote, been accused of threatening to break legs. The reported threats were to break the neighbor's *arms.* Legally, it turns out that broken arms and broken legs are essentially the same; I imagine they hurt about equally. And so the suit against us was dismissed.

There was one additional little bonus for us. To end the legal battle, Liz agreed to pay the *Enquirer* just over $500,000, which we donated to charity—although we *did* allow ourselves a small party to celebrate.

Marriage number eight lasted for a respectable (by Liz standards) five years, and even after the divorce, Fortensky still provided us with some great tabloid material. For instance, he complained in court documents that the $5,000 per month Liz was paying him was not even *close* to sufficient. He needed $850 a month just to dry-clean his Valentino and Versace outfits.

We were sorry to see Larry go, but Liz continued to grace the *Enquirer* throughout the rest of my time with the paper—and beyond.

In 1996, just as the *George* magazine with me on the cover hit the stands, JFK, Jr., was a guest on Oprah Winfrey's TV show. At one point, she asked about the interview, making the comment, "Iain

Calder, who I think I know personally since I am on the cover so much." Kennedy was complimentary about me, and Oprah didn't contradict him or go on the attack—something she could easily have done. After all, we *did* do a lot of stories about Oprah.

In our issue of March 20, 1990, we ran the first of a two-part series featuring her sister Patricia, who revealed the deepest secrets of Oprah's past. The young Oprah had won school trophies for her speaking and debating abilities—a predictor of the great things to come. She had also given birth to an illegitimate baby boy at age fourteen.

A few days later Oprah admitted to the press: "It is true. The baby was born prematurely and died shortly after birth."

Our series revealed all kinds of family details—good and bad—that Oprah might have preferred kept secret. But we also ran a wonderful article headlined: OPRAH'S MISSION OF MERCY.

In 1988, Oprah's beau Stedman Graham had visited the small South African town of Alexandria and told her about the suffering of the town's desperately poor old people. With no fanfare or publicity, Oprah had been spending $50,000 a year to give them a good lunch every single day—she was literally a lifesaver.

The *Enquirer* sent our South African reporter David Barritt to Alexandria with a videotape of the *Oprah* show. Five hundred of the oldsters watched spellbound—and then burst into wild applause for the benefactor they'd never before seen.

Our biggest-selling issue on Oprah was a sneak preview of an upcoming show in 1988. Our headline to the world: OPRAH: HOW I LOST 60 LBS. IN 3 MONTHS. On our cover was the most-beautiful-ever photo of Oprah, at 130 pounds looking slim and glamorous. Readers loved that cover, but they also loved our cover nearly three years later, in June 1991, when we reported that the 5'7" megastar had hit her top weight of a whopping 205 pounds.

We were the oracle on Oprah, whether she was gaining weight, losing weight, planning to marry Graham, or deciding to stay single. It would be understandable if she resented our attention, but she handled it all with style and grace. Nothing shows that better than the story of Oprah's running in the 1994 U.S. Marine Corps Marathon in Washington, D.C. Running alongside her were two *Enquirer* reporters, Peter Burt and David Wright.

Wright had turned out many bylined stories about Oprah. For one, during the Christmas holidays in 1993, he'd followed her and her entourage when she hired a luxury yacht for a Caribbean cruise. He rented a plane and pilot and hopped from island to island with her. At none of the early stops did Oprah actually leave the yacht, so Wright had to get his story from others who came ashore.

On one occasion, our plane passed over the yacht in open waters, and our pilot waggled his wings. Said Wright, "We saw everyone laughing and waving to us." Finally, in Grenada, Oprah came ashore—and was met by Wright. He recalls, "She was friendly and cordial. She told me, 'When we saw the plane fly over, I said to my friends it had to be the *Enquirer*.'" He continued, "She's always surrounded by a corps of staffers protecting her, but when you get past them she really is a delightful person. "

Fast forward to the Marine Corps Marathon, ten months later. Reporter Peter Burt, a young, fit athlete who competes in Ironman triathlons, had no problem running the 26-plus miles with Oprah. Wright, on the other hand, a former marathoner now in his fifties, knew he couldn't complete this one.

Both reporters were wearing *National Enquirer* T-shirts for maximum publicity as dozens of TV cameras and thousands of still cameras focused on Oprah. Burt started alongside Oprah, and Wright stationed himself at the halfway mark, at around 13 miles. No fewer than 16,000 runners were competing in the rain, and Wright wasn't sure he'd even be able to spot the star as she went by. At 13 miles, however, the competitors were strung out into different packs.

David was peering through a group of runners when a familiar voice shouted out: "Hi, David. I'm here."

It was Oprah. Unbelievably, through the sweat, the raindrops, and the crowd, Oprah had recognized our David Wright and called out his name.

Stunned for a moment, Wright recovered and raced to Oprah, to run along with Burt at her side. Her show was filming the whole run from the sidecar of a motorbike, and during the race she talked into the microphone. At one point she pointed to Wright and told the camera: "This is David from the *National Enquirer*." And she used the scene in her subsequent TV show!

Burt, Wright, and Oprah talked throughout the run, giving each other support as the pain barrier kicked in. At 23 miles Oprah "hit the wall"—a phrase distance runners use for when the agony and exhaustion become unbearable.

Says Wright: "Oprah was clearly flagging. She gasped to me: 'Have you ever done this before?' I answered: 'Twice. I know exactly how you're feeling, but hang in there and in another thirty minutes you will be the happiest woman in the world."

The last two-tenths of the Marine Corps Marathon last mile are uphill, toward the Iwo Jima Memorial, and those yards at the end of the 26 miles are heartbreaking. Tears ran down Oprah's face as she courageously refused to give in. She crossed the line to earsplitting cheers from her fans.

After a few moments to catch her breath, Oprah came over to Burt and Wright and posed for pictures with them. She told Wright: "David, you were right. I *am* the happiest woman in the world."

Fantastic photos for the *Enquirer*, and great publicity for us as papers, magazines, and TV shows pictured our *Enquirer* T-shirted reporters right next to Oprah. Plus a nice plug from Oprah on her show.

Bad news for the rival *Globe* tabloid. Their picture editor Ron Haines told Wright later: "We had a heck of a time picking photos. Either you or Burt were in every one."

Oprah was the epitome of class when dealing with the *Enquirer*, and we loved her. Roseanne Barr was anything *but* classy—and we loved her, too.

Roseanne Barr was a gift from God. She exploded onto the celebrity television scene with the force and grace of a drunken elephant. Then, in the 1988–1989 season, her comedy show burst onto TV and soon rocketed into the number-one slot, knocking off the unbeatable Bill Cosby. That's when I knew we'd be guaranteed some fantastic front pages.

Roseanne was our kind of gal. At sixteen she let herself be hit by a car on purpose, cracked her skull, knocked a screw loose, and for a short time was locked up in a mental hospital. At eighteen she had a love child she gave up for adoption. At thirty, she married a Denver motel clerk named Bill Pentland and lived in a mobile home with their three young children.

She was nutty. She was also a brilliant stand-up comedienne and a gifted comic actress who was made for television—and the pages of our illustrious journal.

When Roseanne first got her show she was still married to Bill Pentland. That didn't last long. Roseanne now was making mucho bucks, and the Hollywood man-wolves were circling. She may have been cheated a little by the glamour gods, and she might have weighed twice as much as the flirty showbiz cuties around town. But a top TV star with lots of money and lots of power is a major catch.

Enter Tom Arnold. Good-looking, tall, broad-shouldered, with a great sense of humor and a flashing smile—but not exactly a genius. Arnold was a part-time comedian and full-time party guy who would later need treatment for drug abuse. If a pre-TV Rosie had fallen on the sidewalk, Tom would have stepped over her without a moment's pause. But now she was *the* Roseanne—and Tom began courting her, making her feel like a cross between Raquel Welch and Christie Brinkley.

No contest. Poor hubby Bill was toast.

And we knew a divorce was pending even before Roseanne's husband did.

I'm going to tell you how that happened, but first I have to explain something. Over the years, the *Enquirer* has had literally thousands of secret sources. Our editors and reporters are serious about protecting the identity of those sources. Even in this book, there are secrets I will not reveal.

However, in a couple of special situations, we've reluctantly revealed a confidential source, and this is one of those situations.

As their secret romance blossomed, Tom Arnold was having a wonderful time, enjoying tender rendezvous with Mrs. Roseanne Pentland. His problem: He was broke. How could he pay for all those rendezvous?

The solution was obvious to him. The *National Enquirer* is widely known to pay good money for good stories, good news tips, and good photographs. Tom Arnold knew all that—and he became our secret source on Roseanne.

Keeping his ladylove totally in the dark, Tom called us with stories about their adulterous love affair, complete with the *most* confidential details. And he'd tell us where they were going to be and when.

Early on, I remember telling a photo editor: "Pay him a couple of hundred dollars to kiss Roseanne at exactly the right spot, so our photographer can get the picture." Tom cooperated, even though the pictures didn't work out.

David Perel, now editor in chief of the *Enquirer*, recalls his surprise one day when he answered a ringing telephone on an editorial desk. "It was Tom Arnold on the line, and he was desperate. His usual contact wasn't available, but he recognized my name from a byline, and he said, 'I'm going out on a date tonight with Roseanne. If you promise me five hundred dollars, I'll tell you where it is.'

"It wasn't my story, but I agreed, and we set the whole thing up. It went like clockwork. Tom, at that time, was a man of his word, at least to us."

For Roseanne, the *Enquirer* stories were a puzzling nightmare. She'd rage: "How do these &#@s know what we're doing and where we are all the time?" Tom would pretend to be furious and chase after the offending photographers, threatening them with injury and mayhem.

I knew our great source wouldn't last. Once Tom got his hands on Rosie's money, he wouldn't need us anymore. That was okay—life as usual at the *Enquirer*. Besides, he wasn't our only source, not by a long shot.

By now, Bill Pentland must have realized his future as Rosie's husband was somewhere between bleak and nonexistent. Rosie had given him a job as "script consultant" on the show, but she also hired Tom Arnold as a comedy writer.

In December 1988, hubby Bill was hospitalized with a possible heart attack. Just stress, doctors finally pronounced.

No wonder. Roseanne was on a firing rampage. Her show was a huge hit, but she was in a power-mad frenzy, booting out writers, executives, and all kinds of staff. But not Tom Arnold, of course.

Roseanne was on our cover every few weeks. On March 21, 1989, we revealed that she had put her thirteen-year-old daughter in a psychiatric hospital, blaming husband Bill for causing the emotional problems. She even hinted a divorce was in the air. "This marriage is on the rocks," she told friends.

Finally, Bill Pentland was put out of his misery by our headline of April 11, 1989.

ROSEANNE TO DIVORCE
LOVESICK STAR CHASING NEW GUY WHO KEEPS REJECTING HER

Complete with paparazzi photos of the couple together, we ran a fully detailed story about the Roseanne/Tom romance. Our source—guess who?—said that Arnold was reluctant because he didn't want to be branded as a home-wrecker. We even reported that Roseanne had consulted a divorce lawyer, which was more than husband Bill knew.

Being editor of the *Enquirer* was an emotional roller coaster. If other journalists beat us on a story or if we failed to land a major exclusive, it was a terrible, depressing low. But up to this point, covering Roseanne had been a total high.

I knew I led the best investigative team of editors and reporters in the world. Hollywood flacks, jealous mainstream journalists, and members of the so-called elite might dismiss us, but we continued to break story after story and publish picture after picture, all exclusives. The Roseanne divorce prediction and the story of her new lover had all proved to be true. Our readers knew it, and they appreciated us. That was what mattered.

Tom Arnold's role as an *Enquirer* source would have remained our secret forever—except that Tom, flush with Rosie's cash and his newfound fame, was developing a drug problem. And an ego problem. By this time, he'd stopped being an *Enquirer* source, something we were prepared to deal with. We didn't hold anything against him, but apparently Tom didn't feel the same way. Even before the wedding, he started to appear on TV talk shows and the daily celebrity shows. When the anchors asked the standard question—"What about all those awful tabloids?"—Tom would go on a tirade against us. He attacked the *Enquirer* constantly, harping on our supposedly untrue stories and lack of real sources.

It really upset many of my guys. Here was Mr. Arnold—recipient of our largesse, betrayer of his wife-to-be, and formerly an *Enquirer* secret source—publicly attacking us and telling lies about us. Several editors came to see me, pleading for us to counterattack.

I could see no way to do that. Confidential sources all over the world trusted us. If we lost their confidence, it could hurt us badly. Our only option was to bluff Arnold, telling him that we might "out" him if he didn't stop bad-mouthing us. This threat didn't deter Tom. Finally, after a number of Arnold attacks, a group of editors ganged up on me to ask again. Finally, I agreed. Tell Arnold that this is his last chance. If he says once again that the *Enquirer* has no legitimate sources, we will reveal he was on our payroll.

Arnold got the warning. His response? *Another* attack. He called us liars on *Larry King*, saying we made up our stories.

Bad move. He had finally got me mad.

I called a small editorial strategy meeting to figure out how we could embarrass Arnold and thus stop his attacks. It became clear to everyone that our ace in the hole was gossip editor Mike Walker.

In the early '90s, Mike co-anchored Geraldo Rivera's weekly celebrity program every Friday. (Before the show went off the air, Geraldo figured out Mike had appeared an amazing 264 times—a guest record.) Walker was the guy, and *Geraldo* was the show. As always, I left it to Mike to work out the details.

So one afternoon when Mike was on the show, Geraldo Rivera asked him the $64,000 question: "I saw Tom Arnold on *Larry King* the other night, and, Mike, he said that you and the *Enquirer* make up all this stuff, you print lies, and you invent sources. What gives?"

All over the Lantana office, editorial staffers were watching as Mike prepared to answer. My heart went pitter-patter with satisfaction as Walker prepared to launch his Scud missile—right into the hide of the new Mr. Roseanne.

Said Walker: "Geraldo, I can answer this very easily. We have very good sources, especially on Roseanne." He then reached into his jacket pocket and pulled out a check. The camera zoomed in. It was clearly an *Enquirer* check—and the payee was . . . Tom Arnold. The sum was $1,400.

The audience gasped. Walker then turned over the check. The camera zoomed in. The signature of the person who cashed it . . . Tom Arnold.

Perfect. Crushing. Overpowering. I jumped off my seat in glee, forcing myself not to hop around the room like a kid in a candy store.

Geraldo looked shocked (*what an actor!*) and gasped: "Mike, are you saying what I think you're saying?"

Mike: "Yes, Geraldo. I'm saying that Tom Arnold, who is calling us liars, is the man who has been selling out Roseanne Barr."

Viewers must have been stunned. Certainly the TV audience could hardly believe their ears as Walker explained why he was revealing Arnold's role. Walker said that we *never* reveal the names of sources, but in this case we were forced to name Tom Arnold to protect our reputation. It was the first time we'd named a source in the history of the *Enquirer*, he added.

Walker told the audience that they could believe him 100 percent. "If I'm wrong," he said, "you know that Tom and Rosie will own the *Enquirer*, because they could sue for millions . . . so you know what's at stake here."

Millions saw the show. Tens of millions saw the huge media response as TV and newspapers quoted Walker.

Guess who was the most shocked? My vote would be bride-to-be Roseanne. I would have paid to be a fly on the wall as she tore into Arnold. Years later, in her own book, Roseanne described her anger and disbelief. She wanted to call off the wedding to a man she could no longer trust.

Walker learned how Arnold wriggled out of the situation, through sources and from Roseanne herself some years later.

Says Mike: "You have to hand it to Arnold. As Roseanne screamed at him, 'The marriage is off, you piece of %#@*!', he protested, 'Honey, I did it for you.' 'For me?' said Roseanne. 'Yes,' said Tom. 'I was broke and too proud to admit it. I just wanted to pay for our honeymoon. It was important for me as a man.'"

According to Mike, Roseanne just melted and said: "Aw, honey. You did it for me. You wanted to pay for the honeymoon."

Then everything was hunky-dory. Especially since Tom stopped attacking the *Enquirer*.

Like most major celebrities, Roseanne had a reverse information pipeline into the *Enquirer*. Information about us would come from rival journalists, Hollywood public relations people, and sometimes from freelancers who sold gossip to both sides of the street.

Roseanne and Tom learned that the editor on many of their stories was a young dynamo named Steve Coz. I had hired Coz, a Harvard graduate, as a reporter but promoted him quickly to articles editor, and by 1990 he was on a fast track to the top. Soon he would be running all the news- and photo-gathering as our executive editor, and just as I retired, he took over my old job as editor, a post he held until he was promoted to editorial director of the parent company.

Not long before marrying Arnold, at one of her nuttiest stages, Roseanne actually telephoned Coz in Lantana to ask: "Should I marry Tom Arnold?"

She knew Arnold's background was dodgy, but she also knew Coz knew more than even *she* knew.

Coz was aware that a Roseanne wedding to the equally unstable Arnold was a news bonanza for us, but his pre-*Enquirer* scruples kicked in. He tried, as diplomatically as possible, to steer TV's biggest star away from an obvious mistake. "Maybe I'd think about that," advised Coz.

Fortunately for future headlines, Steve's temporary altruism fell on deaf ears, and Roseanne did dump her hubby for the likeable, energetic, drug-abusing Arnold. It was a decision that, through the years, enlivened the days of our readers and gave us some fun covers.

Later on, it also brought Coz a bloody (nearly broken) nose. My take: It was worth it.

When Tom and Roseanne finally did marry early in January 1990, we learned, through our other sources, that they would honeymoon at the ritzy Las Brisas hotel in Acapulco, Mexico. When they arrived, we were already there. Reporters David Wright and Neil Hitchens had booked a bungalow overlooking the pool and already had some hotel staff on their payroll.

On February 6, 1990, our headline was:

ROSEANNE WEDDING FIASCO—PLUS AMAZING
HONEYMOON SWIMSUIT PICTURES

We had eyewitness accounts of their stay, including complaints about their noisy, boisterous behavior that kept other guests awake. Best of all, we had great photos of them cavorting in the hotel pool on their honeymoon. No one else had even a *clue* where they had been.

I felt especially good knowing that Tom would be baffled about how we got his honeymoon photos without his help.

After marrying Tom, Roseanne seemed to become even more wild and wacky. The set of her TV show was a nightmare for many of the crew and actors. Her TV hubby, John Goodman, was often outraged by her behavior and periodically thought about quitting, even though Roseanne had made him rich and famous. Both Tom and Rosie actually dropped their pants in front of cast and crew to exhibit each other's names tattooed on their butts.

Enquirer readers were treated to stories like Roseanne and Tom trashing a rented mansion in Beverly Hills, causing $100,000 in damage. Or the time the couple stormed into a mental hospital, shouting and shoving people around as they dragged out Rosie's daughter.

Even worse for TV's number-one star was her disgraceful "joke" as she screeched the national anthem at a televised baseball game, then grabbed her crotch as thousands of fans booed and jeered her.

I agonized over whether to run the crotch-grabbing photo on page one. Our readers have always been very conservative when it comes to photos they wouldn't show their children. And supermarkets, especially in the Bible Belt South, are notoriously sensitive.

But the national backlash was so strong—even President Bush

Sr. had called her actions "disgraceful"—that I held my breath and went with the picture. The headline was ROSEANNE DISGRACE, followed by an underline: THE REAL REASON TV'S #1 STAR IS MAKING AMERICA HATE HER.

The dramatic cover sold a ton of copies, and we got bags of mail congratulating us on attacking Roseanne's anti-patriotic antics. Our readers were the heart and soul of America: the "silent majority" of all creeds and political persuasion that President Nixon courted, people who loved their flag and their country.

I just loved editing a publication for them.

In the early '90s, Steve Coz was our main page-one editor, and as such he occasionally visited our West Coast bureau in L.A. On one trip, he stayed at the swanky Bel Age Hotel, and early one morning, there was a knock at his door. Looking through the peephole he saw a man holding a big bunch of flowers.

Steve remembers: "When I opened the door, I saw two very large, tough, and menacing black men, one holding some flowers. Immediately I knew I was in trouble. In a split second they had pushed their way in, and before I could say a word, a huge fist smacked me on the nose. My glasses were broken, and blood spurted from my nose. I went flying backward and crashed into a table.

"I thought they were hit men sent to kill me, so I struggled to maintain my balance and charged them, shoving and wrestling them back toward the door. Somehow I got them out and slammed the door.

"Looking back, it's obvious the goons had been told just to rough me up. They could have overpowered me easily.

"I just sat down, wiped off the blood, and tried to recover. It had been terrifying. I really believed for a moment I was about to be murdered."

The men had left the bouquet of flowers. On it was a note that just said "With Deepest Sympathy." Later tests showed no fingerprints that might provide a clue.

Coz might never have learned who was behind the attack, except that ten minutes later back at his home in Florida his phone rang. His wife, Valerie Virga, our talented photo editor, was at work so the answering machine picked up.

When Valerie listened to the tape later, she heard Roseanne cackling hysterically and saying she was calling Steve to send her "deepest sympathy"—the exact words on the bouquet card.

Tom was shouting in the background: "Sorry about what happened," and Roseanne was yelling: "It couldn't have happened to a nicer guy." For several minutes the two were yelling, laughing hysterically, and having a riotous time.

What did we do about it? Nothing. Steve's a pro. We discussed it and agreed that: (1) It would be tough to prove anything in a court of law; (2) The publicity in Hollywood might make even Roseanne a hero; (3) the story might give other celebrities ideas of their own.

If I thought there was no way the Roseanne story could get any better, I was wrong. Way, way wrong! After less than four years of marriage Rosie began to tire of Tom Arnold, and in 1994 she filed for divorce. A couple of months later, she went on a fantastic $600,000, two-month tour of Europe. Included in her entourage was a bodyguard—and eventually, her new husband—Ben Thomas.

Naturally, the *Enquirer* also went along—unseen and uninvited.

In Rome, our resident Italian photojournalist, Umberto Pizzi, discovered that Roseanne and Ben Thomas were sharing a room.

Flash over to Los Angeles. Alan Braham Smith, a British reporter who joined us in the early '70s, had established himself in Los Angeles as arguably the *Enquirer*'s number-one celebrity reporter. He's been responsible for many of our all-time greatest Hollywood exclusives.

Alan knew exactly what to do with the information from Rome. Alan called Tom Arnold to tell him about the "affair." It seems Roseanne's children had already hinted about the new romance.

Tom was shattered to think his marriage—and his meal ticket—were in danger. He and Alan both concluded that if Tom flew to Europe and confronted Roseanne, he might effect a reconciliation.

In a normal world, Tom Arnold would never have teamed up with an outfit that had written so many nasty (but true) stories about him and embarrassed him worldwide by revealing him as a paid traitor to his wife-to-be. But this is Hollywood, where truth is stranger than fiction—thank the Lord!

Tom Arnold wanted to confront his wife—and we knew where she would be. Tom didn't want to be seen cooperating on this story with the *Enquirer* in case his wife disapproved, so he and Smith made a pact.

Arnold booked a first-class seat on an Alitalia flight to Rome under the name "Bickerstaff" (at the last minute, of course, he had to show airline officials his real passport). Arnold took along his younger brother, Chris. "By accident," Alan was on the same flight—in the row behind him. Somehow they had also booked into the same hotel.

One problem—Roseanne and her party have checked out and left Rome. Tom has no clue where his wife is.

No problem. The *Enquirer* is here. Alan Smith and Umberto Pizzi learn Roseanne has gone to the beautiful Mediterranean island of Sardinia, where she has rented a fabulous cliff-top villa.

Everyone books plane tickets. Smith, not trusting Tom, makes sure he and photographer Pizzi are first off the plane to get to their separate rental cars. But Arnold has one-upped them. He has a limousine waiting and whizzes off without waiting for Alan and Umberto.

No one shakes off Alan Braham Smith that easily. He speeds after them and soon catches up. Pizzi can't get his car started, but he knows the route and once he's on his way, he drives madly, like most Italian drivers, to close the gap, which he finally does.

Arnold's white Mercedes limo sweeps up to the villa and—for some reason—the wooden security barrier is raised. Guards try to close it before Smith and Pizzi squeeze in behind, but they can't do it. Everybody is *in*.

The resulting showdown between Tom Arnold, his cheating wife, Roseanne, and the tough security guard made *fantastic* reading in the next week's *Enquirer*.

The headline:

JEALOUS HUBBY FLIES 6,300 MILES TO ITALIAN ISLAND
TOM ARNOLD AMBUSHES ROSEANNE & NEW LOVE

Our story was accompanied by photographs of the showdown between Mr. and Mrs. Arnold.

Smith recounted: "The first person who met [Tom] on the lawn was Ben Thomas. That's when Tom angrily accused the bodyguard of having sex with Roseanne and ordered him to get out of his way. Ben, a muscular martial arts expert, put his face close to Tom's and snarled back, 'Are you talking to me?'"

Before the two men could come to blows, other bodyguards jumped between them. Then Roseanne came storming out of the villa.

And there, just 30 yards from Alan Smith and furiously clicking photographer Umberto Pizzi, the dramatic confrontation erupted.

Face to face with her husband, Roseanne snapped: "Okay, you got me . . . I want a divorce. I don't even want you in my space." She went on a tirade for several minutes, then spotted our photographer. She was about to protest but then snapped back into her Arnold attack.

Tom pleaded: "I love you, Rosie. We can work it out. I flew all this way because I love you. Come on, honey, calm down."

While he pleaded, Roseanne shouted furiously: "Don't try and change me. You won't."

The argument continued for *thirty minutes*—right in front of the *Enquirer*.

Smith's evaluation: "I've covered celebrities for years, but it was the most amazing sight I'd ever seen."

In the end, *Enquirer* readers were treated to a ringside seat at one of the most extraordinary celebrity showdowns in history.

Whenever my guys pulled off an exclusive this big, I couldn't help but puff up a little with pride. Where else could Americans get stuff like this?

Like most celebrities, Roseanne was happy to be featured in the *Enquirer* during her early showbiz days, began to hate us when she got really big and didn't need the publicity, then finally swung back to loving us as her career slid downhill.

Some years after the Sardinia blowup, Roseanne was no longer number one and had a talk show that needed help in the media. The

Enquirer was there for her. Steve Coz invited her to be guest editor for a week and to compile her choices for the "Twenty Most Beautiful Women" (one was Barbra Streisand!). Rosie then invited Coz to be a guest on her talk show to publicize the issue, and she treated him with fun and warmth.

Steve says: "Off camera, Roseanne was totally sweet and nice to me. She apologized for the attack on me and claimed it was all Tom's idea."

She also told him: "You were so right about Tom."

Mike Walker was also a guest on Rosie's show. This is how she introduced him: "This man has printed the most horrible, the most nasty things about me . . . and they're all true. He's the King of Gossip."

Mike's response? He said to Roseanne: "I used to go to bed at night praying for your safety. Someone like you comes along once in a decade—to make life wonderful for a gossip columnist like me."

By that time she was a true pal of the paper.

Show business wasn't the only source of our most popular celebrities. One of our most flashy personalities of the '80s came from just plain business.

Donald Trump is egotistical, demanding, difficult, and sometimes pompous. At times, he's also colorful, charming, brilliant, and surprisingly warmhearted. Most important, in the late 1980s and early '90s, he was someone our readers *loved* reading about.

Larry Haley, our "Trump Editor," joined us with years of newspaper experience. He'd specialized in covering organized crime, a beat that needed energy and courage. It didn't hurt that he had spent several formative years serving with U.S. Army Special Forces.

After years of covering Trump, Haley's opinion is that deep down, behind the glitz, the Donald is a good guy: "You always smile around him . . . he's such a gregarious showman."

Haley and his team of reporters were in charge of our Donald stories for more than a decade. Recalls Haley: "We first became interested in Donald Trump when his marriage to Ivana was on the rocks. I had just finished a story of how this billionaire had been secretly keeping his beautiful mistress, Marla Maples, for months in

New York's St. Moritz hotel. His wife knew nothing about it, and Donald was so conceited he even brought Marla along when he took his wife and children on a ski trip in Aspen over New Year's, 1990.

"He kept Marla in another Aspen hotel, and from time to time, he'd visit her for some off-slope recreation. Marla was getting impatient to be recognized as his new love and decided to bring things to a boil. She went skiing, right to the area where Donald was with wife Ivana. The result was a big confrontation—frostier than the mountains—which naturally ended in the Trump divorce."

The *Enquirer* had a great exclusive on the Ivana-Marla blowup, but our lawyers insisted we contact Donald for his comments. We reached him in Tokyo, but rather than let the *Enquirer* break the news, Donald called his gossip-column pals in New York to give them the story.

Our loss of the exclusive didn't really hurt us. Our yarn, with its exclusive details, was much better than the competition's. When we published it, on February 17, 1990, the cover read:

TRUMP'S MISTRESS
HE HID HER FOR THREE YEARS—THEN WIFE IVANA FOUND OUT!

We ran an exclusive photo of Ivana look-alike Marla with Donald and a great story of how he'd kept Maples hidden, complete with all the juicy facts our readers loved.

The media, especially in the Big Apple, began covering Trump in a big way, and it was soon evident that we had a new page-one star. Haley was assigned to make sure we broke the best stories.

Spearheading Haley's effort was freelancer Wayne Grover. Grover had some contacts in the Trump camp and knew Donald was proud of his background, which included military school. He set up an interview—and we ran a small, favorable story that Donald loved and that started the love-hate relationship between Donald and the *Enquirer*.

With his stormy personal and public lifestyle, we couldn't avoid running scandal stories that he hated, but, when possible, we'd let Grover tip him off to our plans in advance. In return, Donald would give Grover exclusives.

Once in a while, getting a cover on the sensational couple took good, old-fashioned obstinacy.

After our 1990 MISTRESS cover, Marla ducked the press, and it took us almost a year to get to her. Our reporters Doug Mays and his wife, Sammie, who'd broken many exclusives, were tipped off that Marla was flying out of Aspen alone on December 22. They got behind her in the ticket line and openly introduced themselves as *Enquirer* reporters, then asked for an interview about her romance with Donald.

Marla, a southern beauty, replied, "Y'all sound like you're from my neck of the woods," and when they said they were from Mississippi, Marla became very friendly and began to talk and pose for photos.

After ten minutes, Marla asked Sammie, another blonde beauty, to accompany her to the powder room. They continued the photos and interview for another thirty minutes,

Bingo. We had a MARLA TELLS ALL cover. Inside Marla told our readers that Donald is the world's greatest lover, that he loves talking silly baby talk, and that he went down on one knee to propose marriage to Marla. And she blamed Ivana—not herself—for the breakup of the billionaire's marriage.

We still had to court Donald. The man loves publicity—but only if he controls it. He doesn't care if reporters write that he is a tough SOB who fires people, but he gets angry if a story implies he is softhearted. He'd often call New York reporters, sometimes giving them news tips, sometimes haranguing them about something he didn't like.

Of course, we couldn't let him control the *Enquirer's* work, but sometimes we let him influence an angle or delete something that really infuriated him. As long as his changes didn't weaken the story.

So the relationship Haley and Grover worked out ran like a dream. Trump always returned their calls, gave them interviews, and sometimes gave them exclusives.

Says Haley: "Donald loved having a pipeline into the biggest weekly in America. He loved thinking he could manipulate us, and he knew that, because of our relationship, we would never run a major story without calling him first."

The Haley-Trump bond deepened as the years passed. Larry and

Wayne were invited to several parties at Trump's Mar-a-Lago mansion in Palm Beach.

Remembers Haley: "Inevitably there'd be stacks of nubile young woman; once it was the Dallas Cowboys cheerleaders. There would be a smaller group of men, and Donald loved to have the girls drape themselves all over him, with big kisses and hugs. But the parties were duds, never much fun. They were just a show to prove Donald was irresistible to women."

The Haley-Trump relationship included Donald's occasional angry explosions at Haley. After his divorce from Ivana, Donald and Marla became a live-in couple, and she got pregnant. Grover had great contacts inside the Trump organization, and early in '93 we ran a nice story about the moment Marla told him he was going to be a father (the baby was the little girl named Tiffany). We wrote that Donald, happy at the news, had tears of joy in his eyes.

The following Monday morning Haley's phone rang. It was Trump, spewing a tirade of expletives and insults sprinkled liberally with references to Haley's lineage and sexual habits. Says Haley: "Before I could ask him the problem the phone was slammed down."

Haley waited an hour and called Donald's faithful longtime assistant, Norma Federer. The story had depicted Donald as a nice guy with a heart, so why was her boss so mad?

"Mr. Trump does not cry," contended Ms. Federer. "He does not shed a tear." Apparently Trump felt the mention of joyful tears made him look weak.

The storm soon passed, and Trump and the *Enquirer* were friends again. One night, the billionaire, who called Haley often, phoned Larry at home to ask: "Larry, you know that Marla is pressing to get married. Be honest. Pretend you are me . . . what would you do?"

Recalls Haley: "I was taken aback. How could I pretend to be Donald Trump? But I had to answer. We knew that he and Marla had planned a secret wedding perhaps as early as the following day and had tickets booked for a honeymoon in Paris. I already had three reporters in New York and one in Paris covering all the possibilities.

"It was obvious Donald was having cold feet. So I just gave him my honest answer, which was: 'You're Donald Trump. If you don't want to get married, then don't.'"

Trump hung up. Three hours later he called back saying: "Larry, thanks for the honest advice. No wedding now, but if I ever get married you get a personal invitation."

Maybe Haley influenced him, maybe not, but Donald did not marry Marla at that time. He took her on the planned trip to Paris, and we ran a photo of them getting off the plane. Marla was carrying her wedding dress draped over her arm, fully prepared in case Donald changed his mind. (Trump was as good as his word to Larry. When he finally did marry Marla, both Haley and Wayne Grover were his personal guests at the wedding.)

The Trump-Maples trip to Paris had an odd twist, which demonstrated that Donald did have a big heart, despite his efforts to hide it.

Wayne Grover, waiting for them to arrive in Paris, became very sick. Calling Haley in Florida, he said: "I think I'm dying." Haley quickly arranged for an ambulance to take Grover to the hospital, where he spent several days recovering from a mysterious illness. Haley also called Trump and Maples at their hotel and told them Grover had been hospitalized.

Trump and Marla went to visit Grover in the hospital. Says Larry: "They knew that Wayne had been there to pursue them if they had been married. He had written many stories they hated. Yet they went to see if Wayne was okay. That's the human side of Trump he tries to hide."

Donald called me many times, serving up classic lessons in the art of persuasion, and sometimes the honey seeping over the line just made me smile. I could almost —*almost*—believe him.

Only once did he ever threaten us, saying, "I can always get my lawyers on this." My response: "Donald, you mention lawyers once again and I hang up. You and I can talk on any subject, but if you threaten to bring in attorneys, they'll talk to our attorneys, and our talks end."

He immediately became sweetness and light again.

The cover we ran on Marla's late-night beach activities had the impact of a neutron bomb. It described how local cops had discovered Donald's wife, Marla, on a beach near their Palm Beach home with her attractive young security guard.

By this time I had retired as editor-in-chief and was working part-time for American Media, the new name of the company chosen by chairman Callahan, not long after he took over. I was now in charge of new magazines and projects which would enhance our revenue.

I had promoted Steve Coz to editor, and when he briefed me on the Trump story, I gasped. I advised Coz to call Trump before the story broke. We knew the marriage was in trouble, so the biggest blow to him would not be his tender feelings for his wife but the damage to his ego in public. If we alerted him in advance, at least he could tell his friends that he knew all about the upcoming story and would have time to formulate a response to the other media when they called.

Why was it important to notify Trump? Two reasons: (1) He'd appreciate the early warning, and (2) there's no point in making an implacable enemy of a smart billionaire—unless there's no alternative.

The task of making the phone call fell to Larry Haley. He recalls: "I gulped a little. I was to tell Trump his wife had been caught with her bodyguard. But there was no choice. When I spoke to Donald there was a silence. He was taken by surprise. He said he would call me back.

"Ten minutes later he phoned. He told me he had spoken to Marla, who said it was no big deal—just business and not funny business. I then spelled out the details given to us by the cops, and Donald ended the call.

"I think Donald appreciated our advance notice. After our story came out he was able to spin his version: Marla had gone to the beach to go to the bathroom, and the bodyguard followed to protect her.

"But he was embarrassed. It ended the marriage."

Haley, who was perhaps the number-one Trump-watcher in the media at the time, believes the marriage was a sham from the start. Donald loved their child and had wed Marla out of respect for his parents' old-fashioned values.

Says Haley: "We wrote a very positive follow-up story through his public relations man Richard Fields, saying that Donald was standing by Marla. Fields told us that Donald okayed the words, but after the piece ran, Trump called me on my cell phone and shouted: 'I never said that!' And he hung up. Trump transferred Fields to another job—at least temporarily."

A few months later divorce proceedings began.

Haley is convinced that, if the *Enquirer* had not run the Marla-on-the-beach story, she would still be married to Trump. He adds: "Donald had his marriage, his child, plus the freedom to see other women. He was happy with the deal. Then came the public embarrassment. He just would not tolerate being embarrassed."

★★★

In 1990, my new bosses had been in charge for a year. We had proved to them that they had bought the best editorial investigative team of the twentieth century, but like all good executives, they just wanted to know: What have you done for me lately?

A great opportunity opened up when baseball legend Pete Rose was sent to prison for tax evasion. Now, sports stars were never on the top of our hit list. Ladies in supermarkets mostly don't care about the hottest quarterback or who threw a no-hitter. But there were exceptions: people like Mike Tyson and ultimately O. J. Simpson.

My chairman, Peter Callahan, and my immediate boss, Mike Boylan, were sports nuts.

So when Rose hit the headlines as a prison convict, I knew we really had to impress them.

Pete was sent to the federal penitentiary in Marion, Illinois, a fearsome place where Mafia boss John Gotti spent several years. It's a place you do not escape from.

So when Pete went there, the press went crazy with banner headlines. They wanted to interview the baseball star. They wanted photos.

No dice, said the warden. Nobody gets in to see Rose; nobody talks to him; nobody gets pictures. The end. Finito. The man has spoken.

As boss of the *National Enquirer,* I had an awesome team at my disposal. Some of the greatest news-gatherers from the United States, Britain, Australia, Canada, South Africa, and the rest of the globe were being paid handsomely. By the mid-eighties we were paying reporters up to $100,000 per annum, and some editors double that.

They got the money because they got the stories and the photos.

So I called some of my best people in. This warden says we can't get to Pete. Right? *Wrong.*

Let's do it.

It took four days for the plan to be hatched.

Articles editor Larry Haley happened to have a couple of freelance reporters in Alabama. They were a couple. He was a big tough guy named Doug Mays, and his wife was a glamorous blonde named Sammie.

They had done some good stories for us. But they had one unique asset that was going to be the key to achieving our plan: in effect, breaking *in* to the big, bad federal penitentiary in Marion.

That asset was: Doug and Sammie were singers and musicians who had several times volunteered to give shows to convicts in prisons around the South.

Naturally, their next—and greatest—performance was going to be at Marion, specifically the prison camp area where Rose was incarcerated.

It took a couple of weeks or so to get references and permission to do the show. But finally it was all set up. Officially.

Now, getting into prison with electric guitars, loudspeakers, and equipment means going through security. They don't want anybody smuggling drugs or guns into federal prisons. So getting the camera in was going to take a little bit of thought. A very little bit. Doug just opened a loudspeaker and very carefully taped the camera inside.

Show day was Saturday, so our intrepid team got permission to take their equipment in the night before and set it up in the prison concert room. Everything went perfectly. The camera was in (hidden) place. Then they had to leave for their motel.

It was a restless night. Had the camera been found? Doug and Sammie were very, very nervous Saturday morning as they drove up to the forbidding exterior of the prison. Were they going in as welcomed entertainers? Or would they end up in a locked cell?

Frozen smiles in place, Doug and Sammie passed through the prison gates. But everything was okay, and they started having conversations with guards and prisoners. Since this section was low-security, they were able to wander around—and, as big baseball fans, naturally they wanted to find out about Pete Rose. More easily than they had feared, they were pointed in the direction of Mr. Rose.

Doug managed to extract his camera from the loudspeaker without being seen—and the couple casually sauntered to an indoor recreation area where Pete was sitting, holding court about baseball and watching a baseball game on TV. But he was with two guards, who were fascinated by his baseball stories.

And our dynamic duo needed him unprotected!

How to get rid of the guards? Sammie knew. She is a very attractive woman. So she unbuttoned a couple of top buttons on her blouse, sashayed up to the guards, and asked sweetly if they would show her a very interesting section of the prison.

For a moment it was in the balance. Baseball or sexual attraction. The guards thought for a second. Hallelujah! Sammie won, and as she left with the guards, Doug whipped out the camera and said these most historic words:

Hi, Pete. I'm from the *National Enquirer.*

Pete laughed and laughed. I knew someone would get to me, he said. I just knew it would be you guys. He talked, gave an interview, and posed for pictures to show he was in prison.

The most famous jailbird in America lounged back on a sofa, his feet on a chair—and the photos included several other inmates, plus a wide background to prove without doubt the pictures had been taken in prison. Pete knew he was giving us a major exclusive when he admitted to Doug: "This is the big one . . ."

Total victory! Doug and Sammie had completed Mission Impossible. They had the story. They had the photos. It was done.

Well, almost. They were still in the prison. They still had to give the concert. And Pete—they prayed—had to keep his mouth shut.

So off they go to give the concert. With exhilaration and fear churning his stomach, Doug tapes the camera back into the loud-speaker. But he's in a hurry. He must tape the camera before anyone sees him.

Damn. It is not really secured properly.

So when Doug starts to warm up his electric guitar, a sort of strange vibration comes from the speaker. The sound is vibrating off the camera. One friendly con says he'll help. He's a hi-fi buff, and he can fix it. Doug says thanks, but it's okay. The con insists.

Doug sweats, but—as I said—he's a tough guy. He looks intimidating. And he growls menacingly at the con: You touch my equipment and I'll break your ***** neck.

Whew! Crisis over. Doug and Sammie give a great—if fast—performance (camera vibration and all), then they load the equipment into their little Ford and drive out the prison gates.

Jubilation. They've got the interview. They've got the pix. Finally, it's over.

Sure . . .

Doug and Sammie decide to keep driving until they cross the Illinois state line just to make sure they are safe . . . before they call the *Enquirer* editor with the great news.

So they pull in to a gas station, fill up, and go to a pay phone to make the victory announcement. In their haste and glee they make *one tiny* mistake. They leave the keys in the car ignition.

Haley, their editor, is over the moon. He's on the telephone with Doug and Sammie, listening to them both shrieking: We've got the story, we've got the pictures. Suddenly there's a moment of silence and Doug screams: oh f***. The phone goes dead.

I'm in the newsroom, and a grinning Haley gives me the thumbs up. We've got Rose. Then his face goes dark. I know something terrible has just happened at the other end.

Doug has just spotted a young hippie jumping into his Ford and driving off. Going, going, gone . . . is the car, the musical instruments, the audio equipment, the camera still in the loudspeaker, and the Pete Rose film still in the camera.

He races after the car, which is speeding away. But maybe God was on his side. Traffic lights had stopped a line of cars, and the little Ford came to a halt. In a moment, Doug was pulling open the car door, yanking the hippie out by his hair, and hurling him to the sidewalk.

Afterward, after all the kudos, congratulations, and high-fives, the story and photos went to the printer. Haley told me: My two free-lancers did one of the great reporting jobs of all time.

Before the issue made it to the supermarkets, the news leaked that the *Enquirer* had an exclusive interview, with pictures, of Pete Rose inside the federal prison at Marion, Illinois.

Other news organizations called the warden, who scornfully laughed and proclaimed: "It's phony. Take my word for it. These guys might make up an interview, but they can't have pictures of Pete in here. It just couldn't happen."

When everyone saw the photos, he had to eat those words.

As the early '90s unfolded, the new owners and the old team kept breaking stories and selling zillions of papers. But, like Rodney Dangerfield, we got no respect.

Until O.J.

The O.J. Simpson murders were a watershed for us. Our coverage was so spectacular, sustained, and accurate that our competitors in the media were astonished. The most prestigious newspapers, magazines, and television networks praised the *Enquirer* with accolades we could not have dreamed about years before.

We always knew we were good. Now America's press, competing with us shoulder to shoulder, month after month, on a fascinating story, found out how good we were.

On October 24, 1994, *New York Times* reporter David Margolick wrote: "With accurate, saturation reporting of the killings, evidence and legal maneuvering, The National Enquirer has become the bible of the O.J. Simpson case."

Margolick noted that the O.J. case had been on our front page for sixteen of the previous eighteen weeks, commenting, "In a story made for tabloids, one paper has had a profound impact on the case." His story was headlined: THE *ENQUIRER*: REQUIRED READING IN SIMPSON CASE.

In January 1995, *Time* magazine called us "Leader of the Pack."

And a few weeks later, the *Miami Herald* headlined a front-page story: SCOOPS! ENQUIRER'S JUICY EXCLUSIVES WIN RESPECT—AND READERS. The *Herald* wrote: "Enquirer reporters have beaten the nation's top news organizations again and again . . ."

CNN correspondent Martha Smelgas said on air: "In the O.J. case, if it's in the *Enquirer*, believe it."

The saga began as something sad but nothing huge.

Nicole Brown Simpson, ex-wife of the former NFL superstar, and Ron Goldman were murdered on June 13, 1994. Their bodies were found in pools of blood outside Nicole's house in the Brentwood section of Los Angeles.

Senior editor Steve Coz asked David Perel to mastermind the coverage. It was an inspired choice.

Perel, now editor in chief of the *Enquirer*, reached his pinnacle after years of achievement as a reporter and articles editor. None turned out to be more important than O.J. Says Perel: "It was obviously a good story but not a blockbuster. O.J. had been a great running back, but he'd faded from the public eye, just doing some bit parts in movies." He assigned two reporting teams to the story—one to the murder house and the other to O.J.'s home, about 2 miles away at 360 Rockingham Avenue in Brentwood.

Perel remembers: "Within a few hours it became clear: O.J. Simpson himself was a suspect. I immediately put eight reporters on the story, and we were at O.J.'s house before the coroner arrived."

Less than forty-eight hours later we had a *fantastic* story. At this time I was editor in chief of the *Enquirer*, and my editor was John Cathcart. At our page-one planning meeting, he told me Perel had convinced him to tear up the cover we had originally chosen and go with the headline: THE O.J. MURDERS.

O.J. had not been officially named a suspect, but it was a legitimate label. Simpson was the celebrity: His ex-wife had been murdered and he was being questioned. It was just the way the public would label the killings, even if O.J. didn't do it.

Our attorneys did not agree. Our policy was never, ever, *ever* run with a story or headline not approved by Williams and Connolly.

We fought with, argued with, and pleaded with David Kendall and the other attorneys to find a way to use our major headline. Finally, just before deadline, they asked for some secondary headline changes and inside text fixes. Then they said "go."

The millions of Americans who bought us each week were getting their money's worth. And on some of our biggest O.J. exclusives we were adding three or four hundred thousand extra sales.

From mid-1994, for a full eighteen months, the O.J. story took over Perel's life. He ran the operation, with every newsman, staffer, or stringer reporting directly to him. Perel probably knew more about the case than most of the prosecutors or defense attorneys.

He created massive computer files that cross-checked facts, witnesses, names, dates, key words, and even information we'd already proved false—a database that allowed us to ignore erroneous information often reported by other media. Perel's obsession even led him to read books on molecular biology to help him understand the DNA evidence.

We probably spoke to more witnesses than the cops, which is why we regularly uncovered material they missed.

The first story that really put us on the media map was this cover:

O.J.'s KNIFE
HE BOUGHT THIS DEADLY WEAPON JUST BEFORE MURDERS

A salesman at Ross Cutlery in Los Angeles had reportedly sold a knife that matched the killing weapon—to O.J. Simpson.

Perel assigned Alan Braham Smith to the story. Smith, a transplanted Brit, is one of the greatest newshounds of all time. Since the '70s he's helped break some of the *Enquirer*'s greatest stories, and he's still a phenomenal operator.

When he arrived at the store, the clerk told him the story wasn't true, and he had said the same thing to every reporter who'd called or visited. Smith's other sources, and his instincts, told him the clerk was lying. Smith called him every hour, asking the same question—hour after hour, day after day, never letting up. He told the clerk:

"You're lying. If you tell the truth, we'll pay you lots of money for the exclusive."

After a week, the clerk folded and told us the whole story. He admitted he'd sold the knife to O.J. shortly before the murders, and to prove he was telling the truth this time he pulled out O.J.'s autograph, saying: "I asked Mr. Simpson if he would give me his autograph—and he did." Here was graphic support for the clerk's tale.

Our story stunned America. Prosecutor Marcia Clark immediately sent investigators to check out our story. She verified the account and called the clerk as a witness at the preliminary hearing.

At the nationally broadcast court hearing, prosecutors asked the clerk if he had sold the knife to O.J. and said he answered, "Yes." He was then asked if the *Enquirer* had paid him, and he confirmed he received a check for $17,500 to keep his story exclusive from other media.

When asked why he had finally told the truth to the *Enquirer*, the clerk hesitated and then blurted out: "Because Mr. Alan Smith would not leave me alone."

Perel, watching the witness on TV, says: "When the clerk talked about Smith, I just fell on the floor laughing. Smith was responsible for one of the greatest pieces of reporting ever."

After the hearing, Marcia Clark and the other prosecutors held a press conference outside the courthouse and talked about their witness. He told the truth to the *National Enquirer* for money, she said. He told the truth inside the court for nothing.

That knife story put us on the map. From then on, the other media scrambled to get early editions of the *Enquirer* to find out the latest in the case.

One of our strengths was our ability to put experienced manpower in the field. If Perel wanted a bigger budget or more reporters at any time, neither I nor any of my top executives would say no. In fact, I don't think David ever felt he had a budget. He spent money and resources like crazy—but he always got brilliant results.

Perel was working eighteen hours every day, including weekends. He had unmatched sources inside the police department, the prosecutor's office, and the Hollywood community. At one point, prosecutor Christopher Darden was so upset by the information we were getting from his office that he administered secret lie-detector tests to many of his people in a hunt for the mole. They never found our source—but *we* found out about his secret lie-detector tests.

The amount of information pouring into Lantana was almost too much for one editor to handle, but Perel was a master. Other publications simply didn't have our depth of resources and our news-gathering skills.

When we reported exclusively that Nicole's and Ron Goldman's blood had been found in O.J.'s Bronco, mini-hysteria broke out in the country. Every single day Perel would get phone calls from *Time*, the *New York Times*, and other major media to glean any tidbits.

Says Perel: "From time to time, I gave them some exclusive material. They paid me back by going on TV or writing stories, admitting the *Enquirer* was getting all of the best material. I made a lot of media friends, who were telling the public about how good the *Enquirer* was."

And we *were* good. Just judge for yourself . . .

Prosecutor Marcia Clark needed to decide whether to ask for the death penalty against O.J, so she wanted to try the case with a mock jury. But clearly she couldn't do this in Los Angeles without its leaking to the press.

In the summer of 1994, she set up a mock jury in Phoenix. A local company, under a cloak of total secrecy, hired "jurors" and sent them to a hotel. Each person was paid for working the entire weekend but told almost nothing about what was to transpire, so that nobody could find out. Well, almost nobody.

Marcia Clark and her sidekick Bill Hodgman booked flights for Phoenix. Unfortunately, Marcia forgot she was carrying her gun—and she was stopped by security at Burbank Airport.

Mistake. We were tipped off. The question was: Why in the middle of preparing for the nation's biggest trial would the lead prosecutor fly to Arizona with one of her male colleagues? We were damn sure they weren't heading out for an amorous weekend. On the other hand, you could never be certain.

Perel was now being told it was a mock trial. He assigned reporter Alan Butterfield to the story but keeping the mock trial angle a secret. If Butterfield could confirm the mock trial, he figured that would be a double check.

Recalls Butterfield: "I got to Phoenix as quickly as possible and found Marcia and Bill were staying at the Holiday Inn. I checked in and discovered they'd booked a big conference room for the whole weekend."

It didn't take long for Butterfield to figure it out. The prosecutors had set up a twenty-person focus group, or mock jury, to listen to the evidence. They wanted to know what people believed and what they didn't to help them mold their case for the real jury.

Butterfield decided to wait until the second day, when the final session was over. He sat in his car under the Arizona sun, perspiring in 120-degree heat, waiting for the focus-group people to leave. He wanted to get them outside the hotel, so Marcia Clark wouldn't see him and perhaps warn the "jurors" to keep silent.

The ordeal was worth it. People in the test group were happy to talk about such a famous case. The big news: *None* of them would vote to give O.J. the death penalty. They'd all rather see the charismatic ex-NFL star walk than send him to his death. Marcia Clark was convinced not to ask for the death penalty in the O.J. case.

After getting stacks of quotes and details about the weekend's excitement, Butterfield approached Marcia and Bill. They still thought their trip was top secret, so when he announced: "I'm from the *Enquirer*," they just about fainted. A furious "No comment" was just about all they managed to croak out.

They might as well have done their focus group in L.A.

Now they were flying back, and, unknown to them, Butterfield had arranged for the two prosecutors to sit in one row of three seats, with Marcia at the window and Bill Hodgman on the aisle. Guess who was booked in the middle seat?

Nice try. When the two prosecutors boarded the plane and saw the setup, they blanched, had a quick chat with the flight attendant, and got new seat assignments.

But Butterfield already had his great story—and another exclusive that blew away the competition.

As our exclusives unfolded, the mainstream press was beginning to realize, probably for the first time, that the *Enquirer* had a *great* news-gathering staff, and they began to pay attention to us.

One key reporter they didn't learn about was Peter Burt, younger son of tabloid reporter and editor Bill Burt. Peter, in his early twenties during the Simpson story, was the tall, handsome young guy who had run the Marine Corps Marathon alongside Oprah.

Competing against some of America's best mainstream journalists, Peter was the only reporter to infiltrate the innermost circles around O.J. He had a "Deep Throat" who fed him O.J.'s most intimate secrets, before and during the trial. We knew just about everything. What Simpson told his attorneys in prison, what the lawyers said afterward, the in-fighting and bickering in the Simpson camp— all of it was delivered regularly to young Burt.

Whenever the *Enquirer* ran a page-one exclusive about him, O.J. would rage to his closest associates: "How do they know this?" We not only knew the stories, we also knew his complaints about them.

Remembers Peter: "There's no doubt that O.J. thought he was smarter than all his attorneys. He was calling the shots. Some of his attorneys thought he was arrogant and his ego was out of control. We knew about the fights between lawyers Shapiro and Bailey. When the *Enquirer* ran my 'Deep Throat' exclusives, Shapiro would blame Bailey for the leaks, and Bailey would blame Shapiro." Finally they called in Johnny Cochran, whose smartest move was to let O.J. believe that he would run the trial the way O.J. wanted.

But "Deep Throat" continued to break inside stories—driving O.J. mad about the leaks. He didn't care about the other media, but he was angry that the *Enquirer* often reported his very words.

The *Enquirer* became a must-read for all the mainstream journalists covering the case. One of them, David Margolick of the *New York Times*, was quite impressed. He'd check out our exclusives, and time after time, they would prove correct.

What Margolick didn't know was this: "Deep Throat" would give us an exclusive and, after we hit the newsstands, Margolick would call "Deep Throat" and ask if the *Enquirer* story was true. "Deep Throat" would confirm his own story and say, "I don't know how the *Enquirer* does it, but they're always right."

We *were* always right, and Margolick, to his credit, praised us in America's most prestigious newspaper. He just didn't know he was confirming our stories with our source.

Burt claims he'll never reveal the identity of "Deep Throat"—although some of us in Lantana knew who it was. Burt adds: "We kept it so quiet that we'd use a pseudonym when calling each other. The fake identity was 'Andy Gump,' the name on portable toilets used throughout Los Angeles."

The reason that Burt's bosses, including me, had to know the identity of "Deep Throat"? We wrote him checks that totaled $250,000.

While Burt was sewing up the O.J. end of the story, we had another reporting wizard working the Brown family, the grieving relatives of murder victim Nicole Brown Simpson, O.J.'s ex-wife. Alan Butterfield was a freelance reporter who is as highly regarded as any staffer and who repeatedly—even to this day—turns down *Enquirer* job offers, just to retain his independence.

During the O.J. epic, and working against America's top reporters from the *New York Times, Newsweek,* CBS, NBC, and ABC, he buttoned up the Brown family tightly and exclusively. He turned out major scoops—from the picture of a topless Nicole with a male friend that sent O.J. over the edge to Nicole's diary that from the grave told marriage secrets, including O.J.'s assaults and her fear of him. These *Enquirer* features, courtesy of Butterfield, made rival newsmen writhe in frustration and jealousy.

How the heck did an *Enquirer* reporter get the Browns to give him such a string of exclusives? Hard work, a charismatic personality, and a couple of bucks on occasion. For more than a year, Butterfield became a close friend of the Brown parents, Lou and Judy. He was a frequent guest at their home and sometimes babysat for Justin, O.J.'s young son. And he had romantic flings with Nicole's beautiful sisters, Denise and Dominique.

Butterfield remembers how it all began: "I just began making phone calls to the family—every day, several times a day. At first they really didn't want to know an *Enquirer* reporter. But because my editor fed me tidbits of information from the cops and prosecutors, I was able to give the Browns information they just weren't getting from Marcia Clark and her team."

Because Butterfield's advance information consistently proved accurate, Nicole's mom, Judy, slowly began to trust Butterfield. Recalls Alan: "She began to talk to me and introduced me to her husband and Nicole's sisters, Denise and Dominique. Still, it was all on the telephone. She would never invite me to their home."

At this time, the Browns believed O.J. was innocent. O.J. would call the family and say that after he was cleared he would build a $5 million compound where he and his children would stay. The Brown family would have their own houses in the compound.

But as the evidence built up, the Browns slowly began to suspect that O.J. was guilty—and finally they were convinced.

Butterfield got this information from several family members and, several months after the murder, wrote his first major story: O.J. DID KILL OUR DAUGHTER . . . NICOLE'S GRIEVING PARENTS BAN HIM FROM TALKING TO HIS CHILDREN. The Browns were really angry with Alan. The story was true, but it was a shock to be on the cover of the *Enquirer*.

Alan kept talking to them on the telephone, giving them advance information on the police investigation, and slowly regained their favor.

Then came the big break. Simpson's legal team began trashing Nicole's reputation by leaking stories to their favorite newsmen that she had been a party girl, drinking too much, doing drugs, and neglecting her children.

The Browns needed to defend Nicole. Well, opined Butterfield, who better than the mass-circulation *National Enquirer*? Toward the end of '94, Butterfield was invited to have dinner with Mr. and Mrs. Brown. They loved him. Alan convinced them that having the *Enquirer* in their corner would be a godsend. Not only did three and a half million Americans buy it each week, but 20 million people read it. Everybody who walked through a supermarket checkout saw our covers, and our stories were picked up by newspapers and TV stations all over the country.

The Browns needed a media champion, and we were it. We were given inside information on Nicole and wonderful family pictures to counter the false information being put out by the Simpson "dream team."

By luck, Butterfield stumbled over a major exclusive. One evening Dominique was looking through some old photos. Butterfield's eyes nearly popped out at one in particular—Nicole posing topless with a male friend named Brett Shaves. Dominique mentioned that she had information that O.J. had seen that photo not long before the murder—and he'd exploded in a rage. It was this photo, many people believed, that had finally pushed O.J. over the edge and turned him into a killer.

We *had* to have this photo and the story. It was a blockbuster.

It took Butterfield several months to finally persuade the reluctant family to give it to us.

Eureka! We front-paged it as the photo that pushed O.J. over the edge. As a family paper, we had to block out most of Nicole's boobs—but the picture was still shocking. Our readers loved the picture and the story. (The untouched picture was published in the 2001 *Enquirer* coffee-table photo book *Thirty Years of Unforgettable Images*.) When these major exclusives ran, our circulation jumped by half a million copies.

In a later deposition, Dominique acknowledged that the *Enquirer* had paid her several thousand dollars for the photo. But the Browns weren't cooperating because of money. Says Butterfield: "The family appreciated all the inside information we could give them—and the friendly exposure which let them tell their side of the ongoing story. Everything we told them came true, and they really respected that."

About this time Butterfield took the phrase "journalistic contact" to a new level. He and Denise Brown began a romantic liaison, including a fun weekend away together. But the beautiful Denise was becoming a media celebrity in her own right. Before long, she was a regular on the Geraldo Rivera show—and, by many accounts, she was very friendly with the married TV host.

Nobody ever proved this gossip one way or the other, but Butterfield was given the heave-ho, at least romantically. Not a problem. Dominique, whose knockout figure could have graced a *Playboy* centerfold, willingly stepped in for her sister.

The Brown family's friendship with us really paid off for them when they established the Nicole Brown Simpson Charitable Foundation and hired a professional in Dallas to run it.

Soon after, we received a tip that the man in charge was an alleged wife-beater.

Imagine if the media had broken the story and crucified the Browns for hiring a possible wife-beater to run their charity named for a beaten, murdered wife. Instead, the *Enquirer* ran a story that the Browns had been victimized again, duped into hiring this professional charity organizer. Our sympathetic piece kept other media hounds from attacking the family.

Mr. and Mrs. Brown loved us for that.

Finally came the criminal trial, complete with Johnny Cochran and the dream team. Just before the case started, Denise Brown went to Nicole's grave to pray for justice, a moving, dramatic gesture.

Guess who knew Denise was going? Alan Butterfield. So an *Enquirer* photographer just happened to be at the cemetery to record the moment for history—and our readers. Just great stuff! But there was even better to come.

We all know that O.J. was found not guilty of murder and walked out of court a free man.

The Browns, devastated, went into seclusion to recover from their grief and anger. Not even Butterfield, now a close friend, was included.

Several days afterward, however, Lou Brown telephoned Butterfield. He said: "Alan, I have something that you will like." Lou told him about some pages that Nicole had written before she died.

Butterfield went to the Brown house, where Nicole's father handed him several sheets of paper. Recalls Alan: "As I started to read, my hands began to shake. This was page after page of handwriting by Nicole shortly before her murder. It was almost like she was speaking from beyond the grave. This was history I was holding in my hands."

Nicole had written heart-wrenching details of the living hell she endured at the hands of O.J.—the brutal physical, emotional, and sexual abuse that left her broken.

Back in Lantana, I was floored by this explosive material. Here was the cry of an abused wife calling from the grave and, in her own handwriting, damning a violent man—her husband, O.J.

On October 4, 1995, we ran a five-page special inside the paper and headlined it on the cover:

INSIDE: IN HER HANDWRITING . . .
NICOLE'S DIARY
O.J. BEAT THE HOLY HELL OUT OF ME AND WE LIED AT THE X-RAY LAB
I CALLED THE COPS TO SAVE MY LIFE

Inside, day by day, Nicole described the horror when she told O.J. she was officially splitting with him. She wrote of his threats—"You're going to pay for this, bitch"—and his rages: "New Years eve. Chasing me through house . . . into office into backyard into Michelle house-keepers rm. Beat me on bed. Kept hitting me until police came . . ."

I'm a pretty hard-bitten journalist, but I had never experienced such a powerful indictment from a murder victim, and in her own handwriting.

When that issue was delivered to our office, David Perel, the editor masterminding the whole O.J. saga for us, took a copy home for his wife, Jill. He remembers: "A few minutes later I saw tears streaming down her face. Then she began sobbing. I knew we had hit a home run."

Not only did our readers love the story, but newspapers, magazines, and TV stations picked it up all over the country. Word leaked out from our five printing plants all over the United States. One printing manager called me from his pressroom in Texas, saying, "I've never read anything so moving. My men are angry and furious at O.J. A couple of them were even in tears after reading Nicole's words."

Domestic violence experts all over the country concluded that Nicole's diary demonstrated that O.J. was a classic wife-beater.

After the second, civil trial, in which a jury found that O.J. had indeed killed Nicole and Ronald Goldman, the furor finally began to subside.

Said Butterfield, "It was almost a relief. For more than a year the Simpson story and the Brown family was my whole life, my obsession. It was an incredible experience, but it was a relief, in some ways, to move on."

A wonderful irony ensued after O.J. was found not guilty at the criminal trial. He needed money and was willing to sell the exclusive story and photos of his homecoming. But *not*, said Simpson, to the *Enquirer*, which had obviously penetrated his secret groups of friends and attorneys.

Under normal circumstances that would have meant Peter Burt, who had broken so many O.J. stories, would have no access to this material. Except these weren't normal times.

For one thing, Peter had always insisted there be no bylines on his Simpson exclusives, so that no one would suspect anything if he was seen with his secret source.

For another, our sister tabloid weekly *Star*, also owned by American Media Inc., had offered him a job as an editor at about the time of the Simpson verdict. I didn't want to lose Peter, but I couldn't stand in the way of his being promoted to editor at *Star*.

Peter's move had important consequences for the Simpson saga. Knowing that O.J. hated the *Enquirer* because of Burt's stories, "Deep Throat" made sure that O.J. knew the *Enquirer* would pay the most for the exclusive on his return home from jail.

"Deep Throat" then suggested that they take the *Star* offer of around $1 million. He arranged for O.J. to be told it could be set up through a friendly *Star* editor who could be trusted. That editor, of course, was Peter Burt. Holding out on his buddy O.J., "Deep Throat" didn't mention that young Burt had been Media Enemy Number One.

So Peter, the secret author of all the *Enquirer* stories that enraged O.J., ended up as the only journalist in his Brentwood house, representing *Star*.

Says Burt: "O.J. had no idea of my connection to the *Enquirer* or he would have kicked me out. The media was in a frenzy outside the house when he drove in from court, after being found not guilty. He shook my hand warmly but gave me a strange look. I was worried for a second, then I realized he was giving *everyone* the same strange look. It was almost like he was sizing up people to guess whether they really believed he was innocent."

As the world's press and TV journalists surged and shouted outside the gates, Burt walked about the house freely, directing top freelance photographer Kathy Amerman as she shot dozens of film rolls—O.J. smiling, O.J. celebrating, O.J. hugging his friends and attorneys.

Peter was in heaven. The phone was constantly ringing. Friends would shout, "O.J., it's Larry King on the phone . . . O.J., Barbara Walters wants a quick word . . . it's Diane Sawyer . . . Maria Shriver." All the big TV names were calling. But O.J., now under contract, could talk with only one person—Peter Burt.

The *Star* pressrun was due to begin the following morning, so as the photographer finished every three rolls, Peter took them out to the front gate. As rivals screamed for a crumb of information, Burt handed the film over to a waiting messenger—his wife, Tricia, who happened to be the daughter of America Media chairman Peter Callahan. A professional driver rushed Tricia to a secret photo lab in Los Angeles and then brought her back to the gate to await Peter's next package.

What a coup for *Star*. As sorry as I was that this wonderful, world-exclusive photo shoot hadn't appeared in the *Enquirer*, I was also executive vice president of *Star*'s American Media parent company and owned a small piece of it. So, all in all, it was a happy time.

After O.J. Simpson's acquittal at his criminal trial, Lou Brown, father of Nicole, and Fred Goldman, father of murdered Ron Goldman, brought a civil suit against Simpson in 1997—and won a $33.5 million judgment.

Many legal observers consider the key piece of evidence in the civil suit a photo of O.J. wearing Bruno Magli shoes.

At the murder scene, detectives had found bloody footprints made by a pair of rare, very expensive Italian-made Bruno Magli shoes with an unusual sole. The footprints showed the wearer was pigeon-toed (as is O.J.).

Under oath in a deposition, Simpson denied he ever even owned a pair of these "ugly ass" shoes. Did the cops check out his denial? They didn't bother, so nobody at the criminal trial challenged his statement.

The *Enquirer* did. After the not-guilty criminal verdict and before the civil trial, the *Enquirer* proved conclusively that O.J. had indeed lied about owning Bruno Magli shoes. Our evidence made a stunning cover story in the *Enquirer* and was later presented as damning evidence by attorney Daniel Petrocelli in the parents' civil case.

In his book *Triumph of Justice*, Petrocelli praised our Bruno Magli photographs as a key piece of evidence that nailed O.J.

It all began with a phone call to editor Larry Haley in Lantana from a high school kid in Colorado who had seen Haley's byline on O.J. stories. The teenager said he had photographed Simpson in Denver's Mile-High Stadium before the murders. Could he be wearing the Bruno Magli shoes mentioned in all the newspapers? he asked.

Interested, Haley asked the kid to mail the photo forthwith. Disappointment. The photo was taken through a chain-link fence, and O.J. was way off in the distance—almost a dot. His image was so tiny he could have been wearing boots, tennis sneakers, or no shoes at all. It was a dead end, one of thousands our reporters encountered during the investigation.

But the photo gave Haley an idea. O.J. had been a TV commentator at numerous football games before the murders. If we searched through enough photos, we just *might* find a picture of him wearing those Bruno Maglis.

Haley and photo editor Ray Farrell got executive permission to follow the lead and conduct a photo "sweep." They asked photographers and photo agencies all over the country to send in pictures of O.J. taken at football games before the murders.

Thousands of pictures poured in, including one big pile from the official NFL photographer. Haley and Farrell were soon red-eyed from scanning photo after photo. Nothing seemed promising until— bingo—one shot looked possible. Using a magnifying glass they found one picture of Simpson wearing shoes that looked an awful lot like Bruno Maglis.

Said Haley: "We got excited, but there are no shoe experts at the *Enquirer*, so we called the Bruno Magli company for help. They just didn't want to know. They clearly didn't want their exclusive footwear to be tied to the world's most famous murder case. They refused to cooperate."

Haley tracked down the closest local shoe store that specialized in Bruno Maglis. We took them copies of our photos with the top half hidden so the store personnel wouldn't know that the feet they were identifying belonged to Simpson. That might have made them nervous. After looking at a blown-up print of anonymous legs and feet, they pronounced the shoes Bruno Magli Lorenzi Model I with Silga soles, probably size 12, Simpson's shoe size. Only 200 pairs of these shoes had been imported to the United States.

Still not enough. A major national story like this needs to be nailed down solidly.

The photo had come from the official NFL photographer, who then sent in more pictures from the sequence, plus the original negatives. Haley located a top Florida expert in footwear and footprints who'd been trained by the FBI and often gave evidence in criminal court cases.

The expert asked to see the whole series of photos in different sizes. It took him three days, but his verdict was that these were Bruno Magli shoes with Silga soles.

In the meantime, photo editor Ray Farrell was working with one of the world's greatest experts on photo imaging. He was a professor at the Rochester Institute of Technology and a consultant to NASA, and he agreed to inspect the prints and negatives.

Haley flew to Rochester with the evidence. The professor, who had also worked with the U.S. Senate on JFK assassination photos, spent three and a half hours in his lab as Haley waited nervously. Finally the professor walked out and said: The photos are genuine.

Recalls Haley: "Our expert was very careful. He knew the press would grill him. In fact, when we ran the story, O.J.'s lawyers called the photos fake. 'It was just the *Enquirer*,' they said. But our expert went on the *Geraldo* TV show and pronounced them genuine."

We kept looking for more O.J. photos. It turned out a football newsletter in Buffalo had taken photos the same day and printed them. O.J. was seen in the published newsletter wearing the same shoes some nine months *before* the murders. Eventually we amassed a total of thirty-three shots of O.J. wearing the Bruno Maglis. His lawyers stopped talking about *Enquirer* fakes.

Said Haley: "It was good detective work—a lot better than the L.A. police did. It showed O.J. had lied, and the Browns' lawyer was generous enough to announce that this key piece of evidence helped him win the case for the Browns and Goldmans."

Some time after we ran the O.J./Bruno Magli photo, the National Association of Chiefs of Police awarded Haley their most prestigious anti-crime accolade, the J. Edgar Hoover Award. Haley received a pewter plaque inscribed: "Distinguished Public Service: 1996 Outstanding Investigative Reporting in O.J. Simpson Case— Larry Haley, *National Enquirer*."

Haley was also nominated for a Pulitzer. Naturally he didn't win. The chances of a mainstream group of journalists and professors awarding their most prestigious honor to the *Enquirer* was as likely as the Republican National Committee naming Bill Clinton "Man of the Year."

What about the Colorado teenager who came up with the original idea? Haley sent him a check for $1,500. So the kid not only helped present the civil trial jury with the evidence to nail O.J., he also made a nice bit of change.

One more O.J. postscript: Some women's groups took the press to task for not publicizing O.J.'s earlier beatings of Nicole. If they had, some claimed, the football star might have been shamed into seeking treatment. And perhaps the lives of Nicole and Goldman would have been spared.

Excuse me, ladies. The *Enquirer* did run the story of O.J. beating Nicole and her calling the cops. It was in our issue of February 21, 1989.

In fact, writer Katy Butler praised us in the *Los Angeles Times* magazine, December 10, 1995. Under the headline "The Accidental Feminist," her piece had an interesting subhead: "If the *National Enquirer* Proved Nothing Else during the O.J. Trial, It Reaffirmed Its Surprising Pro-Woman, Anti-Abuse Stance."

Butler made note of our 1989 O.J. wife-beating story and added: "If other newspapers had taken the Simpsons' violent marriage as seriously as the *Enquirer* did, said Dr. Joyce Brothers in one story, Nicole Brown Simpson might well be alive today."

Butler may have been surprised by our "pro-woman" stance, but all of us who worked there knew it made perfect sense. After all, about 90 percent of *Enquirer* buyers were women.

IT ALL CATCHES UP WITH ME

I hardly ever get sick. From the time we moved to Florida in 1971, I had had the flu once and maybe a couple of bouts with colds or sore throats. But that was it. Missing a day's work for illness was something that happened to me maybe twice a decade.

So, in 1994, when I began to get dizzy spells, I was shocked.

Usually it happened in my office. The vision in one eye would suddenly buzz with wavy, jagged lines. Then I would feel dizzy, as if the room were spinning. Each episode could last from five to fifteen minutes.

If I was talking with staff, I'd manage to camouflage my symptoms until they left. The only person in the office I couldn't fool was my principal assistant, Judi Walsh. She knew something was wrong—and I leveled with her.

My first thought was a problem was my eyes, but after an examination, my ophthalmologist told me I had "ocular migraines"—migraine headaches without the pain. Lucky you, he joked.

But when I mentioned this condition to my regular internist, a friend for many years, he blanched. He immediately sent me to a neurologist who put me through a battery of tests, including an MRI scan.

The MRI revealed that one-sixth of my brain was filled with a huge mass. The neurologist tried to calm me by saying it wasn't as bad as it looked. But it looked *really* bad. As I peered at the MRI films, half of my brain looked okay, and two-thirds of the other half was fine, too. But you didn't have to be an M.D. to see that the big, dense-looking mass in that final one-sixth was bad news.

It was an arachnoid cyst—"arachnoid" means related to spiders and the cyst apparently resembled a spider web. The good news, said the doc, was that it looked like it had been there for many, many years. Perhaps I'd been born with it. His advice was: Forget about it; it's not causing the dizzy spells, and it doesn't seem to be doing anything harmful, so just ignore it.

That's easy to say when *you* don't have one-sixth of your skull filled with a spidery mass. I wanted a second opinion—from the best.

Through friends and contacts, I was able to make an appointment at Memorial Sloan-Kettering Cancer Center in New York City, arguably the number-one cancer center in the world. There, Dr. Clifford Solomon, a young neurologist, the son of a good friend, took me under his wing and set up an appointment with the chief of neurology, who spent an hour or so testing me and looking at my MRI. He also had the case reviewed by a team of specialists.

Their conclusion: Forget about it. It's not causing the dizzy spells, and it doesn't seem to be doing anything harmful, so just forget about it.

The chief neurologist told me the mass had either been there since birth or had been caused by an early childhood injury. I should take several MRI scans over the next year or so, to make it sure it wasn't growing. Other than that, I was fine.

I tried to joke with the doctor: "I've done okay with five-sixths of my brain. Just think how successful I would have been with six-sixths."

His response: "Sir, it doesn't work like that."

The best brain expert in the world, he might have been. But not much of a sense of humor.

Just to be sure, Dr. Solomon also sent the case file over to the neurology department at Cornell Medical Center, and they agreed with the diagnosis. So now I had a confirming *third* opinion.

Relief. But none of these top doctors could find any reason for my dizzy spells.

So back to my Florida internist I went, and he referred me to a new neurologist, reputed to be the best in the county.

He put me through all kinds of tests, including measuring blood flow to the brain, listening to a variety of loud noises through earphones, and watching flashing colored lights in a dark room. The doc could find nothing wrong.

"I believe it's stress," he said one day.

I laughed out loud and replied, "I don't get stress. I *give* stress." It was crazy. *Nobody* handled stress like I did. Throughout my career, I could read a story, talk on the telephone, and answer questions from people in my office—all at once. I loved the high-tension lifestyle.

Most of my staff knew nothing about my dizzy spells as I continued to work normally, but I did confide in Mike Boylan, who, as my boss, had a right to know. Mike didn't believe the dizziness was related to stress, either: "I've never seen anyone handle stress as well as you."

Still, I *had* been working continuously, under enormous pressure, from the age of sixteen—nearly forty years. I had been the top executive at the *Enquirer* for twenty years, without a single vacation that hadn't included calls to and from the office several times each week. Maybe it was time for a break.

I asked Boylan and chairman Callahan for a long break—with no interruptions. As always, they were very generous and gave me eight weeks to relax and unwind.

I went back to Scotland—in style. I rented a two-hundred-year-old mansion located on an estate of 2,000 acres near Edinburgh. Included in the rental fee were a housekeeper, an amazing chef, and several part-time maids. Once, my wife asked the chef if we could serve forty relatives for lunch in the dining room. He replied, "No problem. Let's go over the menu."

This was living. I felt like a character in a fairy tale—the poor little Scottish boy coming back from America like a lord of the manor. We were there for six weeks, and the place certainly impressed our Scots relatives, and our sons, who visited us for a short golfing trip.

I'll probably never have a vacation like it again, and the effect was magical. My dizzy spells disappeared within a few days. I felt relaxed and refreshed. When I returned, I called my neurologist to say, "I'm cured." After a couple of weeks back at my job, the dizzy spells returned.

This time my neurologist refused to treat me anymore. "There's nothing wrong with you physically. I'm sending you to a stress specialist."

I knew what he meant—a psychiatrist who sent people to the funny farm. This was awful. I was desperate to be well again, so I went.

Dr. McKinley Cheshire was a psychiatric expert on stress. (He was also one of Palm Beach County's top experts on killers who claimed to be insane.)

For one session a week, we discussed my symptoms, my job, the pressures, and anything else I wanted to discuss. I was pleasantly surprised to find he was not like the movie shrinks who want to know about any sexual attractions you had for your grade school teacher or your pet hamster. He also interviewed my wife.

After six weeks, he rendered his verdict: "You have a severe case of stress. Your body is giving you a message. Unless you get rid of the stress you might become quite ill. It could be heart disease, cancer, or some other illness. But you must change your life."

That meant changing my job. But I loved my job. Plus it paid me $600,000 per year.

I thought about it and then asked if I reduced my duties significantly, could I keep working? He thought the answer was yes.

In December 1995, I told Mike Boylan I had to resign as president and editor in chief. If he wanted, I would stay on as executive vice president and board member, working on new projects and increasing revenues. I suggested working 50 percent of the time for 50 percent of the money. Clearly, I would also be available to run editorial in any emergency.

The decision, of course, belonged to the chairman. I always respected Callahan, and still do, but we didn't always click personally. I perhaps fought some of his *Enquirer* decisions too vigorously, although I always followed his final orders. I thought, in later years, he was cutting staff too severely, for example, and I probably rubbed him the wrong way at times.

However, Peter was generous and considerate as usual. He said he felt I was still a valuable asset to the company, gave me my choice of new offices, and signed a new contract.

In the year after Gene died, the *Enquirer* had average sales of over 4.25 million copies per week. By the latter part of 1991 it was 3.75 million per week, and in the last six months of 1995 we were averaging fewer than 2.75 million copies per week.

Of course, we were now charging $1.29 instead of 75 cents, and our readers got 48 pages per issue instead of 64. Because of editorial cutbacks, we had to change the mix of stories, with expensive non-celebrity features biting the dust. It was no longer the authentic Gene Pope *Enquirer* but it was still number one in weekly circulation, and finance-wise it was a big success. The bankers loved us.

Our falling numbers were also part of a general circulation drop among the biggest American magazines. All publications—from *TV Guide* to the women's magazines—were seeing a decline in single-copy sales. Even the TV networks were losing viewers at an unprecedented rate, because consumers were becoming more selective.

As more cable channels gave viewers more choices, thousands opted for the Food Channel, the Golf Channel, MTV, CNN, and dozens of others, defecting from their old triple standby—NBC, CBS, and ABC.

The same thing happened in print. Literally hundreds of small specialty magazines burst onto the scene, stealing customers from *McCalls*, *Reader's Digest*, and all the other biggies.

We had one additional problem. Our very success had made all kinds of general interest magazines run personality stories, and TV was awash with celebrity programs. We had generated our own competition.

On November 22, 1995, I officially stepped down as president and editor in chief of the *Enquirer*. For the first time in forty years, I was no longer a full-time journalist, which was upsetting. I moved into a specially built, smaller office. My job now was coming up with ideas to grow the company. We initiated the *National Enquirer* syndicated TV show, kept the British *Enquirer* growing, and worked on improving circulation of our smaller magazines.

My step down from editor in chief rated a lot of ink in papers around the country. One story began: "Had aliens whisked Iain Calder from the top spot at the *National Enquirer*, it might have caused less of a stir.

"Calder, 56, told the staff of the Lantana-based tabloid Friday that he was resigning as president and editor-in-chief to sidestep the stress that's apparently responsible for recent medical problems."

They quoted a competitor calling it an "epic moment in tabloid history."

Later, a massive story in the *Palm Beach Post*, our local daily, did their version of an exposé, which I rather liked. They interviewed my family and staffers who'd worked for me, asking what I was like. My friend Bill Burt described me as "demanding" and added, "He wants everything done the Iain way, you know."

Another editor, who asked for anonymity, said: "He'd torture you over the details. [He's] very demanding, almost overbearing."

My own son Douglas was quoted as saying, "My father absolutely hates to lose. I don't care whether it's playing me at tennis, watching *Jeopardy*—he's got to get the question before anyone else—or a 2-foot putt on the golf course. It's anathema for him to lose."

The paper's headline conclusion: "For 32 years, he's been a demanding, driving force at the *National Enquirer*."

All true—but it was strange to be at the other end of the journalist's pen.

Editor & Publisher, the magazine written for professional journalists, did the same kind of piece. They quoted reporter Joe Mullins saying about me: "He's a guy who'd probably toss his granny off the trolley for a scoop."

The piece concluded that I was a "results-driven, tough taskmaster, part ogre, part genius." Wrong on one count. The only *Enquirer* genius ever was Gene Pope.

★★★

In twenty-five years with the *Enquirer*, I met countless movie stars, TV bigwigs, sports figures, and people who were famous for being famous. As with most groups of people, I liked some and didn't like others. One of the people I like and admire most is Bill Cosby.

Cosby is one of the smartest celebrities around. He found, over the years, that by taking our calls and being honest—usually directly with us, and not through his agents—that we would take his word. I do not believe he ever lied to us or tried to spin his way out of controversy, even in "bad publicity" circumstances.

His honesty paid off—even in a tough story in which his daughter admitted to being hooked on drugs and booze. But in some ways it hurt him. Rumors circulated in Hollywood that we "had something" on Cosby. Even some of our newer editors and reporters would ask me why Bill cooperated with us. Luckily, Cosby was big enough to ignore the rumors, which were simply not true. We had nothing on Cosby.

An incident in the early '80s had opened the bond of trust between us.

One of my editors asked me to approve a lead, saying that Bill Cosby was romancing a Las Vegas showgirl behind his wife's back. I approved it to be checked out—one level lower than a firm approval.

Cosby had been an Emmy-winning star with *I Spy* some years earlier, but at that time he was known mainly for his kids' TV cartoon *Fat Albert*, some appearances on Johnny Carson, and a major Las Vegas comedy act. Talented, successful, but not a major cover celebrity for us.

Then came an odd call from Edward Bennett Williams, founder of our law firm, Williams and Connolly, and one of the best-connected people in America.

"Iain, I got an interesting phone call today. From the Reverend Jesse Jackson. He says you're doing a story on Bill Cosby," said Ed.

"We are?" I had forgotten. We worked maybe 500 stories at any one time—and only ten or twenty of the most important would be in the front of my brain.

Ed Williams continued: "Bill Cosby has told Jesse Jackson that the story is not true. He is up for something major, and if you run a false story it could cost him millions. I've known Jesse Jackson for a long time, and he says Cosby would never lie to him."

Williams said Jackson had not asked that the *Enquirer* kill the story—just to look at it very carefully. The potential for harm was really great.

No kidding. I couldn't know that Cosby was on the edge of signing a huge new deal to be spokesman for Jell-O and close to beginning one of the biggest-grossing TV series of all time.

I called for the file and didn't find it totally convincing. We had no photos—usually a must in features like this. The story didn't seem worth fighting for. It would need a lot more work and, at best, was a small inside-the-book piece.

I decided to drop it, but because Williams was involved, I told Mr. Pope. He didn't like killing a story because of influence, but since we didn't know if the story was solid, GP didn't care.

When I called Ed to say the story was dead, he thanked me.

The next day, my secretary called to say Mr. Bill Cosby was on the line. "Iain," he said, "I just want to call to thank you . . ." I stopped him: "You have nothing to thank me for."

Cosby went on: "You have my word, it is not true. But you have shown me I can trust your paper, and I will remember that."

Conversation over. Big deal. Bill Cosby trusted us. Bill *who*? How could I ever have imagined he'd become Mr. Television and the most-watched star on American TV.

Stars often turn on "old friends" in the media. Bill Cosby never turned on us in all the years I was editor. Cosby, I believe, cooperated with us in the years to follow for two reasons: (1) He did trust us, and (2) we reached more than 20 million people each week. The killed story was a non-event. We didn't even know if it was true and, even if it had been, we could never have constructed a file to pass our legal requirements.

Cosby usually worked with reporter David Duffy, but once in a while he'd call me.

One time when Jane and I went out for the evening, we left teenaged Douglas at home to look after our younger son, Glen. Normally, they took turns answering the telephone, but once Glen refused his turn, claiming to be too busy. Douglas picked up the phone. It was Bill Cosby, at the height of his TV career, asking for me. Cosby talked with Douglas for about five minutes, asking him questions and just being a nice guy.

When Glen heard about this, he was crushed, green with envy. He had just missed a chance to tell his school pals he had talked with Bill Cosby. When we returned home our younger son was really down in the dumps.

Some days later, when I spoke to Bill I mentioned the story in passing. Cosby said, "What time can I call your home tonight and speak with Glen?" It was hard to believe. This was Bill Cosby—who could make network presidents jump, who could call the White House and get through to the president.

At the prescribed time, our home telephone rang. I asked Glen to get it. When he picked up, the voice said, "Hi, Glen. This is Bill Cosby." For the next five minutes my son's face lit up like a full moon.

Years later, in the spring of 1989, reporter David Wright had dinner with Bill Cosby's daughter Erinn and her fiancé at a top New York City restaurant. This attractive young woman had left home to make a life for herself away from her rich and powerful dad.

Wright, interviewing Erinn about her family, had promised to pay her $1,000 or more if she gave us a good story. The young woman was enchanting. Bright-eyed and articulate, she was charming but really had no story for us. At the end of the dinner David thought, she's far too nice for the *Enquirer*.

Recalls Wright: "When I returned home, I told my wife Carol that Erinn was delightful. I'd be proud to have Erinn as a daughter."

The young lady, a skilled actress, had successfully concealed a deep, dark secret from one of our most potent reporters.

He learned the truth six months later when Erinn Cosby called his home. Her message was: "I'm in rehab and coming out Friday. How much will you pay for my story?"

This news really shocked me. It was the first hint of trouble in the Cosby household, which had seemed a model all-American, up-standing family.

Obviously, the first step was to meet with Erinn and find out what had gone wrong. Wright flew to meet with her and found a different girl than the one he'd met six months earlier.

Her story was heartbreaking. She'd begun drinking secretly nine years before, at age fourteen. At sixteen her parents had discovered her bombed out on booze and pot. Recognizing her as a rebellious youngster, her parents thought she might straighten out at a prestigious all-girls boarding school.

This choice was a disaster. The school introduced her to a life of partying, sex, and drugs. She dropped out and disappeared for weeks, and when she finally called her mom and dad, they were frantic and wanted her to come home to L.A. Instead, Erinn chose a life of booze and drugs in New York City. At nineteen she was supporting a $200-a-day cocaine habit.

Wright asked: "When we had dinner together, were you on drugs at that time?" "Big time," she said. He was floored.

Now Erinn wanted to dump on her famous dad, saying that he wouldn't support her financially or emotionally. She wanted to expose TV's perfect dad as an uncaring, neglectful father.

When I read Wright's copy, I was touched by this searing story of a young woman who should have been on top of the world, but who just couldn't handle her terrible problems. But the father she was describing just didn't resemble the Bill Cosby I had known for the past few years.

I knew we'd have to call Cosby to give him a chance to respond. Celebrities often had skeletons in their closets, and we'd contact them for their comments. Most of them were either stupid or took bad advice. Invariably their public relations flacks would dissemble ("lie" is such a harsh word) or their lawyers would threaten to sue. That was the *worst* way to handle the *National Enquirer*.

Bill Cosby, as we knew, was totally different. There is a reason he became the richest and most successful TV star in the 1980s.

He openly admitted his daughter's problems and told us the heartbreaking story of how, over the years, they had suffered with her, tried everything to straighten her out, given her comfort, love, counseling sessions with experts. Everything a loving family could do.

Now, after conferring with the best psychiatrists and counselors available, they had to try "tough love." He told us, on the record, "We have to take a very firm, tough stand that forces her to realize that no one can fix things for her. She has to beat this on her own."

Our cover story on October 10, 1989, was a blockbuster:

Cosby Heartbreak—His Daughter Is a Drug Addict

An underline said: *Her Own Story Plus Exclusive Interview with TV's #1 Dad.*

The result was a huge sale and a story that the media all over America picked up. By cooperating with us, Cosby came across as he really was—a caring, loving father trying to save his daughter.

The mainstream press praised him. Famed *Washington Post* columnist William Raspberry wrote about Erinn: "I hope Cosby will go on being Cliff Huxtable, model husband and father. I like to think I have learned some important things from his TV portrayal: things like patience and wisdom.

"But I also hope he will go on along his path of 'tough love.' There are valuable lessons in that, too—chief among them the limits of what even the most loving of parents can do."

This story should have been a lesson for Hollywood. Cooperating with us, even on tough stories, is a big plus for celebrities. Lying, attacking us, or threatening to sue—such tactics just bring more grief, but few stars understood this message.

As a by-product of our story, it looked like Erinn might reconcile with her parents. She had successfully completed the rehab program, had talked with her parents on the phone, and was hoping to make up for all the heartache she had caused.

Sadly, it wasn't to be. In our December 26 issue, just a few weeks later, we revealed:

Bill Cosby's Daughter Back on Booze and Drugs
Now TV's #1 Dad says, 'If She Wants to Sleep in the Gutter,
That's Her Choice'

Erinn had stayed clean for just a few weeks before selling a valuable watch, a gift from her parents, and using the money to buy drugs and booze. It was a sorrowful ending for the Cosby family and our readers who had written to us, hoping for a happy reunion.

★★★

I wish the next big Cosby story had never happened. But since it did, I'm glad we were able to bring a killer to justice, so the Cosbys wouldn't wonder if their son's murderer was still out on the streets.

In 1997, I was no longer president or editor in chief of the *Enquirer*, but I was still working on new projects for American Media. The new *Enquirer* editor, Steve Coz—a kind of protégé of mine, I suppose—kept me up to date on major stories, would listen to my occasional advice, and even asked me questions once in a while. And my counsel still seemed valued by my friend and boss Michael Boylan, vice chairman and uber-boss of all American Media editorial.

I liked to think I still had some gas left in the old think tank, that I wasn't just a senile old duffer wandering around the office. I got a chance to prove it when we learned that Bill Cosby's son, Ennis, had been shot to death in California.

Ennis, a smart, handsome young man, with his mother's looks and his father's brilliant smile, was a graduate student at Columbia University and planned to be a teacher. On January 16, 1997, Ennis was home in L.A. on winter break. Early that morning, he was driving down a deserted Los Angeles freeway to visit a friend, Stephanie Crane. His Mercedes suddenly had a flat tire, and Ennis called Stephanie, who said she'd drive to where he was while he changed the tire.

When Crane arrived in her Jaguar, a stranger in a knit cap ordered her: "Get out of the car or I will kill you." Terrified, she sped away, then circled back. When she returned she saw the man—who turned out to be the killer—run off and Cosby lying by the side of the road. She could not identify the man in the knit cap.

The cops seemed baffled. They were under the glaring searchlight of media all over the United States. They had to find the killer but had almost no evidence to work with.

I knew how to help. I immediately typed a memo to Steve Coz. "We need to immediately offer a reward of $100,000 for information leading to the capture of the Cosbys' son's killer. Clearly we should clear this with Bill Cosby and the cops, but I think they would be thrilled."

Coz was given permission for the reward by Mike Boylan and

chairman Callahan. It would look better for the *Enquirer* if we reported that Bill Cosby actually suggested the reward—and we had leaped at the chance to help justice. So Bill Cosby dutifully asked for our help.

We solved the case. It was simple. After we offered the reward, a witness contacted our office in Los Angeles and told us the whole story.

A Ukrainian immigrant named Mikail Markhasev and two associates, stopping to make a phone call to drug connections, saw Ennis Cosby changing a tire.

Markhasev walked across the highway to rob Cosby and ended up shooting him to death. The three ditched the weapon by wrapping it in the knit cap and throwing it away. Markhasev, a gang member known for his hatred of blacks, might never have been caught, but the day after the murder he made a mistake.

He called a Korean friend named Michael Chang to help him find the gun and dispose of it permanently. Chang had no car, so he asked a pal named Christopher So to drive them.

So heard Markhasev boast to Chang: "I shot the nigger. It's all over the news."

After our reward was offered, Christopher So called our Los Angeles office and spoke to two reporters, John South and Marc Cettner. He said he knew something about the Cosby killing and asked about the reward.

Was he believable? Absolutely. The cops had put out a false story to the media giving the wrong caliber of gun—a .45. Our witness knew the real gun was a .38 caliber.

Cettner, one of the bureau's aces, took over the story and called the LAPD. The correct gun caliber excited them, and they immediately picked up So. He led the cops to the gun in some grass near the Los Angeles River in North Hollywood. It was wrapped in a knit cap that contained hair fibers that matched Markhasev's.

Very quickly the cops arrested their man. But we didn't have our story. Christopher So, who had been reluctant to meet with *Enquirer* reporters, finally agreed to meet with Marc Cettner.

Recalls Cettner: "I told the guy I would meet him in a restaurant, give him some money for the full story—and promised him the hundred-thousand-dollar reward if Markhasev was found guilty.

"I was very nervous. These were dangerous guys, and I had no idea what might happen to me. I arranged for another reporter to sit in a car nearby with two thousand dollars in cash and wait for my phone call.

"Within minutes I knew I had the story of a lifetime. The cops believed Christopher So, and within a short time it was clear he was telling me the truth. My spine tingled with excitement, and my ears felt like they were on fire as So described how the murder had taken place."

The Enquirer *had actually caught the Cosby killer.*

Cettner's story was the stuff journalists just *dream* about. The following year Markhasev was tried, convicted, and sentenced to life without parole.

But not before the cops needed us again. The day before So was due to give critical evidence, he disappeared, and the prosecution was worried he was too scared to testify against a dangerous gang member. In court, the lead detective, a guy named Garcia, went over to Marc Cettner and whispered: "Where is the man?"

Outside the courtroom, Garcia begged Cettner to find their key witness. No problem. Our reporter made a few phone calls and talked to So. He still wanted the reward.

Cettner told his detective pal: "You'll find So at home." Three cop cars sirened their way to the witness and kept him safe overnight to ensure his testimony—which helped put the killer behind bars. And So received a whopping $100G *Enquirer* check.

Steve Coz recalls: "The police and district attorney's office gave us full credit. Media all over the country picked up the story, and even *Time* magazine praised us."

Not all the mainstream media could overcome their bash-the-*Enquirer* instincts. The *New York Times* published a fairly major story giving critics a forum. The editor of the *Columbia Journalism Review* (a mighty organ if there ever was one) said he frowned on rewards by news organizations since "it tempts the news organization to give the story more play . . . than they otherwise would." What did he think—we should catch a killer, then run it as two paragraphs on page 36?

Of course, our readers didn't know where the original idea had come from, and they didn't care. They paid for us at the checkout—

and that was the best thanks of all. Quietly, though, I couldn't help a little smile of satisfaction. I still hadn't lost the touch.

You might have thought that the *Enquirer*'s role in catching the killer would have endeared us to the Cosby family. Instead, the opposite happened.

While the investigation was under way, the *Enquirer* ran a headline saying that Cosby's wife had hired gunmen to find the truth. It *was* a bit of a stretch. What Bill's wife, Camille, had hired were gun-toting private detectives, and she was rip-roaring furious with us. She gave media interviews stating she would *never* hire gangsters.

Then our editors decided to add another Cosby story to the mix. The headline:

THE MISTRESS: SHOCKING STORY OF LOVE, LIES—AND MONEY

A young woman who claimed to be Cosby's illegitimate daughter had been arrested for allegedly trying to extort $24 million from him. We found the girl's mother, who said she had been Cosby's secret mistress. He'd paid her $3,000 per month but lied when he promised to make her his number-one woman.

This was all too much for the Cosby family. From that point on, they refused to cooperate with us again, despite all kinds of friendly overtures from us.

Their attitude probably cost us millions of dollars in future revenues. In my post-editor job, my main assignment was to find new sources of income. I'd already launched two successful new magazines and begun the British edition of the *Enquirer*, which was making a profit of $1 million-plus per annum. Now I had blueprints to launch a weekly tabloid-size magazine targeting the African-American community.

Working with Michael Forsyth, a talented black journalist from *Weekly World News*, I'd conceived a publication we were sure would work. It was to be a weekly newspaper focusing on stories and photos that would inspire pride and confidence within the African-American community. We'd include coverage of black celebrities, but the main interest would be ordinary African-Americans who had uplifting and exciting stories to tell.

Many publishers will tell you "good news" doesn't sell. Not true. You just need to spin your news with interesting new angles. I'm certain this new magazine would have attracted a huge readership. The African-American community has become more prosperous, with consumers spending billions of dollars on products. This new publication, sold in supermarkets, would reach millions of black consumers and be a great vehicle for advertisers.

It was clear that this publication had to have the goodwill of the black community—normally a "white" publishing company like us would be viewed with suspicion. So I contacted one of our major investors, a black-owned, very successful investment company, and convinced them the new publication would be an asset to their community. They agreed to help us find a solid African-American publishing partner.

Michael Forsyth and I then visited one of America's top black-owned advertising agencies, showed them our concept, and got their enthusiastic support.

In the last move, I began discussions with a major African-American publisher to form a partnership. A number of fine black-owned magazines were already established in the marketplace, but everyone we contacted agreed that our weekly concept was different enough to be successful.

That's when the bombshell hit. Camille Cosby happened to be best friends with the wife of the publisher we planned to partner with. Camille had been enraged by the *Enquirer*'s "gunmen" and "mistress" stories. The deal blew up.

I'm sorry about this on many levels. I'm sorry the Cosby friendship with the *Enquirer* ended. I'm sorry about the potential millions we *didn't* make. And I'm sorry African-Americans don't have this weekly publication that would have helped engender hope, joy, and pride in their community's achievements.

While I was developing new projects for American Media, I had many ideas, and a few worked out. But I was the wrong person at the wrong time. Boston Ventures, getting itchy to cash out their very successful investment, wanted to sell the company. This was not the time to spend big bucks on new expansion. Never mind that the extra income from the British *Enquirer* alone paid for my salary several times over. But Callahan and I had never been close. I wasn't finding much enthusiasm for my ideas.

Unknown to me, the sand was running out of my hourglass when I had to travel back to Britain. Bill Ness, the husband of my younger sister Sandra, had just died after a long, painful bout with cancer. I went to the funeral, flew home, and, still grief-stricken, walked into my office.

In the mail on my desk was a letter. It was like an electric shock when I read the words from my boss, Peter Callahan.

Dated October 1, 1997, the letter read: "I have not been completely satisfied with your contribution to the operating cash flow and general development of the company in 1997, and I suspect that you do not disagree.

"Accordingly, I hereby give you notice as required by your amended employment agreement. . . . Effective, April 1, 1998, you will become a consultant to the company. . . ."

I'd been fired. After thirty-three years, it was all over. After thirty-three years, I didn't even rate a face-to-face firing. Just a letter. Neither Callahan nor his two vice chairmen were in town, so there was no office I could storm into.

To be fair, Peter probably did the right thing. If an employee isn't working out, let him go. But he should have told me in person. Callahan later agreed with me and gave me an apology, which I accepted. How long can you hold a grudge against a man whose abilities you respect—and who made you a millionaire?

American Media entered into a tough period, which had nothing to do with my departure.

On August 31, 1997, Princess Diana was killed in a car crash with Dodi Fayed. The spotlight was turned onto the paparazzi who had been chasing them. The photographers were responsible, cried critics—a stupid idea when you consider the driver was drunk and speeding at over 60 m.p.h. in a 35-m.p.h. zone when he lost control and smashed into the concrete pillar of a traffic tunnel.

A French judge, who blamed alcohol, drugs, and excessive speed, cleared the photographers of causing the crash. But that didn't matter to the journalist critics. The American media screamed "paparazzi," and in the United States "paparazzi" implied tabloids, the most prominent of which was the *Enquirer*. To make things worse, the very week of Di's death we had run a cover story about her, with her photo, headlined: DI GOES SEX MAD. The cover had been printed days before the tragedy, but no one thinks about a paper's print schedule, and we looked unbelievably insensitive.

All this furor was sweet music for our Hollywood enemies, despite the fact that the French photographers were not working for the *Enquirer*. Entertainers like Tom Cruise, George Clooney, Madonna, Michael Jackson, and Alec Baldwin jumped on the criticism bandwagon, joyously bashing the *Enquirer*. Even Patsy Ramsey got in on the act. Yeah, the Patsy Ramsey who just missed being voted mom-of-the-year after daughter JonBenet was murdered.

Liz Smith, America's best-known celebrity columnist, pointedly observed that even after it was determined that Di's limo driver had almost four times the legal limit of alcohol in his system, "no celebrity crusades were organized against drunk driving."

However unfair the attacks, the damage was severe. Says Mike Boylan: "Supermarkets were getting demands from customers to take tabloids off the racks. Almost all resisted, but sales plummeted. That week was a disaster, and a couple of months later, when the dust had settled, we had permanently lost about 250,000 per week in circulation."

It was the worst disaster in tabloid history at that time. Despite my being fired, I felt bad for the paper and all my friends there.

They say that for a type-A personality, retirement can be disastrous. For me, it was like a release from prison. From the age of sixteen on, I had been a slave to deadlines. From the early '70s on, I couldn't be too far from a telephone, in case a great story broke.

Now I could go to lunch for as long as I wanted. Just browsing aimlessly in a bookstore seemed like sybaritic luxury. I could play golf or tennis without having to answer to anybody (except my wife, of course). Jane and I could take a cruise whenever we wanted.

I just loved it. Even when I received a million-dollar package offer from my friend Harry Evans to edit a major New York publication, I turned it down without a second thought.

The only downside of my retirement is that I can't turn off my editor's mind. When I read a publication or watch a news show on television, I can't help but marvel at how often they miss the angle or fail to understand what their customer really wants. I want to call the editor or producer and scream, "*Here's* how you do it!"

But I don't. And the urge fades a little as the years pass.

I still give advice when people ask, do a little consulting here and there, give occasional magazine interviews, and serve as a director on a hospital foundation board, and our local university has given me the title of distinguished lecturer. So far, *Who's Who in America* hasn't thrown me out of their latest edition.

Even in retirement, I watched as interesting events unfolded at my old company. After the first sale to Boston Ventures, I lost touch with Austin Beutner, Pete Peterson's young partner who had helped me reassure the panicky staffers before the original sale. It turns out he'd had an interesting decade. After a stint with the U.S. government, Austin joined former assistant secretary of the treasury Roger Altman to form Evercore Partners, a fund established for the purpose of buying, expanding, and selling companies to make wealthy investors even wealthier.

In 1999, Boston Ventures and the Callahan trio were well past their original target date to sell the company, take their profits, and ride off into the sunset. Mike Boylan, super-salesman and raconteur extraordinaire, started shopping American Media around on Wall Street and in the publishing industry.

That caught the attention of David Pecker, the highly regarded North American president of Hachette Filipacchi, the international publishing company; he'd been involved in one of the also-ran bids for the *Enquirer* in 1989. Word also reached Austin Beutner.

Recalls Austin: "I was told David Pecker was interested, and I had been watching the progress of the *Enquirer* group ever since the original sale. Pecker was a world-class talent, and the *Enquirer* people were impressive. Put that together with my opinion that the *National Enquirer* is one of the best media franchises in the world, and it took about one and a half minutes to really confirm my interest."

Within a few months the deal was done, and Evercore was the new owner of American Media Inc. David Pecker resigned from Hachette and is now chairman, president, and CEO of American Media. Under his management, American Media shrewdly bought its last remaining tabloid, the *Globe*, and moved most of the company into spacious offices in nearby Boca Raton (the building would later be the center of the 2001 anthrax tragedy). *Enquirer* investigative journalism flourished. Very quickly they broke a number of major stories. In January 2001, Coz and his guys hit the racks with a bombshell headline:

JESSE JACKSON'S LOVE CHILD

On the cover was a picture of Jesse with his mistress—and a picture of the little girl, with her face erased for privacy.

Less than two months later the *Enquirer* ran another exclusive exposé, this one involving Hillary Clinton's brother, Hugh Rodham. The headline:

CLINTON PARDON PAYOFF EXPOSED
$200,000 DEPOSITED IN SECRET FAMILY BANK ACCOUNT

Rodham's law firm received a huge payment from a convicted perjurer and mail fraud felon—just one business day after the criminal received a pardon from president/brother-in-law Bill Clinton. The *Enquirer* even had a copy of the money transfer.

Both these stories—and a number of others—were widely praised by the mainstream media and helped David Pecker persuade his wide contact list of New York–based advertisers that the *Enquirer* was worthy of their business. Even the business press paid attention now that a successful former magazine executive was running the tabloid empire.

In February 2001, Coz was invited onto the CNN journalism program *Reliable Sources*, and was practically lionized by major journalists who admired the presidential pardon exclusive. Michael Isikoff of *Newsweek* called it a "slam dunk" of a story and added, "My hat is off to him [Coz]. . . . Any mainstream news organization, from the *Washington Post* to *Newsweek* to CNN would have gone with it in a minute."

Howard Kurtz, *Washington Post* and CNN media expert, had earlier commented on CNN that the Jesse Jackson and Clinton stories had been "rock solid" and that the *Enquirer* had handled them "in a very professional manner."

In the midst of all this glory, a wild disaster struck the *Enquirer*. A few weeks after September 11, when the country was still distraught from the terrorist attacks on New York and the Pentagon, someone—possibly a terrorist—sent a package containing deadly anthrax spores to one of the tabloids in the new building. A friend of mine, retouch artist Robert Stevens, exhibited the first signs of exposure and died in early October. Another employee, mailroom worker Ernest Blanco, became ill but recovered.

Panic—controlled, but nevertheless panic—ensued when the anthrax spores were discovered. The building was evacuated and barricaded shut, and all employees, plus anyone who'd visited for weeks before, were tested by local health authorities and given supplies of the powerful antibiotic Cipro.

Health officials found anthrax in ninety different locations within the building. Employees and their families, many suffering from severe side effects from the Cipro, were bewildered when health authorities could provide little information about the dangers posed by this kind of exposure to anthrax.

Out-of-state employees who'd recently been in the building received even less support from the medical profession. It took Mike Walker nearly two days to get treatment in Los Angeles. He called hospitals, health authorities, and doctors, but nobody wanted to treat him. Most didn't even want him to *visit*. This, despite all the statements from Washington that everything was under control.

Don't believe the bureaucrats. We're still not prepared for a bioterror attack.

Am I sorry I was gone before this worst-ever catastrophe for my paper? Obviously, I am relieved that my family and I had no contact with a deadly disease. But part of me hurts not to have been at the side of my friends and colleagues as they struggled for survival. And I think that, like many action-scarred war veterans, I missed being in the biggest battle of all.

AFTERWORD

Modern mainstream journalists aspire to winning the Pulitzer Prize, named after Joseph Pulitzer, the feisty publisher who made a success of the *New York World* in the 1880s. Today his prizes go to the likes of the *New York Times*, the *Washington Post*, and the *Los Angeles Times*. The *Enquirer* isn't even in the running. (However, we *did* once fire a Pulitzer Prize–winning reporter—but that's another story.) But I bet old Joseph would rather champion my *National Enquirer*.

According to Elizabeth Bird's scholarly book *For Enquiring Minds*, Pulitzer's paper became an enormous success when he followed his vow to concentrate on "what is original, distinctive, dramatic, romantic, thrilling, unique, curious, quaint, humorous, odd, apt to be talked about."

Which modern newspaper could he be describing? The *Times*, the *Post*, the *Herald*? Looks to me like he could have been devising the blueprint for the *Enquirer* that Gene and I created over the years.

William Randolph Hearst began copying Pulitzer when he bought the *New York Journal* in 1896. His editor, Arthur McEwen (sounds like another Scotsman), defined the essential element of journalism as the "gee whiz emotion." Drat. I thought I'd made up that phrase myself.

So at the end of the day I'm proud of following the leads of Joseph Pulitzer and William Randolph Hearst and helping to keep their inspiration alive.

What of the future? Will interest in gossip fade? In an age of email and the Internet, will magazines go the way of horse-drawn trolleys?

Lacking the abilities of the many psychics I published, my answers may be suspect. But I believe gossip is as old as civilization. In the days before television, neighbors would be shocked and entertained by such tidbits as: "Mrs. Jones down the road has run off with the milkman."

These days the neighbor would have no idea who Mrs. Jones is. Most people hardly even know their next-door neighbor. They do know Oprah, Rosie, Tom Cruise, Britney Spears, and Regis. They want gossip about *them*. When an *Enquirer* reader learns something new, it's fun, and it gives her a feeling of power to call a friend and say: "Did you know . . ."

This, I submit, is human nature.

Magazines will still be around in a hundred years, but maybe not on paper. Consider this: A publisher could send you a survey to find out what kinds of stories interest you alone—instead of everyone. A magazine specially designed for your individual taste could be beamed to your home electronically. It could be published on a special small printer right in your living room or kitchen. Or even more sci-fi, it could be transferred onto a 3-D hologram, so you could feel you are reading a real magazine, turning the pages and enjoying the words and pictures. Yet all you'd be holding would be a ghostly image of electrons, light, and gizmos.

I've seen these 3-D holograms of images at Disney World. Surely it would be possible to turn these into "magazines" and beam them to your home. Environmentalists would love it. Think of all the trees that wouldn't have to perish.

I won't be around to find out if this happens. But I will try to beam myself down—or up—to take a peek.